Individuals seem to make decisions using a wide variety of strategies, ranging from careful and reasoned examination of alternatives to simple and fast rules of thumb. How do people decide how to decide? What factors determine the strategy a decision maker will use in one situation as opposed to another? Answers to such questions are crucial for building a theoretical and empirical account of decision making.

The Adaptive Decision Maker provides a new framework for answering these questions; in addition, the authors present compelling new evidence consistent with this framework. Drawing upon their own programmatic research and the latest insights from other research on decision making in a variety of disciplines, the authors propose that people have a repertoire of strategies for making judgments and choices and that the use of these strategies is contingent upon a variety of task, context, and individual difference factors. The authors' framework for explaining these contingencies focuses on the accuracy and cognitive effort characterizing the available strategies. In particular, they provide new methodological approaches and extensive empirical evidence for their hypothesis that individuals select the particular strategy that represents the best accuracy–effort tradeoff for the task at hand. This research shows that individuals are often impressively adaptive in their responses to different decision situations. The authors also extend their framework to consider on-the-spot, constructive decision processes and discuss when decision makers may not be adaptive. Finally, insights about how to improve decisions and about opportunities for future research are offered.

In sum, the authors show that an accuracy–effort approach to understanding how people decide to decide is a powerful one for understanding decision-making processes. Their framework should be of interest to psychologists, other academics studying decision making, policy and decision analysts, economists, managers, and policy makers.

The adaptive decision maker

The adaptive decision maker

John W. Payne
Fuqua School of Business
Duke University

James R. Bettman
Fuqua School of Business
Duke University

Eric J. Johnson
The Wharton School
University of Pennsylvania

Published by the Press Syndicate of the University of Cambridge
The Pitt Building, Trumpington Street, Cambridge CB2 1RP
40 West 20th Street, New York, NY 10011-4211, USA
10 Stamford Road, Oakleigh, Victoria 3166, Australia

First published 1993

Printed in the United States of America

Library of Congress Cataloging-in-Publication Data
Payne, John W.
The adaptive decision maker / John W. Payne, James R. Bettman,
Eric J. Johnson
   p.   cm.
Includes bibliographical references and indexes.
ISBN 0–521–41505–5. – ISBN 0–521–42526–3 (pbk.)
1. Decision-making. 2. Adaptability (Psychology)   I. Bettman,
James R.   II. Johnson, Eric J.   III. Title.
BF448.P39   1993   92–21581
153.8′3–dc20   CIP

A catalog record for this book is available from the British Library.

ISBN 0–521–41505–5 hardback
ISBN 0–521–42526–3 paperback

To

Suzanne, Alan, and David (JWP)

My mother, Virginia Bettman, and the memory of my father, Roland Bettman (JRB)

Jeanne Johnson, my mother, and the memory of Milton Johnson, my father (EJJ)

Contents

Preface

Choice among alternative courses of action lies at the heart of the decision-making process. The study of how people make preferential choices and judgments has been of great interest to psychologists, economists, and researchers in many other fields, and over the past 20 years a number of different strategies used by people to solve decision problems have been identified. Some of those strategies involve the processing of all relevant information about the available alternatives and explicit consideration of tradeoffs among values, whereas other strategies (heuristics) use information more selectively and tend to avoid tradeoffs. As a consequence of using such selective heuristics, people sometimes make substantial decision errors.

Prior decision research has also shown that human decision behavior is highly sensitive to a wide variety of task and context factors. For example, the same individual often uses different processes for making choices rather than judgments, for choosing among a few versus many alternatives, or for deciding among a set of good versus a set of bad options. Strategy selection, in other words, is highly contingent on the properties of the decision problem.

The purpose of this book is to present a framework for understanding how people adapt their strategies for solving decision problems to the demands of the tasks they face. In attempting to understand contingent decision behavior, we view the decision maker as a limited-capacity information processor with multiple goals for the decision process. In particular, we emphasize the goals of attaining decision accuracy and limiting cognitive effort. Our hypothesis is that the contingent use of strategies (heuristics) represents an intelligent response to decision problems by an individual willing to trade off accuracy and effort. That is, we propose that observed decision processes often reflect a reasonable compromise between the desire to make a good decision and the desire to minimize the cognitive resources used in making the decision. In short, we believe that individuals are adaptive decision makers.

In addition to our framework, we present empirical evidence of human adaptivity in decision making. We also acknowledge, however, that there can at times be important constraints on such adaptivity. Thus, we discuss these constraints and also consider how our concepts about contingent decision making may be used to develop methods for improving judgments and choices.

This book reflects a research program that began almost 15 years ago. John Payne began a program of research on contingent strategy usage (e.g., Payne, 1976) that led to a review of the field and suggestions for several possible conceptual frameworks, one of which was a cost–benefit approach (Payne, 1982). Eric Johnson then joined with Payne to develop a full-fledged accuracy–effort approach, leading to computer simulations of the accuracy and effort of various strategies in different task environments (E. Johnson & Payne, 1985). Jim Bettman joined the team at about this time, and the collaboration turned to empirical demonstrations of the usefulness of the framework (e.g., Payne, Bettman, & Johnson, 1988). All three of us have been fascinated by the enormous flexibility people display in making decisions, and our research efforts have increased our appreciation for the adaptive decision maker. Our work over the years has also led us to value the benefits of a collaborative approach.

This book owes a great deal to many others, without whose contributions it could never have been written. There is an obvious intellectual debt to the work of other researchers on decision behavior. We have tried to reference explicitly the work of colleagues as it relates to our ideas when possible. However, we would like to recognize specifically several pioneering articles and books that greatly influenced our formative thinking on decision making and adaptivity: Simon (1955), Slovic and Lichtenstein (1968), Tversky (1969), Einhorn (1970), Newell and Simon (1972), Kahneman (1973), and Russo (1977).

We would also like to acknowledge our colleagues, both at our own institutions and elsewhere, with whom we have discussed and sometimes debated our ideas over the years. We have gotten many insights from these interactions.

Over the past 10 years, we have also benefited greatly from discussions with many of our doctoral students at Duke University, Carnegie Mellon University, and the University of Pennsylvania. Our students have helped us carry out our research, have contributed fresh ideas, and have done their own work on adaptive decision making. We wish to especially thank Eloise Coupey, Elizabeth Creyer, Scott Hawkins, Mary Frances Luce, David Schkade, Sankar Sen, and Itamar Simonson for their contributions to our research program.

Several secretaries at Duke University have been remarkably congenial in typing the manuscript. We thank Kathy Wheeley, Tammy Wills, and Anne Jenkins, all of whom performed magnificently in processing many drafts.

Support of the research reported in this book was provided by the Office of Naval Research; the National Science Foundation; our respective institutions, including the Isle Maligne Society of the Fuqua School of Business and a Joseph Wharton term chair at the University of Pennsylvania; and the Graduate School of Management, University of California, Irvine. Their backing is gratefully acknowledged.

We also wish to acknowledge the kind permission of the American Psychological Association, IEEE, Prentice-Hall, Harvard University Press, The Institute of Management Sciences, John Wiley and Sons, Ltd., and Academic Press to incorporate into this book portions of several of our prior publications.

Finally, each of us would like to make note of several very special sets of contributions to this book. John Payne expresses his deep appreciation to his wife Suzanne and his sons Alan and David for their love and support during the writing of this book. The family atmosphere they provided was, and continues to be, a great gift. Jim Bettman gives profound thanks to his wife Joan and his son David for their love, encouragement, and understanding throughout this program of research. Eric Johnson would like to express his gratitude to Deborah Mitchell, his wife, for sharing the stress of deadlines and the excitement of research.

1

Adaptive decision behavior: An introduction

> Human rational behavior is shaped by a scissors whose two blades are the structure of task environments and the computational capabilities of the actor.
>
> (Simon, 1990, p. 7)

Flexibility in decision making

One of the most fascinating aspects of human decision behavior is the flexibility with which individuals respond to a wide variety of task conditions. Preference judgments, assessments of uncertainty, and choices among alternative courses of action all can be affected by minor changes in the task environment. To illustrate, imagine that you are a senior member of the faculty of a psychology department at a private university. One of your responsibilities is to help in the hiring of new faculty. One day, the chairperson of your department drops the files of two job applicants on your desk. She would like to know which one of the two job applicants you would prefer to invite in for a job interview. The files contain information on each applicant's educational background, prior publication record, current research and teaching interests, and evaluations of prior teaching performance, among other information. How would you go about processing the information about the two applicants in order to make a choice? How would you solve the choice problem if one applicant seemed to offer more potential as a teacher whereas the other applicant offered more potential as a researcher and colleague?

Now imagine that you are in the same situation as just described, except that your chairperson puts the files of a dozen applicants on your desk. She still wants you to choose the single applicant you would most prefer to bring in for a job interview. Again, some applicants seem better on some dimensions (e.g., current research interests), whereas others seem better on other dimensions (e.g., prior teaching record). How would you go about processing the information about the dozen applicants in order to make a choice? Is your strategy for making the decision the same regardless of whether the number of alternatives is 2 or 12?

Much research suggests that your strategy for processing information will differ depending upon the number of alternatives to be considered. When faced with decision problems involving just two or three alternatives, people often use decision strategies that process all relevant information and require one to decide explicitly the extent to which one is willing to trade off less of one valued attribute or dimension (e.g., research potential) for more of another valued attribute (e.g., teaching potential). Such a decision process, involving the use of all relevant information and making explicit tradeoffs, is often associated with normative theories of preferential choice (see, e.g., Keeney & Raiffa, 1976).

When faced with more complex choice problems involving many alternatives, people often adopt simplifying (heuristic) strategies that are much more selective in the use of information. Further, the strategies adopted tend to be noncompensatory, in that excellent values on some attributes cannot compensate for poor values on other attributes. As an example, you might decide when faced with 12 applicants to eliminate from further consideration any applicant who has not had a research publication. Tversky (1972) refers to such a strategy as an elimination-by-aspects process.

The basic thesis of this book is that an individual's use of multiple decision strategies in different situations, including various simplifying methods or choice heuristics, is an adaptive response of a limited-capacity information processor to the demands of complex decision tasks. Further, we argue that the specific strategies used to solve particular decision problems are usually *intelligent* responses under the assumption that people have multiple goals for decisions, including both the desire to be accurate and the desire to conserve limited cognitive responses. Thus, we believe that how people decide how to decide is predictable when both the benefits and costs of specific decision strategies in particular task environments are taken into account and that people often select strategies that are appropriate to the circumstances.

Factors influencing contingent decision behavior

The two potential decision strategies described in the preceding example – that is, the use of explicit tradeoffs and the use of elimination rules – illustrate processing that is contingent on variations in the properties of the decision problem, such as the number of alternatives available. Throughout this book, our emphasis will be on the interaction of such properties of decision tasks and the limited processing capabilities of the decision maker in determining the strategies used and preferences we observe. This emphasis is consistent with the view expressed by Simon (1990) on the primacy of task and computational capabilities in determining human rational behavior.

However, factors other than properties of the decision task can also effect how a person decides how to solve a particular decision problem. For example, the reactions to a given problem can be moderated by a host of individual difference variables. Prior task knowledge and expertise in a problem domain represent two individual level factors, which can significantly affect how information is processed (Alba & Hutchinson, 1987; Chi, Glaser, & Farr, 1988). Shanteau (1988), for instance, argues that experts almost always follow some sort of divide-and-conquer process in which large problems are broken down into smaller parts, which are then solved, and then the partial solutions are put back together again. Individuals are also likely to differ with respect to the difficulty they experience with different types of reasoning operations (e.g., qualitative vs. quantitative). An example of a qualitative operation is determining whether an applicant has or has not had a prior research publication. An example of a more quantitative operation is determining how many additional publications would be needed to compensate for a poor prior teaching record.

Finally, decisions are generally not made in a social vacuum; rather, many social factors can influence decision making (Tetlock, 1985). For instance, even if an individual is making a decision, he or she may feel accountable to others such as family members or superiors in a business organization. Such feelings of accountability can affect how one makes a decision; Simonson (1989), for example, has shown that the need to justify a decision to others causes the choice to be more sensitive to certain aspects of the decision task.

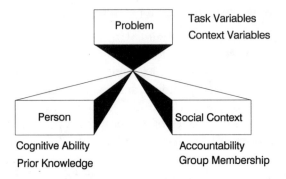

Figure 1.1. Contingent strategy selection.

Figure 1.1 illustrates the three major classes of factors that we believe influence which strategy is used to solve a particular decision problem: characteristics of the decision problem, characteristics of the person, and characteristics of the social context.

At a more detailed psychological level of analysis, these three major types of factors influencing strategy choice affect the availability, accessibility, processability, and perceived benefits of various decision strategies. For instance, prior knowledge, obtained either through experience or training, will determine which strategies are available to a decision maker in his or her memory. Experience in a decision domain also may impact the frequency and recency with which available strategies have been used, thus affecting the accessibility of various strategies. That is, experiences with strategies will affect the likelihood of recalling a particular strategy when a person faces a new decision problem. Characteristics of the problem, such as how information is displayed, can affect how much cognitive effort is needed to implement various strategies (processability). Finally, the characteristics of the social context can influence the relative importance of such factors as the justifiability of a decision in determining strategy selection.

The benefits and costs of contingent decision behavior

This brief discussion has stressed that decision behavior is contingent upon a variety of factors: Decision makers adapt to different situations. Perhaps this flexibility is not that surprising; there are potential benefits to adaptivity. At a macro level, the flexibility of early man (e.g., willingness to eat a variety of foods) may have played a major role in the survival of the species (Calvin, 1986). At a more micro level, the flexibility of organizations can determine their chances for success in a competitive and turbulent environment (Peters, 1987). Finally, at the individual level, flexibility of response (adaptivity) is generally viewed as a mark of intelligence. Specifically, Feldman and Lindell (1990) have emphasized that flexibility of response to decision tasks is a key to the survivability of an organism. Further, they argue that "irrationality observed in any given instance is evidence of the variation in behavior that must occur if adaptation to a given environment is to take place" (pp. 107–108). Thus, a particular decision error or bias, as indicated by a deviation between behavior and a normative model, may not really be an error from a long-run, adaptive point of view. Individuals may try different behaviors and observe the results as part of a process of learning about their environment and learning how to adapt to that environment over time.

Flexibility in response may have long-run value; however, it unfortunately can also lead to short-run errors in judgment. For instance, the use of noncompensatory processes in multialternative choice can lead to the elimination of potentially good alternatives early in the decision process. Another example of how flexibility in decision making can lead to difficulties is the now classic preference reversal phenomenon (Lichtenstein & Slovic, 1971). Common sense suggests that good decisions are consistent decisions, in that small changes in the way in which a question is asked should not change what we prefer. However, Sarah Lichtenstein and Paul Slovic (1971) showed more than 20 years ago that the expressed preference order between two gambles often reverses, contingent upon whether the response requested is a direct choice between the gambles or a bidding price for each gamble. That is, the same individual would choose gamble A over gamble B and would bid more for gamble B than for gamble A, a reversal in preference. Such reversals were even replicated in a Las Vegas casino setting (Lichtenstein & Slovic, 1973), where individuals could win or lose substantial amounts of their own money.

Tversky, Sattath, and Slovic (1988) have shown more recently that people's tradeoffs between attributes (e.g., lives vs. dollars) also are contingent on the nature of the response. The more prominent dimension (i.e., lives for most people) looms larger when the decision maker responds by making a choice as compared with when he or she responds by making a matching response, in which an aspect of one option is adjusted so that this option matches another option in overall value.[1] Hence, the tradeoff between lives and dollars is different for matching and choice. Tversky, Sattath, and Slovic suggest that choice tends to elicit qualitative types of reasoning strategies that focus on the most important attribute, whereas matching tasks elicit more quantitative types of reasoning.

If one's preferences or beliefs are affected by subtle changes in the presentation of information or changes in the way questions are asked, decision makers may be vulnerable to strategic manipulation by others. Tversky and Sattath (1979), for example, discuss how placing constraints on the order in which elements of a choice set are considered by an individual (i.e., an agenda) can affect the preference order of that individual. Thus, the flexible use of cognitive processes to make decisions, contingent on task factors, has both benefits and costs for the individual.

The highly contingent nature of decision behavior also poses problems (costs) and creates opportunities (benefits) for decision researchers. At a theoretical level, the fact that decision processes are not invariant across task environments complicates the search for a small set of underlying principles that can describe observed behavior. The research question becomes not what is *the* cognitive process used to make decisions, but instead *when* are different decision processes most likely to be used. More specifically, the cognitive control or metacognitive question of how one decides how to decide becomes crucial. This question is a major focus of our book.

The importance and pervasiveness of task and context effects also may create a view of decision research as a fragmented and chaotic field. As one answer to that problem, Hogarth and Einhorn (1992) suggest focusing on the effects of task variables on simple psychological processes like the sequential processing of information. They

---

[1] To illustrate a matching response, imagine that you are asked to consider the following two programs for dealing with traffic accidents, described in terms of yearly costs (in millions of dollars) and the number of casualties per year: Program X is expected to lead to 570 casualties and cost $12 million, while program Y is expected to lead to 500 casualties and cost $??. Your task is to provide a value for the cost of program Y, presumably some amount greater than $12 million, that would make it equal in overall value to program X.

believe that a wide range of judgmental effects can be explained in terms of the interaction of task variables with simple information-processing strategies. We agree with Hogarth and Einhorn's emphasis on the effects of task variables on decision strategies.

The contingent nature of decision behavior has important implications at a more applied level as well. The lack of invariance across tasks that are seemingly similar (e.g., choice vs. bidding for the same lotteries) calls into question the validity of the judgmental inputs needed to operationalize such decision-aiding techniques as decision analysis (Watson & Buede, 1987). On the other hand, as noted by Tversky (1988b), it could be argued that the evidence of contingent decision processes shows that people may greatly benefit from various decision aids. He suggests that rather than abandoning decision analysis, we try to make it more responsive to the complexities and limitations of the human mind.

Because individuals adjust their decision strategies depending upon the decision task, decisions can sometimes be improved by rather straightforward, inexpensive changes to the information environments within which individuals make judgments and choices. For example, in the 1970s the provision of unit price information in supermarkets was promoted as a way of increasing consumer welfare. However, several studies showed that people were either not aware of the unit price information or were not using it. Jay Russo (1977) argued that people would like to compare alternatives directly on important attributes like unit prices; however, he also argued that it was difficult for most consumers to process unit price information because of the way in which the information was displayed. Each unit price typically was available only under each item on a shelf. Russo then argued that people would tend to ignore unit price information that was not easy to process. Thus, making information available was not sufficient to change consumer behavior; the available information also had to be processable. Russo demonstrated the power of this argument by showing that consumers' actual purchase decisions could be altered by making a simple change in the format used to present unit price information – putting all the available information on unit prices together in an easy-to-read list with unit prices ranked from lowest to highest. An important area of public policy that is currently greatly concerned with information provision issues is the communication of risk information to people about such hazards as radon levels in homes.

More generally, Arkes (1991) argues that efforts to improve (debias) intuitive judgments can be facilitated by considering the costs and benefits of various cognitive processes underlying those judgments.

Finally, the contingent nature of decision behavior has important implications for those whose job it is to measure and predict preferences. Market researchers, for example, have begun to wonder how robust their methods are to changes in decision tasks and contexts (Green & Srinivasan, 1990). More generally, recent decision research argues that preferences for objects of any complexity are often constructed – not merely revealed – in the generation of a response to a judgment or choice task (Slovic, Griffin, & Tversky, 1990). Thus, the preferences that are measured, in at least some situations, may reflect labile values, that is, values that depend on how the questions are asked.

The idea of constructive preferences means more than simply that observed choices and judgments are not the result of a reference to a master list of values in memory. Hand in hand with the notion of constructive preferences is the idea that preferences also are not necessarily generated by some consistent and task-invariant algorithm such as expected value calculation[2] (Tversky, Sattath, & Slovic, 1988). Instead, it appears that decision makers have a repertoire of methods for identifying their preferences. March (1978) attributes the constructiveness of preferences to limits on the information-processing capacity of individuals. In his words, "human beings have unstable, inconsistent, incompletely evoked, and imprecise goals at least in part because human abilities limit preference orderliness" (March, 1978, p. 598). A key research question is to understand what elements of the judgment or choice task cause different methods to be used in construction of the observed preferences.[3]

---

[2] The expected value algorithm involves the multiplication of the value (payoff) of each outcome that might occur if a particular course of action is selected by its associated probability of occurrence, adding the payoff-probability products across all the outcomes of an alternative course of action. The expected value decision rule is to select that alternative course of action with the largest expected value. As a strategy for making decisions, the expected value rule has been in existence for at least several centuries.

[3] The notion of constructed preferences is consistent with the "philosophy of basic values," which holds that people lack well-differentiated values for all but the most familiar of evaluation tasks (Fischhoff, 1991). Fischhoff draws an interesting comparison between the philosophy of basic values and the "philosophy of articulated values," which assumes that people have values for all (most) evaluation questions and that the trick is just to ask the right question in the right way.

Overview of a framework for adaptive decision behavior

Given the extensive evidence that human decision behavior is a highly contingent form of information processing, there is a need for a framework within which such contingent behavior might be understood. A major purpose of this book is to offer such a framework. We are concerned with the task conditions and psychological mechanisms that lead to the selection of one cognitive process rather than another in solving a particular decision problem. The theoretical framework we offer allows us to answer the question of when different strategies will be used by a decision maker; we also provide evidence for that framework.

As noted earlier, our basic thesis is that the use of various decision strategies is an adaptive response of a limited-capacity information processor to the demands of complex task environments. In particular, we emphasize understanding adaptive strategy use in terms of the accuracy of and the cognitive effort required by various available strategies. That is, we believe that the two primary considerations underlying contingent decision behavior are the desire to achieve a good decision and the desire to minimize the cognitive effort needed to reach a decision. Although we believe that decision processing generally reflects reasonable effort and accuracy trade-offs, there are also important constraints on human adaptivity in decision making. People do make errors in judgments and choices. Thus two additional focuses of the book are limits on adaptivity in decision making and how decision making might be improved.

Decision strategies and problem solving

We have used the term *decision strategy* a number of times already without offering a specific definition. Within our framework, we define a decision strategy as a sequence of mental and effector (actions on the environment) operations used to transform an initial state of knowledge into a final goal state of knowledge where the decision maker views the particular decision problem as solved. For example, the cognitive operations used to transform knowledge states might include such operations as acquiring an item of information from the external environment or comparing two quantities to determine which is larger.

Included in the initial state of knowledge are facts about the problem. For example, in the decision problem posed at the beginning of the chapter, there are a dozen job candidates available, there are uncertainties to be considered, and there is information available about how well the alternative job candidates meet various objectives, such as good teaching and good research performance. The initial state of knowledge will also include general goal statements regarding the task, such as "choose the most preferred candidate to invite for a job interview." Of course, sometimes the initial problem state is not that well defined, and the decision maker is faced with the need to set up subgoals and evoke processes to accomplish such subtasks as the generation of new alternatives.

As the decision maker applies operators to states of knowledge, new intermediate states of knowledge about the decision problem are generated. The decision maker might learn, for instance, that the first several faculty job candidates have no prior teaching experience. As another example, after applying a set of elimination operators to the faculty hiring problem described earlier, one might reach an intermediate state of knowledge in which the original problem is transformed into a choice among only a few candidates who have prior publication records. Note that this view of decision processing argues that the problem situation is constantly being redefined by the decision maker. After the application of additional operators, an intermediate state of knowledge could be transformed into the final goal state, in which the preferred alternative has been identified.

One distinction between decision making and other types of problem-solving tasks is that decision problems are generally ill-defined about exactly how the final goal state is to be characterized. For example, at the beginning of the problem of selecting among job candidates, you may not have a good sense of how much you are prepared to trade off research potential for teaching potential, or even if such tradeoffs are required. Thus, your task of identifying which candidate best meets the goal state requires, in part, that the goal state be clarified during the decision process. Hogarth (1987) argues that people often prefer not to directly confront the conflict of trading off more of one valued attribute for less of another valued attribute, which is inherent in many decision problems. Thus, he argues that people may sometimes use noncompensatory decision strategies to solve even simple decision problems as a way to avoid conflict. Hogarth's argument points out that accuracy and effort considerations may not be the only determinants of strategy choice;

we agree. However, we believe that accuracy and effort are the *primary* determinants of contingent strategy use.

The view of decision making as the application of a series of operators to knowledge states is not unique to us. A similar conception of decision processing, for example, is offered by O. Huber (1989). More generally, our view of decision strategies is closely related to views of problem solving as the application of a sequence of mental operators (see, e.g., Newell & Simon, 1972; Holland, Holyoak, Nisbett, & Thagard, 1986).

For some decision problems, the strategy used to solve the problem will be a simple memory retrieval process. As an example, when asked the question, What is your favorite college basketball team? the answer – Duke – is drawn readily from the memories of the first two authors of this book. This type of strategy for solving decision problems is called affect referral (P. Wright, 1975). No information is processed about the characteristics of the alternatives being considered; instead, the answer is simply based on prior evaluations of the alternatives. This book is concerned, however, with the strategies people use to solve decision problems for which affect referral does not provide an acceptable solution. That is, we are interested in decision behavior when a person is faced with a decision problem of some novelty and complexity. We also assume that more than one sequence of operators (strategies) is available to the decision maker for decision problems of any complexity.

We assume further that the operators used to transform knowledge states in decision making can be represented as productions of the form IF (condition 1, . . . , condition n) THEN (action 1, . . . , action m). An example of a production might be "If there are more than four alternatives, then eliminate those alternatives that cost more than some target amount, say $100." The conditions can include goals and subgoals (e.g., If the goal is to please the chairperson then . . .) as well as information on problem states. The presence of goals and subgoals in the condition side of productions provides the basis for a hierarchical structure to decision behavior. Further, as acknowledged by J. Anderson (1983), the setting of goals can be used to favor special modes of processing, such as efficiency. The actions can include actions on the environment (e.g., then eliminate alternative X) and the creation of new knowledge states (e.g., then alternative Y is better on the cost attribute than alternative Z). Satisfaction of the conditions depends on the match between the conditions and active information in a person's working memory. Like Holland et al. (1986) and others, we assume that active information may come directly from perceptual input, from the previous actions of other operators, or from a more permanent memory store.

This idea that the conditions of operators are matched against active information in working memory, coupled with the notion expressed previously that the problem situation is constantly being redefined by the decision maker, usually implies that decision making is very sequential and dynamic. That is, which operations a person performs next in solving a decision problem will depend on the information active in memory as the result of the actions of prior mental operations. Further, given that working memory has limited capacity, the information in working memory will likely reflect the most recently performed operations. As a result, the preferences we observe will depend on the particular sequence of operations used to solve a decision problem, and the performance of some operation at time t may inhibit or facilitate the performance of another operation at time $t+1$. Kahneman and Tversky (1979b) make a related point, arguing that the order in which simplifying procedures (what they call "editing operations") are applied to a risky choice problem may permit or prevent the later application of other editing operations. As noted by Kahneman and Tversky, the sequence of operations is likely to vary as a function of variables like information display and the particular set of alternatives in the choice set. Thus, the preference order among alternatives need not be invariant across contexts.

Cognitive effort and accuracy

We also believe that the operators used in performing the types of decision tasks in which we are interested take cognitive resources to execute and that different operators may require different amounts of cognitive resources. For example, working memory limitations may often make certain kinds of cognitive processes (e.g., the mental multiplication of large numbers) very difficult to perform. There may also be circumstances in which some operators may not be feasible given the constraints of the human information-processing system. Because cognitive resources are needed to implement individual mental operations, increasing the number of operators or using more demanding operators to reach the goal state creates a more effortful decision process. All else being equal (e.g., for a given level of accuracy), a key assumption of our framework for understanding contingent decision behavior is that people are motivated to use as little effort as necessary to solve a problem. Often people seem to behave according to Zipf's (1949) principle of least effort, in which a strategy is selected that ensures that the minimum effort will be involved in reaching a specific desired result.

Finally, we assume that different strategies are characterized by differing levels of accuracy. That is, a strategy that eliminates some alternatives on the basis of just one piece of information, such as prior publication record, may result in an alternative that would in fact have been a more preferred option not being chosen. A strategy that examines all the information, on the other hand, might more accurately reflect the decision maker's preferences. All else being equal (e.g., given a desired effort level), our assumption is that a decision maker wants to maximize his or her chances of making the most accurate judgment or choice.

The fundamental assumption of our framework is that individuals decide how to decide by considering both the cognitive effort and the accuracy of various strategies. Individuals try to find strategies that will yield high degrees of accuracy for reasonable amounts of effort in any given decision task. Often, however, individuals must make tradeoffs between accuracy and effort in selecting a strategy. Our view is that the relative accuracy and effort levels of various strategies change with task demands; therefore, individuals must be flexible in strategy use across tasks. In later chapters we characterize strategies in terms of their accuracy and effort levels, using these results to predict which strategies are more likely to be used for a given task.

A key issue within an accuracy–effort framework is to under-stand the factors that influence the relative weight placed on accuracy versus effort. Increasing the importance (payoffs) of a decision is generally expected to increase the amount of effort you put into a decision. That is, one would be expected to work harder. However, would one also work smarter in the sense of shifting decision strategies toward ones that reduce the chance of decision errors? We see at least three ways in which a decision maker may adapt his or her behavior to changes in the importance of a decision task: (1) the decision maker may do more of what he or she is already doing; (2) the decision maker might change some parameter of the

Table 1.1. *Major assumptions of our framework for adaptive decision making*

Decision strategies are sequences of mental operations that can be usefully represented as productions of the form IF (condition 1,..., condition n) THEN (action 1,..., action m).

The cognitive effort needed to reach a decision using a particular strategy is a function of the number and the type of operators (productions) used by that strategy, with the relative effort levels of various strategies contingent upon task environments.

Different strategies are characterized by different levels of accuracy, with the relative accuracy levels of various strategies contingent upon task environments.

As a result of prior experiences and training, a decision maker is assumed to have more than one strategy (sequence of operations) available to solve a decision problem of any complexity.

Individuals decide how to decide primarily by considering both the cognitive effort and the accuracy of various strategies.

Additional considerations, such as the need to justify a decision to others or the need to minimize the conflict inherent in a decision problem, may also impact strategy selection.

The decision of how to decide is sometimes a conscious choice and sometimes a learned contingency between elements of the task and the relative effort and accuracy of decision strategies.

Strategy selection is generally adaptive and intelligent, if not optimal.

current decision strategy (e.g., increase the cutoff levels for the number of prior publications required to be considered for a faculty position); and/or (3) the decision maker may change from a selective, noncompensatory decision strategy to a more compensatory process. We believe that increased incentives will generally lead to greater effort but not necessarily to the increased use of more optimal (reduced error) decision strategies. More discussion of incentive effects can be found in chapters 3 and 6.

We believe that the decision about how to decide is sometimes a conscious choice. Often, however, the selection of strategies may reflect learned contingencies between elements of a decision task (e.g., the number of alternatives available) and the accuracy and effort of particular strategies (e.g., elimination-by-aspects). Thus, the concept of contingent strategy use often does not require the assumption of a conscious decision about how to decide.

Finally, as suggested earlier, other considerations beyond accuracy and effort may also be relevant in strategy selection. For example, in some circumstances minimizing conflict or justifying the decision to others may be of primary importance.

Obviously, we have only briefly outlined our framework; more details are presented in chapters 3 and 4. Table 1.1 summarizes the major points of our theoretical perspective.

Because much of human behavior appears to be contingent, we hope that the framework for understanding adaptive decision behavior presented in this book will be of value to those researchers in psychology and other areas who are trying to understand these contingencies in human behavior. We briefly consider such related research on contingent processing in the next section.

Research on contingent behavior in other areas of psychology

As noted already, our approach is closely related to research on human problem solving (Newell & Simon, 1972). Beyond this general relationship between our approach to understanding decision behavior and problem-solving research, however, we see relationships to a number of other more specific topics in psychology where the issue of contingent behavior has arisen. For example, Reder (1987) argues that people use contingent strategies for question answering. One strategy, direct retrieval, attempts to find the answer in memory; another, the plausibility strategy, attempts to compute a plausible answer given facts in memory. According to Reder, the more familiar the words in the question, the more likely one is to try direct retrieval.

Siegler (1988) has investigated contingent strategy selection in children's arithmetic, although, unlike our approach, he argues that such contingent processing is not necessarily governed by explicit consideration of alternative strategies and their characteristics. He argues that in some situations children will use retrieval strategies and in others they will resort to more effortful counting or calculating approaches. This contingency is dependent upon the associative strength in memory between a potential answer and the stated problem. More specifically, Siegler argues that a retrieval strategy will always be tried first; more effortful backup strategies like counting are used only if the retrieval strategy involves more than some predetermined maximum number of retrieval efforts or does not produce an answer that exceeds some confidence criterion.

Contingent processing notions also appear in social psychology. For example, Petty and Cacioppo (1986) have proposed the elaboration likelihood model (ELM) of attitude change. The elaboration likelihood of a communication situation is a function of the motivation and ability of the communication recipients. If conditions are such that people are motivated and able to process the communication message, the elaboration likelihood is high, and recipients will scrutinize and process message arguments (the central route to persuasion). On the other hand, when elaboration likelihood is low due to lack of motivation and/or lack of ability to process, recipients will form attitudes based not on processing of message arguments but on processing of simple cues associated with the message, such as the source (the peripheral route to persuasion). The ELM view of attitude change processes implies, at least implicitly, a concern with both accuracy and effort.

As another example, Fiske (1982; Fiske & Pavelchak, 1986) has proposed that individuals may evaluate stimuli in two basic modes. In piecemeal processing, the evaluation of a stimulus is based upon combination of the evaluations of the individual elements or attributes of that stimulus. In category-based processing, if a stimulus is successfully categorized in an existing category, the evaluation associated with that category is associated with the stimulus. Fiske and Pavelchak hypothesize a two-stage process. If the first categorization stage succeeds, then category-based evaluation processing ensues. If categorization fails, piecemeal processing is invoked. This categorization approach has been examined by Sujan (1985) in a consumer setting. Sujan shows that when the information in a print advertisement matches expectations, there is evidence of category-based processing; when the information does not match expectations, there is evidence for piecemeal processing. These effects are more pronounced for experts than for novices. Thus, there is some very interesting evidence that prior knowledge can affect contingent processing.

Those examples certainly do not exhaust the other areas in which contingent processing has been investigated. However, they do demonstrate that contingent use of strategies is a widespread phenomenon. As noted, we hope that the ideas and methods we present for understanding the contingent use of strategies in decision making can contribute to insights into contingent processing in these other areas of psychology.

Finally, as evidenced by the following recent quote from an economist, we also believe that an understanding of the contingent use of strategies may prove useful to investigators in disciplines other than psychology as well:

It may be that any attempt to find a single unified model of individual decision making under risk and uncertainty will fail *simply because no such model actually exists.* Given that there are a number of alternative decision models that can claim to represent rational behavior, at the very least we should not rule out the possibility that different individuals have learned to handle risk and uncertainty in different ways, so that no single model can accommodate them all.

But there is an even more radical possibility, namely that the *same* individual may use different models to deal with different problems. The idea here is that human beings learn how to handle (and perhaps mishandle) risky decisions of various kinds not by introspecting about axioms but as a result of the piecemeal experience of having to deal with different types of problems encountered at different times. When presented with a fresh problem, they may recall the type(s) of problem from their previous experience that most resemble the one that now confronts them and apply whatever approach they considered successful (or at least satisfactory). (Loomes, 1991, p. 105).

As discussed earlier and documented extensively in the next chapter, the data are now clear: The *same* individual *will* use different models (strategies or methods) to deal with different problems. Thus, understanding the basis of adaptive strategy use is crucial to understanding human decision behavior in many arenas.

The organization of the book

The rest of this book is organized as follows: In chapter 2, we characterize a number of the strategies that people use when making choices and judgments, identify some of the important features of the decision task environment that have been shown to influence how people process information when making judgments and choices, and briefly examine constraints on the information-processing abilities of decision makers. Then we review research showing how task properties and processing limitations interact to produce contingent decision behavior.

Next, we present our framework for understanding when a particular decision strategy is likely to be selected by an individual (chapter 3). As noted, the heart of that framework is the idea that the use of multiple strategies for decision making may often be an adaptive way for an individual to balance the need to make a good decision (accuracy) with the need to minimize the cognitive effort involved in the decision process. We also consider, however, how other factors such as the avoidance of conflict (Hogarth, 1987) may impact strategy use. In chapter 3 we also consider how to measure cognitive effort and accuracy, evidence for our proposed measure of effort, the nature of effort–accuracy tradeoffs, and the relationship of our framework to others concerned with contingencies in decision behavior.

We then describe several tests of our framework, using a unique combination of several techniques for studying decision behavior (chapter 4). We show, for example, how the use of production system representations of decision strategies and Monte Carlo computer simulation techniques can be used to characterize the effort and accuracy (or error) levels of various strategies in different types of decision environments. Using the simulation results as a guide for generating hypotheses, we describe several empirical tests of the effort–accuracy framework. For example, we examine whether people use decision strategies in environments with time pressure in ways that seem to make sense in terms of the effort and accuracy levels characterizing those strategies. In describing these tests, we outline various innovative empirical methodologies for studying decision processes at the level of detail necessary for examining strategy selection. Chapters 3 and 4 present the core of our approach to understanding contingent decision behavior.

In the next portion of the book, we examine several extensions to the basic framework. In chapter 5, we explore how individuals may construct strategies on the spot instead of selecting strategies a priori. The idea is that individuals often process opportunistically and will change their processing on the spur of moment, depending upon the information they encounter. We argue, however, that such opportunistic information processing still involves accuracy–effort tradeoffs. Included in chapter 5 is a discussion of how people may restructure decision problems in order to reduce effort and improve accuracy. The question of how adaptivity in decision making might fail is addressed in chapter 6. We explore failures in adaptivity due to deficits in the knowledge of strategies, in the knowledge of task structures, and in the ability to execute strategies.

In chapter 7, we consider how understanding strategy selection in contingent judgment and choice behavior might be used to improve human decisions. Some of the applied implications of the adaptive nature of human decision behavior for the design of information environments, the practice of decision analysis, the design of man–model decision systems, and the measurement of values are outlined. Finally, chapter 8 provides a summary of where we think our framework has succeeded, where we see it as needing extensions, and proposals for further research on adaptive decision making.

2

Contingencies in decision making

Introduction

By now, our basic premise is apparent: Individuals display a great deal of flexibility in making decisions. In their highly influential review of behavioral decision theory, Einhorn and Hogarth (1981) noted that "the most important empirical results in the period under review have shown the sensitivity of judgment and choice to seemingly minor changes in tasks" (p. 61). More than a decade of research since Einhorn and Hogarth's review has strongly reaffirmed that information processing in decision making, as in other areas of cognition, is highly contingent on the demands of the task. The same individual will use many different kinds of strategies in making a decision, contingent upon such factors as how information is displayed, the nature of the response, and the complexity of the problem. This chapter has two purposes. First, we briefly define a number of decision strategies that have been proposed to describe judgment and choice. Second, we review the research showing the impact of different task and context variables on the use of decision strategies by an individual.

Before we review the literature, several aspects of our point of view need to be made explicit. First, in order to keep the scope of the chapter manageable, we focus on preferential decisions; inferences and forecasts receive much more limited attention. Preferential decision problems are typically described using three basic components: (1) the alternatives available to the decision maker; (2) events or contingencies that relate actions to outcomes, as well as the associated probabilities of those events; and (3) the values associated with the outcomes. Values are often based on multiple objectives, such as maximizing safety and minimizing cost. These informational elements, along with a goal statement (such as "choose the preferred alternative"), represent the task environment presented to a decision maker. Outside the laboratory, decision problems often are not presented in a completed form. For example, alternatives may not be given but may have to be generated (Keller & Ho, 1988; Gettys, Pliske, Manning, & Casey, 1987). Nevertheless, it remains useful to define decision problems in terms of these three basic components of alternatives, uncertainties, and values.

The decision maker's internal representation of the task environment is the individual's problem space (or set of knowledge states) (Newell & Simon, 1972). A typical example of a decision problem is the selection of an automobile. Each car is characterized by different mileage, attractiveness, safety record, passenger capacity, and so forth. The values of some of these attributes may be known with reasonable certainty (e.g., a specific car's engine size). However, the value of other attributes is uncertain, such as the reliability or durability of a newly introduced car. Of course, the individual's representation will generally be selective and will not include all features of the car. Another example is the choice among two simple lotteries or gambles. Each lottery is defined by a probability of winning or losing and a specified amount to be won or lost.

When presented to subjects, such preferential choice problems are usually "well structured" (Langley, Simon, Bradshaw, & Zytkow, 1987). That is, subjects are typically given a specified set of alternatives and a set of attribute values to be used in solving the problem. It is important to note, however, that preferential problems often have elements that make their solution difficult. For example, conflict is typically present, in the sense that no one option is best on all attributes of value, and conflict has long been recognized as a major source of decision difficulty (Shepard, 1964). The task also may be unfamiliar in the sense that a rule for resolving the conflict cannot readily be drawn from memory. Thus, solving decision problems often is not the kind of "recognize and calculate" process associated with expertise in a task domain (Chi et al., 1988). This is true even for the simplest laboratory decision tasks. Rather, decision making is often characterized by *tentativeness, search,* and the *use of relatively "weak" methods (heuristics)* that are more representative of novicelike problem solving (Langley et al., 1987).

A second aspect of our viewpoint concerns the terms *task effects* and *context effects,* which have often been used interchangeably in the literature. For the purposes of this book, we distinguish between the two. Task effects describe those factors associated with the general structural characteristics of the decision problem, including response mode, number of alternatives, number of outcomes or attributes, time pressure, information display mode, and agenda constraints. Context effects refer to those factors associated with the particular values of the objects in the specific decision set under consideration, including similarity and the overall attractiveness of alternatives. In general, the values of context factors are more dependent on individual perceptions than the values of task factors.

Finally, we view decision making as consisting of such interrelated subprocesses as information acquisition, evaluation of information, and the expression of a decision. The literature review focuses on those task and context influences that result in (1) a change in the salience and use of information in the environment, and/or (2) a change in the processes used to combine information into a judgment or choice.[1] For example, a change in response mode may result in the same evaluation (combination) strategy being used but with attention focused on different information. Alternatively, the change in response mode may result in the use of a different evaluation process. Thus, observed contingent decisions may result from the effect of a task or context variable on the acquisition (salience) of the information used or on the strategy used to combine the information or both. Mellers, Ordóñez, and Birnbaum (1992) have recently emphasized a similar distinction between the encoding (salience) of information and the integration (evaluation) of multiple items of information in their examination of preference reversals (see the section on response mode effects in this chapter).

Decision strategies

Before considering how individuals flexibly use various strategies in response to different decision tasks, we outline some of the more

---

[1] Goldstein and Busemeyer (1992) have suggested that rather than affecting either the encoding or combination of attribute information, task and context factors impact the criterion used by a decision maker to decide whether the evidence in favor of one alternative or another is sufficient to warrant an expressed preference. Although we do not doubt that the use of a criterion for deciding is sometimes part of the decision-making process, we feel that the evidence presented here is overwhelmingly supportive of the use of multiple decision strategies rather than use of a single criterion-dependent strategy. Further discussion of this point can be found in chapter 3.

common strategies used. A variety of such decision-making strategies has been identified, and descriptions of some of these strategies and their properties are given here. Each strategy can be thought of as a method (a sequence of operations) for searching through the decision problem space. That search may reflect information about such aspects as the relative importance of an attribute – weight or salience (e.g., safety is more important that comfort); cutoff values specifying a minimal acceptable level for attributes (e.g., the gas mileage cannot be less than 20 miles per gallon); and differential preferences across attribute levels (e.g., a loss of $10 hurts worse than the pleasure of a gain of $10). Search is often selective, and different strategies limit the amount or type of information processed in various ways.

Before examining the specific strategies, however, some general aspects of decision processes need to be addressed. First, as noted earlier, decision problems often involve conflict among values, because no one option best meets all of our objectives. Some of the decision strategies used by people can be thought of as conflict confronting and others as conflict avoiding (Hogarth, 1987). That is, some decision processes confront and resolve conflict by considering the extent to which one is willing to trade off more of one valued attribute (e.g., economy) for less of another valued attribute (e.g., safety). Other strategies do not as explicitly confront and resolve tradeoffs among valued attributes. Second, particular evaluation strategies can either be used alone or in combination with other strategies. Some typical combinations are discussed after the individual strategies have been presented. Third, strategies can be either constructed on the spot or their use could be planned a priori (see chapter 5 for further details). For example, Bettman (1979, p. 33) has suggested that "choice heuristics may not be stored in their entirety in memory, but may exist only as fragments – subparts which are put together constructively at the time of making a decision." Fourth, strategies differ in both how effortful they are to use and how accurate they are likely to be (see chapter 3). For example, a heuristic that only considered information on one attribute (e.g., the lexicographic heuristic) might be less effortful and less accurate for some types of decisions than a heuristic that examined a larger proportion of the available information.

Descriptions of choice processes

The weighted additive (WADD) rule. The weighted additive rule considers the values of each alternative on *all* the relevant attributes and considers *all* the relative importances or weights of the attributes to the decision maker. Further, the conflict among values is assumed to be confronted and resolved by explicitly considering the extent to which one is willing to trade off attribute values, as reflected by the relative importances or weights. A rule like WADD involves substantial computational processing of the information. The WADD rule develops an overall evaluation of an alternative by multiplying the weight times the attribute value for each attribute and summing these weighted attribute values over all attributes. It is assumed that the alternative with the highest overall evaluation is chosen. Given that the weighted additive rule processes all of the relevant problem information and resolves conflicting values explicitly by considering tradeoffs, the WADD rule (or some variant of it) is often viewed as a normative procedure for dealing with preferential decision problems of the type considered in this book (see, e.g., Keeney & Raiffa, 1976).

Exactly how people think of "weights" within the context of the WADD rule is the subject of investigation. There is some evidence that weights are sometimes local in interpretation, in that the relative weights reflect the ranges of attribute values across the alternatives in the choice set – that is, the greater the range, the greater the importance of the attribute (Goldstein, 1990). At other times, the weight given to an attribute seems to be interpreted by subjects more globally, for example, safety might always be viewed as much more important than costs, without much consideration of local ranges of values (Beattie & Baron, 1991). Another issue related to weights is whether the influence of the weights on preferences reflects an adding or averaging process. In an averaging model, the weights are constrained to sum to one; that is, they are normalized (see Stevenson, Busemeyer, & Naylor, 1990, for a discussion of adding vs. averaging models).

Two strategies related to the WADD rule may be used in making decisions under risk, the expected value and expected utility rules. The expected value rule involves multiplying the value (i.e., monetary amount) of each possible outcome of a lottery by its probability of occurrence. These products of the values and probabilities are then summed over the outcomes to arrive at the expected value of the lottery. This multiplying and summing process is assumed to be repeated for all the lotteries in a choice set. It is further assumed that the lottery or gamble with the highest EV will be chosen. The expected utility rule differs from the EV rule in that the utility of each outcome is substituted for its monetary value. This valuation (utility assessment) aspect of the EU rule expands the domain to which the EU rule applies beyond monetary gambles; it may also require additional processing effort. However, the general processing assumptions of both models are very similar.

The EV rule, and especially the EU role, are also viewed as normative rules for choice. Thus, in the literature one can see the EV and EU rules used as both proposed descriptions of actual behavior and as normative prescriptions for behavior. However, while people sometimes make decisions in ways consistent with procedures like the WADD, EV, and EU rules, more often people appear to make decisions using simpler choice processes (heuristics). Some of the more common choice heuristics are described in this chapter. Each heuristic represents a different method for simplifying search through the decision problem space by limiting the amount of information processed and/or making how information is processed easier.

The equal weight (EQW) heuristic. This processing strategy examines all the alternatives and all the attribute values for each alternative. However, the equal weight strategy simplifies decision making by ignoring information about the relative importance or probability of each attribute. An overall value for each alternative is obtained by simply summing the values for each attribute for that alternative. This assumes that the attribute values are expressed, or can be expressed, on a common scale of value. Hence this heuristic is a special case of the weighted additive rule. The equal weight rule has been advocated as a highly accurate simplification of the decision-making process (Dawes, 1979; Einhorn & Hogarth, 1975). A variation of this rule that has been advocated for use in risky choice is the equiprobable procedure, in which probability information is ignored and the alternative with the highest average payoff selected (Thorngate, 1980). O. Huber (1989) references empirical work documenting the use of an equal weight heuristic in risky choice.

The satisficing (SAT) heuristic. Satisficing is one of the oldest heuristics identified in the decision-making literature (Simon, 1955). With this strategy, alternatives are considered one at a time, in the order they occur in the set. This heuristic compares the value of each attribute of an alternative to a predefined cutoff level, often thought of as an aspiration level. If any attribute value is below the cutoff, then that alternative is rejected. The first alternative that has values that meet the cutoffs for all attributes is chosen. If no alternatives pass all the cutoffs, the cutoffs can be relaxed and the process repeated, or an alternative can be randomly selected. An implication of the satisficing heuristic is that choice will be a function of the order in which a decision maker evaluates alternatives. That is, if alternative A and alternative B both pass the cutoffs, then whether A or B is chosen will depend on whether A or B is evaluated first. There will be no comparison of the relative merit of alternative A as compared with alternative B. A variation of this procedure is the conjunctive model proposed by Coombs (1964), Dawes (1964), and Einhorn (1970).

The lexicographic (LEX) heuristic. The lexicographic procedure determines the most important attribute and then examines the values of all alternatives on that attribute. The alternative with the best value on the most important attribute is selected. If two alternatives have tied values, the second most important attribute is considered, and so on, until the tie is broken. For example, a consumer may always buy the cheapest brand. Sometimes the LEX strategy includes the notion of a just-noticeable difference (JND). If several alternatives are within a JND of the best alternative on the most important attribute (or any attributes considered subsequently), they are considered to be tied (Tversky, 1969). This version of the LEX rule is sometimes called lexicographic-semiorder (LEXSEMI).

A consequence of using a lexicographic-semiorder decision rule is that a person may exhibit intransitivities in preferences in which $X > Y$, $Y > Z$, and $Z > X$. The following example decision problem, adapted from Fishburn (1991), illustrates that potential. Professor P is about to change jobs. She knows that if two offers are far apart on salary (e.g., more than $10,000 apart), then salary will be the determining factor in her choice. Otherwise, the prestige of the university will be dominant. She eventually receives three offers, described in part as follows:

	Salary	Prestige
X	$65,000	Low
Y	$50,000	High
Z	$58,000	Medium

She prefers X to Y on the basis of the better salary of X. Because Y and Z are less than $10,000 apart in salary, she prefers Y to Z on the basis of the greater prestige. She also prefers Z to X on the basis of prestige. Thus, $X > Y$, $Y > Z$, and $Z > X$, an intransitive pattern of preferences. The general assumption is that rationality in choice requires transitivity in preferences, although Fishburn (1991) presents some arguments why it may be reasonable for people to sometimes violate transitivity.

The elimination-by-aspects (EBA) heuristic. First described by Tversky (1972), an EBA choice strategy begins with determination of the most important attribute (Tversky actually assumed that the attribute is selected probabilistically, with the probability that an attribute is selected being a function of its weight or importance). Then, the cutoff value for that attribute is retrieved, and all alternatives with values for that attribute below the cutoff are eliminated. One can interpret this process as rejecting or eliminating alternatives that do not possess an "aspect"; the "aspect" is defined as having a value on the selected attribute that is greater than or equal to the cutoff level. The EBA process continues with the second most important attribute, then the third, and so on, until one alternative remains. Note that while an EBA process violates the idea that one should use all relevant information in making a decision, it does reflect rationality in the ordered use of the attributes. This "partial" rationality in processing characterizes most choice heuristics.

The majority of confirming dimensions (MCD) heuristic. Described by Russo and Dosher (1983), the MCD heuristic involves processing pairs of alternatives. The values for each of the two alternatives are compared on each attribute, and the alternative with a majority of winning (better) attribute values is retained. The retained alternative is then compared with the next alternative among the set of alternatives. The process of pairwise comparison repeats until all alternatives have been evaluated and the final winning alternative has been identified.

The MCD heuristic is a simplified version of a more general model of choice called the additive difference (ADDIF) model (Tversky, 1969). In that processing strategy, the alternatives are compared directly on each dimension, and the difference between the subjective values of the two alternatives on that dimension is determined. Then a weighting function is applied to each difference and the results are summed over all dimensions to obtain an overall relative evaluation of the two alternatives. Under some conditions, the additive difference rule and the WADD rule will produce identical preference orderings, although the two rules differ in some aspects of processing (see Tversky, 1969, for a further discussion of how the ADDIF and WADD models are related). The MCD heuristic simplifies the additive difference model both by ignoring attribute weights and by coding the attribute differences in a binary fashion, so that only the direction of the difference, but not its magnitude, is considered.

A variation on the additive difference process, proposed by Aschenbrenner, Bockenholt, Albert, and Schmalhofer (1986), is to process the attribute differences sequentially, accumulating the summed differences until the summed advantage of one option over another exceeds some criterion value. Bockenholt, Albert, Aschenbrenner, and Schmalhofer (1991) suggest that the criterion value may reflect the balance the decision maker desires between the effort involved in a decision process and the quality of the choice process.

The frequency of good and bad features (FRQ) heuristic. Alba and Marmorstein (1987) suggest that decision makers may evaluate or choose alternatives based simply upon counts of the good or bad features the alternatives possess. To implement this heuristic, a person would need to develop cutoffs for specifying good and bad features. Then the decision maker would count the number of such features. Depending upon whether the decision maker focused on good features, bad features, or both, different variants of the heuristic would arise. Note that this heuristic could be viewed as the application of a voting rule to multiattribute choice, where the attributes can be viewed as the voters.

Combined strategies. Individuals sometimes use combinations of strategies. Typically, combined decision strategies have an initial phase, where poor alternatives are eliminated, and then a second phase examining the remaining alternatives in more detail (Payne, 1976). One such combined heuristic that is frequently observed in decision behavior is an elimination-by-aspects plus weighted additive strategy. EBA is used to reduce the number of alternatives to some small number (e.g., two or three), and then a weighted additive rule is used to select among those remaining alternatives.

Other heuristics. Several even simpler heuristics also have been proposed. A frequent strategy for choice of this sort is the habitual heuristic: Choose what one chose last time. A related heuristic, mentioned in chapter 1 and suggested by P. Wright (1975), is *affect referral.* An individual simply elicits a previously formed evaluation for each alternative from memory and selects the most highly evaluated alternative. No detailed attribute information is considered. Note that both of these heuristics are only relevant for repeated choices.

General properties of choice strategies

The strategies we have discussed are just some of those proposed to describe choice behavior. These strategies have come from a number of disciplines and have been described using very different kinds of formalisms. As a result, in order to compare and contrast strategies for choice, researchers have often described them using fairly broad and global characteristics. Several of these characteristics are considered next.

Compensatory versus noncompensatory. A central distinction among strategies is the extent to which they make tradeoffs among attributes. Decision strategies (such as weighted additive) that make tradeoffs are called compensatory strategies, whereas strategies (such as lexicographic) that do not make tradeoffs are called noncompensatory. The key to this distinction is the ability of a good value on one attribute to make up for bad values on other attributes. A lexicographic strategy is noncompensatory because a bad value on the most important attribute will ensure that an alternative would never be chosen, no matter how good it is on another attribute. A weighted additive model is compensatory because good values on one attribute can offset bad values on another. Finally, some rules, like the majority of confirming dimensions (MCD) rule, are partially compensatory in that the total number of advantages for an alternative does matter, but the relative sizes of the advantages do not.

This distinction between compensatory and noncompensatory rules is related to how a strategy deals with conflict. Compensatory rules confront conflict, whereas noncompensatory rules avoid it. Hogarth (1987) has suggested that people find making explicit tradeoffs emotionally uncomfortable. Thus, decision makers may avoid strategies that are compensatory not only because they are difficult to execute (cognitive effort) but also because they require the explicit resolution of difficult value tradeoffs (conflicts)[2].

Consistent versus selective processing. A related aspect of choice strategies is the degree to which the amount of processing is consistent or selective across alternatives or attributes. That is, is the same amount of information examined for each alternative or attribute, or does the amount vary? In general, it has been assumed that more consistent processing across alternatives is indicative of a more compensatory decision strategy (Payne, 1976). Consistent processing sometimes involves examination of all information for every alternative and attribute. A more variable (selective) processing pattern, on the other hand, indicates a strategy of eliminating alternatives or attributes using only part of the information available, without considering whether additional information might change the decision.

Amount of processing. A third general processing characteristic is the total amount of processing. A key distinction among decision rules is whether they explicitly ignore potentially relevant information in solving a decision problem, and thus reduce the amount of information processed, or attempt to process all relevant information. Whether processing is consistent or not, the total amount of information examined can vary, from quite cursory to exhaustive. For some strategies, such as EBA, lexicographic, and satisficing, the total amount of information processed is contingent upon the particular values of the alternatives and cutoffs.

---

[2] As an example of this avoidance of tradeoffs, Gregory, Kunreuther, Easterling, and Richards (1991) note that the unwillingness of people to consider trading off increases in environmental risks for money (economic benefits) is one reason why the siting of hazardous waste disposal facilities is so controversial.

Alternative-based versus attribute-based processing. A fourth aspect of processing concerns whether the search and processing of alternatives proceeds across or within attributes or dimensions. The former is often called holistic or alternative-based and the latter dimensional or attribute-based processing. In alternative-based processing, multiple attributes of a single alternative are considered before information about a second alternative is processed. In contrast, in attribute-based processing, the values of several alternatives on a single attribute are processed before information about a second attribute is processed. Russo and Dosher (1983) suggest that attribute-based processing is cognitively easier.

Formation of evaluations. The strategies differ in terms of whether or not an overall evaluation for each alternative is explicitly formed. In the equal weight or weighted additive rules, for example, each alternative is given a score that represents its overall evaluation. On the other hand, rules such as lexicographic or EBA eliminate some alternatives and select others without directly forming an overall evaluation.

Quantitative versus qualitative reasoning. Finally, the strategies also differ in terms of the degree of quantitative versus qualitative reasoning used. Some strategies include quantitative reasoning operations. For example, the equal weight method involves a summing of values, and the frequency heuristic requires counts. The weighted adding rule includes the even more quantitative operation of multiplying two values. In contrast, the reasoning contained in the other strategies described previously is more qualitative in nature. That is, most of the operations for a strategy such as EBA involve simple comparisons of values. Tversky et al. (1988) make a similar distinction between qualitative and quantitative thinking. Hegarty, Just, and Morrison (1988) also have recently explored strategy differences that involve a distinction between qualitative and quantitative reasoning in making inferences about mechanical systems.

The various decision strategies or rules we have described represent different combinations of these general properties. Table 2.1 characterizes each of the major strategies in terms of five of these properties. Consistent with our conception of strategies as particular sequences of mental and effector operations (see chapter 1),

Table 2.1. *General properties of choice heuristics*

Heuristics	Compensatory (C) versus non-compensatory (N)	Information ignored? (Y or N)	Consistent (C) versus selective (S)	Attribute-based (AT) versus alternative-based (AL)	Evaluation formed? (Y or N)	Quantitative (QN) versus qualitative (QL)
WADD	C	N	C	AL	Y	QN
ADDIF	C	N	C	AT	Y	QN
EQW	C	Y	C	AL	Y	QN
EBA	N	Y	S	AT	N	QL
SAT	N	Y	S	AL	N	QL
LEX	N	Y	S	AT	N	QL
MCD	C	Y	C	AT	Y	QN
FRQ	C	Y	C	AL	Y	QN

Note: WADD = weighted additive; ADDIF = additive difference; EQW = equal weight; EBA = elimination-by-aspects; SAT = satisficing; LEX = lexicographic; MCD = majority of confirming dimensions; FRQ = frequency of good and bad features.

Table 2.2. *Operations used by choice heuristics*

Heuristics	Comparisons	Eliminations	Concatenations
WADD	+		+ + +
ADDIF	+	+	+ + +
EQW	+		+ +
EBA	+ +	+	
SAT	+ +	+	
LEX	+ +	+	
MCD	+ +	+	+
FRQ	+ +		+

Note: Within each type of operation, the number of pluses indicates the relative extent to which each heuristic utilizes that type of operation. For key to abbreviations, see Table 2.1.

the various strategies can also be classified in terms of different combinations of operations. For example, the WADD rule obviously involves operations that concatenate the values of two or more attributes, for example, adding two values together. The lexicographic decision rule, on the other hand, does not include explicit concatenation operations, but does involve many comparisons of one alternative's value on an attribute against the value of another alternative on the same attribute. Further, some rules, such as EBA or SAT, include explicit elimination operations. Table 2.2 offers a classification of each of the major decision strategies in terms of the extent to which such operations as comparisons, eliminations, and concatenation processes are utilized. In chapter 3, we will expand upon the set of operators used to describe the various strategies in order to develop a measure of decision effort.

These strategies may be differentially available across individuals. A person's repertoire of strategies may depend upon many factors, such as cognitive development, experience, and more formal training and education. By 12 years of age, for example, children know many strategies, but they apply them less consistently than adults (Klayman, 1985). Individuals may also acquire new strategies through experience with a broad variety of choice tasks. Finally, formal teaching can provide individuals with new strategies they can use (e.g., Larrick, Morgan, & Nisbett, 1990).

While we have discussed many different decision-making strategies, we have not specified the conditions where one rule or another would be used. As noted earlier, there is much evidence showing that decision behavior is a highly contingent form of information processing. In the next section of this chapter, we review some of the problem characteristics that have been shown to influence decision making. Where relevant research has been done, we also explore in individual subsections how problem characteristics and characteristics of the person (e.g., expertise) interact in determining strategy use.

Decision problem characteristics: Task effects

Task complexity

The complexity of a decision task is influenced by a number of variables, such as the number of alternatives available, the number of attributes or dimensions of information on which the alternatives vary, and time pressure. In general, as decisions become more complex, people will tend to use simplifying decision heuristics. As discussed in this section, much evidence supports that belief.

Number of alternatives. A series of experiments over the past 15 years indicates that choice strategies are sensitive to the number of alternatives (Biggs, Bedard, Gaber, & Linsmeier, 1985; Billings & Marcus, 1983; Klayman, 1985; Olshavsky, 1979; Onken, Hastie, & Revelle, 1985; Payne, 1976; Payne & Braustein, 1978; Shields, 1980). When faced with two alternatives, subjects use compensatory types of decision strategies, such as WADD. When faced with more complex (multialternative) decision tasks, subjects prefer noncompensatory strategies, such as elimination-by-aspects (Tversky, 1972) and the conjunctive model (Einhorn, 1970).

In an early study by Payne (1976), a shift in strategies due to the number of alternatives was found for 17 of the 18 subjects studied. Subsequent studies have also reported a shift from compensatory to noncompensatory strategies for the substantial majority of subjects. Payne (1976) also found, however, that individuals differed in whether they used alternative-based versus attribute-based processing for their compensatory strategies.

There is also some evidence that the information acquisition phase of decision making becomes more attribute-based as the number of alternatives increases, although this effect does not appear to be as strong as the shift from compensatory to noncompensatory strategies (Payne & Braustein, 1978). Finally, there is also evidence to suggest that the processing in complex decision problems is generally more attribute-based early in the process and more alternative-based later in the process (Bettman & Park, 1980). The latter finding suggests that one response to task complexity may be to use mixtures of choice strategies. Payne (1976) also finds evidence for such phased strategy use.

As noted, early work on the effect of variation in the number of alternatives available showed that the shift from compensatory to noncompensatory processing was general across subjects. Some more recent studies, however, have sought to determine if task complexity effects will be mediated by such personal characteristics as age and expertise.

Klayman (1985), for example, examined the decision strategies of 12-year-olds in response to changes in task complexity. He found that by 12 years of age, children understand many of the basic concepts of decision making, such as compensation and elimination. Further, the children adapt their strategies to task complexity in ways similar to those found with adults, although the children made frequent use of simplifying decision strategies for even the smallest decision task. Finally, Klayman (1985) reports some data suggesting that there is an interaction between cognitive capabilities, decision importance, and the effects of the number of alternatives. Specifically, the difference in search between problems with few alternatives and problems with more alternatives is less for more important decisions (e.g., choosing a bicycle) and for the more cognitively capable children (i.e., those with larger memory capacity).

Although children's making decisions about bicycles and lunch could be viewed as instances of expert decision making, studies by Biggs et al. (1985) and Shields (1980) have more directly addressed the question of the effects of expertise and task size on decision processing. In the Biggs et al. study, the subjects were experienced bank loan officers who were asked to make loan decisions. In the Shields study, business executives were asked to analyze the performance reports of a fictitious manufacturing company. In both studies the experts responded to increased task complexity by using more noncompensatory processing, although the Biggs et al. results for the number of alternatives were not as strong as have generally been reported in the literature.

Number of attributes. Numerous studies have investigated the effects of the number of attributes or dimensions of information on decisions, as well as the effect of number of alternatives (e.g., Hendrick, Mills, & Kiesler, 1968; Jacoby, Speller, & Kohn, 1974; Keller & Staelin, 1987; Malhotra, 1982; Shields, 1983; Sundstrom, 1987). Whereas these studies show that increasing the amount of attribute information about alternatives increases both subjects' confidence in their judgments and the variability of responses (Slovic & Lichtenstein, 1971), the picture for the effects of the number of attributes on the quality of the decision is less clear. Several of these studies, though not all, indicate that decision quality decreases with increases in attributes after a certain level of complexity has been reached. The idea is that people can be "overloaded" with information.

The evidence for this overload effect has been questioned on various methodological grounds, however. For instance, Meyer and Johnson (1989) have argued that a major problem with the research on information overload has been the identification of what constitutes a good decision. Most research uses individuals' ratings of attribute importance to determine the best alternative, and such ratings are subject to error. Because this error often covaries with the amount of information, defining an accurate choice in these studies is difficult. Nonetheless, the evidence for increased variability in response, the fact that some studies do report decreases in decision quality, and the fact that individuals have limited information-processing capacities suggest that information load will have an effect on decision making.

In part, information overload effects may result from mechanisms of selective information acquisition. For example, the enlarged set of information may be attended to only on a selective (perhaps probabilistic) basis. The question then becomes the extent to which that selection reflects the value, salience, or relevance of the attribute information. That is, do people respond to complex information environments by focusing on the most important information or do they get distracted by irrelevant or less important information? Grether and Wilde (Grether & Wilde, 1983; Grether, Schwartz, & Wilde, 1986) have argued that for most "real" tasks consumers are able to ignore the less relevant information, and hence that over-load is irrelevant for public policy purposes. On the other hand, Gaeth and Shanteau (1984) found that expert judgments were adversely influenced by irrelevant factors, although that influence could be reduced with training. Nisbett, Zukier, and Lemley (1981) also have found that nondiagnostic (useless) information can "dilute" the effects of diagnostic information on judgments.

In addition to selectivity in attending to a subset of the presented information, a decision maker might shift evaluation strategies. Although Grether and Wilde argued that information overload is not that important because decision makers could shift to simpli-fying strategies that generally produced good decisions, the evidence for strategy shifts as a function of number of attributes is mixed. Payne (1976) and Olshavsky (1979), for instance, found no evidence that increases in the number of attributes affected the underlying decision strategies. Biggs et al. (1985) and Sundstrom (1987), on the other hand, did find that the use of noncompensatory strategies increased with increases in the number of attributes.

Finally, there are suggestions that increases in the number of outcomes possible for risky options (gambles or lotteries) may impact choice through a change in how information is represented. Payne (1980), for example, suggested that a decision maker might respond to multiple-outcome gambles by treating all outcomes below and above a certain target level or reference point as similar. A decision maker might then combine the probabilities associated with outcomes below the target into a composite probability of failure to meet the target, and similarly for outcomes above the target. (See Lopes, 1984; S. Schneider & Lopes, 1986; and Tversky & Kahneman, 1990, for more on how people respond to multiout-come risky choice problems.)

Taken together, the research on number of alternatives and number of attributes is very consistent in demonstrating contingent decision behavior. People respond to increases in task size both by selective attention to information and by shifts in decision strategies. Simpler, noncompensatory strategies are used increasingly as task size increases.

Time pressure. As an alternative to increasing task complexity through increases in the number of alternatives and/or attributes, P. Wright (1974) suggested that complexity could be varied by changing the time available to make a decision. Generally, the less the time available, the greater the complexity. Further, time pressure is assumed to be experienced whenever the time available for the completion of a task is perceived as being shorter than normally required for the activity (Svenson & Edland, 1987). As noted by Svenson and Edland, under severe time constraints, a person might experience time pressure as being similar to other stress experiences, such as noise levels or electric shock. (An annotated bibliography of recent research on stress and decision making is provided by Mross & Hammond, 1989.)

In addition to its possible effect on task complexity, time pressure is an interesting task variable for other reasons. First, time pressure often characterizes some very important decision situations. Second, people may use simplifying heuristics under time pressure because they have no other choice (Simon, 1981a). A more normative decision strategy like expected value maximization may exceed the information processing capabilities of even the most motivated decision maker under time pressure.

In spite of its potential importance, relatively little research has focused on how time pressure affects decisions about multi-attribute alternatives. Nonetheless, the evidence available suggests that people cope with time stress in several ways. One way to respond to time pressure is to *accelerate* processing (Ben Zur & Breznitz, 1981; Miller, 1960) by trying to process the same information at a faster rate. Another way to cope with time constraints is to process only a subset of the most important information, an idea referred to as *filtration* (Miller, 1960). The idea of filtration is related to the concept of *perceptual narrowing* as a response to stress – that is, a reduction in the range of hypotheses or actions considered (Keinan, 1987). Finally, one could shift decision-processing strategies. At the extreme, this could involve random choice or *avoidance* (Ben Zur & Breznitz, 1981; Janis & Mann, 1977; Miller, 1960). A less extreme form of strategy shifting would involve the use of a noncompensatory rather than compensatory decision rule.

The hypothesis of acceleration of processing was supported in a study by Payne, Bettman, and Johnson (1988; see also chapter 4 of this book). As the time constraints were made severer, the amount of time spent processing an item of information decreased substantially. Similar findings were reported by Ben Zur and Breznitz (1981).

The hypothesis of filtration has been supported in several studies. For example, P. Wright (1974; P. Wright & Weitz, 1977) found that more weight was placed on negative information about alternatives under time pressure. Similarly, Ben Zur and Breznitz (1981) observed that under time pressure, subjects tended to spend more time examining the information about negative outcomes of gambles (amount to lose and probability of losing). Wallsten and Barton (1982) and Payne et al. (1988) also report that the focus of attention shifts to the more important information as time pressure increases. Rothstein's (1986) finding that cognitive control decreases under time pressure is related to this notion of selective use of information. Rothstein finds that the same judgment strategy is employed in a less consistent fashion. Ben Zur and Breznitz (1981) have argued that combining acceleration and filtration "can be viewed as the optimal decision making strategy when the [decision maker] is confronted with information overload while pressured by deadlines" (p. 102).

Finally, there is some evidence to suggest that decision strategies may shift as a function of time pressure. Zakay (1985) hypothesized that the use of noncompensatory strategies would increase under time pressure (a similar hypothesis had been proposed by P. Wright, 1974) and found greater use of a lexicographic choice strategy under time pressure. The design of Zakay's experiments, however, makes it hard to distinguish shift in strategies from filtration. The study by Payne et al. (1988), on the other hand, found that processing was more attribute-based as well as more selective under severe levels of time pressure. The shift to more attribute-based processing under time pressure is a fairly clear indication of a shift in decision strategy. The Payne et al. results also indicate a possible hierarchy of responses to time pressure. Under moderate time pressure, subjects accelerated their processing and became somewhat more selective in processing. Under severe time pressure, people accelerated processing, focused on a subset of the information, and changed toward more attribute-based processing.

The foregoing hypotheses deal with processing information. Accuracy under time pressure was addressed by Zakay and Wooler (1984). They found that under time pressure the alternative that had been measured as having the greatest additive value was chosen a smaller proportion of the time. Similar results are reported by Payne et al. (1988), although they also found that performance under time pressure improved with experience with the decision task.

Lastly, P. Wright and Weitz (1977) demonstrated an effect of time horizon on decisions. When the outcomes of a choice were to be experienced in the near future, subjects were more averse to risk than when the outcomes were to be experienced at a more distant point in time. In a related study, Christensen-Szalanski (1984) found that women's preferences for anesthesia in childbirth changed with the time horizon. Perhaps not surprisingly, women preferred to avoid anesthesia prior to active childbirth, preferred anesthesia during childbirth, and once again turned against anesthesia one month after childbirth.

In summary, there is much evidence to suggest that decision behavior is highly contingent on task factors that impact task complexity, such as number of alternatives, number of attributes, and time constraints. As the number of alternatives varies, there is strong support for a change in evaluation strategies. As number of attributes and time pressure change, there is considerable evidence for increased selectivity in processing with increases in either variable. There is also at least some evidence for changes in the form of processing as well. Finally, these task complexity factors appear to impact the quality of decisions as well as the method for processing information.

Response mode

Variations in response mode are responsible for many of the most striking examples of contingent decision behavior. With one response mode, a decision maker may indicate that option A is preferred to option B, yet with another response mode, that same decision maker may indicate that option B is preferred to option A. As noted by Tversky et al. (1988), such a reversal in preference violates a fundamental principle of rational decision theory called *procedure invariance*. Procedure invariance denotes the idea that strategically equivalent ways of eliciting a decision maker's preferences should result in the same revealed preferences. The idea of procedure invariance is related to the notion that a decision maker has a set of preferences (values) that are "read off" from some master list when a person is asked to indicate direction or intensity of preference. However, evidence that preferences are contingent upon response mode suggests that values are actually constructed in the elicitation process instead of simply being read off (Tversky et al.,

Choice Mode:	Matching Mode:
Prob Amount	Prob Amount
H: 32/36 $4	H: 32/36 $4
L: 4/36 $40	L: 4/36 -?-
Which gamble do you prefer?	Complete the missing value so that the two gambles are equal in value.

Bidding Mode:	Rating Mode:
Prob Amount	Prob Amount
L: 4/36 $40	H: 32/36 $4
What is the minimum amount for which you would sell the gamble?	How attractive is this gamble?
	1 ———————————— 20
	Unattractive Attractive

Figure 2.1. Examples of response modes.

1988). Thus, observed preferences are likely to reflect both a decision maker's values *and* the heuristics used to construct the required response in a particular situation.

Decision research has used two general types of response modes. The first, a choice task, involves presenting two or more alternatives and asking the subject to select the alternative(s) most preferred. The other response mode, a judgment task, generally involves the successive presentation of individual alternatives, to each of which the subject assigns a value reflecting its psychological worth. Sometimes the value is in terms of a rating scale (e.g., 1–100); sometimes it might be in terms of the amount of money a subject would pay for the alternative (a bidding mode). A variation of a judgment task that involves the presentation of two alternatives is the matching response mode. In a matching procedure, the subject is required to fill in a missing value for one option in a pair so as to make the two options in the pair be of equal value. Examples of response modes are given in Figure 2.1.

Preference reversals. As mentioned previously, the judged relative worth of an alternative can sometimes change as a function of whether a judgment or choice is called for. One of the most dramatic demonstrations of such response mode effects is the change in preferences for simple gambles depending on how these preferences are assessed. In a series of experiments, Lichtenstein and Slovic (1971) and Lindman (1971) found that subjects would often indicate preference for one gamble over a second gamble when a choice procedure was used but would pay more to play the second gamble when a bidding procedure was used. Choices tended to favor the gamble with the higher probability of winning but a smaller amount to be won (called the P-Bet or H-Bet); the higher bids were made for the gambles with the larger amounts to win but a lower probability of winning (called the $-Bet or L-Bet). This pattern of results has been termed a preference reversal. The results from these early studies have been replicated in a Las Vegas casino setting using nonstudent subjects and real money (Lichtenstein & Slovic, 1973), by economists seeking to discredit the earlier results (Grether & Plott, 1979), and in the context of group discussion (Mowen & Gentry, 1980) and experimental markets (Berg, Dickhaut, & O'Brien, 1985).

The explanation offered by Lichtenstein and Slovic (1971, 1973) for preference reversals is that variations in response mode cause a *fundamental change in the way people process information about gambles.* In the choice mode, it is suggested, the processing is primarily dimensional (Tversky, 1969). That is, each dimension of one gamble might be compared with the same dimension of the other gamble. Furthermore, it is suggested, for many subjects the most important dimensions in such a comparison are the probabilities of winning and losing. In contrast, the bidding response and the successive presentation format are seen as leading to an "anchoring and adjustment" process, which is an alternative-based procedure. Anchoring and adjustment involves using one item of information about an alternative as an anchor or starting point for a judgment and then adjusting that anchor to take into account additional information. It is generally believed that the adjustment is insufficient (Slovic & Lichtenstein, 1971; Tversky & Kahneman, 1974). The amount to win often serves as the anchor for a gamble that is basically attractive. Because the adjustment to an anchor is usually insufficient, the gamble with the larger amount to win would be assigned a higher bid. This explanation of the preference reversal phenomenon involves a task influence on the salience of information, probabilities versus amounts, and also a change in the strategy for processing information, dimensional versus alternative. Similarly, Tversky et al. (1988) have argued that "different elicitation procedures highlight different aspects of options *and* suggest alternative heuristics" (emphasis added, p. 371).

Considerations of cognitive effort played a central role in the earliest explanations of preference reversals. For instance, Slovic (1967) states in relation to bidding responses that "it seems plausible that the cognitive effort involved in making this sort of compatibility transformation discouraged [subjects]... from relying on probabilities in a precise manner" (p. 34). More recently, Slovic et al. (1990) have advanced a "compatibility hypothesis," which states that the weight of a stimulus attribute (e.g., the payoff) is enhanced by its compatibility with the response (e.g., a dollar bid). One rationale for this hypothesis is that noncompatibility "requires additional mental operations, which often increase effort and error and may reduce impact" (Slovic et al., 1990, p. 5). Thus, one speculation is that the more compatible attribute would tend to serve as a preliminary *anchor* response because it is easier to use.

While most early research compared choices and prices, Slovic and Lichtenstein (1968) also found inconsistencies between bids and another response mode, ratings of attractiveness. Goldstein (1984) later extended these results in experiments in which subjects were asked to make choices, state prices, and give attractiveness ratings for the same bets that Lichtenstein and Slovic (1971) used. Not only did judgments and choices produce systematic reversals, as before, but ratings and prices produced reversals as well. Furthermore, the most extreme reversals occurred between the two judgment modes: $-Bets were strongly preferred in pricing, P-Bets were strongly preferred in rating, and choices were about evenly distributed between the two. Subsequently replicated (E. Johnson, Payne, & Bettman, 1988), these new reversals indicate that preference reversal not only is due to the comparison of choice with judgment but perhaps is due to other processes as well.

Goldstein and Einhorn (1987), for example, suggest in their *expression theory* that the evaluation process is the same for all response modes. They locate the principal source of procedural variance in the expression of the underlying evaluation onto different response scales.

Hershey and Schoemaker (1985) suggest that preference reversals also may be understood in terms of how individuals reframe decisions with certain response modes. Suppose that a person is given a sure thing option and a gamble offering the possibility of either a specified greater amount or a specified lesser amount, and that the person is asked to set (match) a probability p of obtaining the greater amount in order to make the sure thing option and the gamble equal in value. Hershey and Schoemaker suggest that the person uses the amount of the sure thing as a reference point, with the two outcomes of the gamble then coded as a gain and as a loss. With other response modes the framing of the problem is assumed to be different (see Bell, 1985, for the suggestion that the EV of a gamble serves as a natural reference point in a bidding mode). Casey (1991) emphasized the related idea of an aspiration level in his explanation of a new form of preference reversal. Similarly, Wedell and Bockenholt (1990) emphasize the concept of an aspiration level in both choice and bidding in interpreting their finding that the frequency of preference reversals is less under repeated play conditions. Finally, E. Johnson and Schkade (1989) show that the more an individual uses a reframing and an anchoring and adjustment strategy, the greater the extent to which value assessments differ across response modes.

The past few years have seen a number of experiments conducted to understand better which mechanisms underlie preference reversals. Tversky, Slovic, and Kahneman (1990) have found that the most important determinant of risky preference reversals appears to be an overpricing of the $-Bet. Bostic, Herrnstein, and Luce (1990) also identify the responses to $-Bets as a major difficulty for subjects. A general explanation offered for the overpricing of $-Bets is the "compatibility" hypothesis discussed earlier (Slovic et al., 1990). Support for such an attentional or compatibility mechanism in preference reversals is provided by Schkade and Johnson (1989). Using the Mouselab system (see the Appendix), they found that the percentage of time spent on payoffs was significantly greater in pricing than in choice. The attentional difference was particularly pronounced for those subjects who produced preference reversals.

The Schkade and Johnson study also found evidence of strategy differences between choice and judgment behavior. They showed that in choice (relative to judgment), subjects take much less time, use different patterns of information search, and often use evaluation strategies that directly compare alternatives. Similarly, Billings and Scherer (1988) found that when subjects were asked to make choices, they collected less information, were more selective, and processed more by attribute than when asked to make explicit judgments about each alternative. Interestingly, the importance of the decision task had essentially no effect on the process differences between judgment and choice. Finally, Mellers, Chang, Birnbaum, and Ordóñez (1992) examine the different preference orders resulting from varying response modes and conclude that people use different decision strategies for combining information depending upon the response mode used to elicit preferences.

Additional evidence that judgment and choice evoke different information processing strategies is provided by studies that relate response mode to memory for alternatives and attribute values (E. Johnson & Russo, 1981, 1984). For the choice response mode, memory is more variable across alternatives and concentrated on the preferred option.

In summary, different explanations for preference reversals place the cause of the phenomenon at different decision stages – either the framing, strategy selection, weighting of information, or expression of preferences. As several authors suggest (e.g., Goldstein & Einhorn 1987), however, the preference reversal phenomenon may be robust because there are many possible underlying causes, each of which may be operative in some situations but not in others. In any event, it is quite clear that how much an individual likes a decision option depends greatly on how the question is asked.

Other effects of judgment versus choice. Compatibility effects and strategy effects due to response mode also have been shown for nonrisky as well as risky decision tasks. Slovic et al. (1990), for instance, gave subjects information on 12 well-known U.S. companies taken from the 1987 *Business Week* Top 100. The information consisted of the 1986 market value (i.e., the total value of the outstanding shares) and 1987 profit standing (the rank of the company in terms of its 1987 earnings among the top 100). Half the subjects then predicted the 1987 market value of the companies in dollars. The other half predicted the ranks of the companies in market value for 1987. When the response was in terms of market value (dollars), the greater weight was given to the market value information in dollars. When the responses were in market value *ranks,* the greater weight was given to the ranks in terms of profit, as implied by the compatibility hypothesis. E. Johnson, Payne, and Bettman (1990) have replicated the Slovic et al. finding and have also shown that the compatibility effects are related to differences in attention to information and to the initial starting point (anchor) used by subjects in generating a judgment response.

Tversky et al. (1988) and Fischer and Hawkins (1993) also provide evidence for possible strategy shifts related to compatibility. Tversky et al. (1988) distinguish between response modes that evoke *qualitative* thinking (the location of apartment A is better than that of apartment B) and those that evoke more *quantitative* thinking (e.g., how much will I pay for a quieter apartment). Fischer and Hawkins (1993) have extended that argument in assuming that tasks that require qualitative responses evoke qualitative strategies based on ordinal judgments, whereas tasks that require quantitative responses evoke quantitative strategies based on cardinal judgments. Choice is a response task that evokes qualitative strategies. Ranking may also evoke more qualitative reasoning. Response tasks such as rating, minimum selling price, and matching, on the other hand, evoke quantitative strategies (Fischer & Hawkins, 1993).

As a consequence of their assumptions that different heuristics are used in choice and matching and that choice involves more lexicographic processing, Tversky et al. (1988) formulated the *prominence hypothesis*. That hypothesis states that the more prominent attribute distinguishing two options will weigh more heavily in choice than in matching. Evidence in support of the prominence hypothesis is presented in Tversky et al. (1988) and Fischer and Hawkins (1993).

Additional factors may also contribute to differences between judgment and choice. One factor relates to a distinction developed by Tversky (1977) between similarity and dissimilarity judgments. Tversky defined the similarity between objects a and b with feature sets denoted by A and B, respectively, in terms of a similarity measure $S(a,b)$ given by the following equation:

$$S(a,b) = \theta f(A \cap B) - \alpha f(A - B) - \beta f(B - A), \qquad (1)$$

where $(A \cap B)$ represents features that a and b have in common, and $(A - B)$ and $(B - A)$ represent features that are distinctive to a and b, respectively. In this equation, θ, α and β are parameters that affect the salience of the various feature sets. Tversky argued that the focus is on the distinctive features, $(A - B)$ and $(B - A)$, for judgments of dissimilarity. Choice is more related to a dissimilarity response. That is, what determines a choice between a and b is the distinctive features of a and b, not the features held in common. In fact, some models of risky choice, such as prospect theory (Kahneman

& Tversky, 1979b), suggest that probability–outcome combinations held in common by two prospects will be edited out of the decision problem. Note that with the typical rating or bidding judgment, however, all the features of an alternative are likely to be considered. This explanation of judgment-versus-choice differences emphasizes the effect of task demands on the salience of information used in decision making. Furthermore, it suggests a close connection between an important task variable, response mode, and an often-studied context effect, similarity among alternatives.

Another possible component of the judgment-versus-choice difference has been suggested by Slovic, Fischhoff, and Lichtenstein (1982). They argue that choice often includes a justification process (see also Tversky, 1972; and Simonson, 1989). Part of the deliberations prior to choice are said to consist of finding reasons that justify the selection of one option instead of the others (Slovic et al., 1982). Because justification is not a major part of a judgmental response, the inconsistencies between judgments and choices may be caused in part by the justification process.

Hogarth (1981) also discussed how the differences between judgment and choice may be mediated by the degree to which the decision environment is static or dynamic. It may be, for example, that the degree of commitment required in a dynamic decision will affect the degree to which behavior is more or less judgmental in nature. The more a commitment is required, the more choicelike will be the response.

Other response mode effects. One individual difference factor that may mediate response mode effects is the knowledge or familiarity the decision maker has in the domain for which preferences are being elicited. As noted by Tversky et al. (1988), "if one likes opera but not ballet, for example, this preference is likely to emerge regardless of whether one compares the two directly or evaluates them independently" (p. 371). Similarly, response mode effects will likely disappear if one has an algorithm for computing value, such as expected value (Tversky et al., 1988). The effects of individual differences such as knowledge or familiarity on the extent of procedural invariance would be an interesting area of research.

In addition to the basic judgment-versus-choice comparison, several other response mode effects have been demonstrated. For instance, Coombs, Donnell, and Kirk (1978) found that "substantial and significantly different levels of inconsistency of choice" were obtained under instructions to pick one of three gambles as compared with instructions to reject one of three gambles. Although the final preference orderings were similar, the reject response mode yielded more consistent preference orders. Explanations offered for this effect included the possibility that the different response modes changed the salience of the various components of a gamble. Another response mode effect that has been of great interest to economists has been the apparent difference between willingness-to-pay and willingness-to-sell prices (Knetsch & Sinden, 1984). Often people demand over twice as much to sell an item as they would pay for the item.

To summarize, response mode phenomena have proved to be some of the most robust in decision research. This robustness is likely due to the fact that many of the phenomena are the result of multiple effects such as the compatibility between stimulus values and response, different heuristics used for choice and judgment, and possibly bias in the expression of an evaluation onto a required response. Given the great importance of response mode effects for both theoretical and applied activities, this form of contingent decision behavior is likely to be the subject of much continued research interest.

Information display

A third set of task variables concerns how information is displayed to the decision maker. Tversky (1969), for example, suggested that the use of an additive versus an additive difference rule in comparing two alternatives would be affected by how the alternatives were displayed, with the additive rule being more likely when alternatives were presented sequentially and the additive difference rule being more likely when they were presented simultaneously.

The concreteness principle. Slovic (1972) suggested a "concreteness" principle, namely that decision makers will tend to use only that information that is explicitly displayed in the stimulus object and will use it only in the form in which it is displayed. The argument is that in order to reduce the cognitive strain of integrating information, any information that has to be stored in memory, inferred from the display, or transformed will be discounted or ignored. Note that this explanation of a display effect on decision behavior involves the same information-processing considerations used in explaining the effects of task complexity on choice.

A study by Aschenbrenner (1978) nicely illustrates such concreteness effects on preferences among gambles. He asked subjects to indicate preferences for gambles presented in the form $(x, p; y, 1 - p)$, where one wins amount x with probability p or loses amount y with probability $1 - p$. He also asked subjects to indicate preferences for gambles of the form $(y, p, x + y)$, where one pays the stake y, in advance, in order to play the game involving a p chance of winning $x + y$ or winning nothing with probability $1 - p$. For given values of x, y, and p, both forms of gamble are equivalent in terms of final outcomes and probabilities. Nonetheless, Aschenbrenner reported that the preference orders obtained under the two presentation modes showed "hardly any relation for the same gambles" (p. 519).

Aschenbrenner (1978) interpreted his results as showing that subjects use the dimensions of gambles "as they are presented to them rather than transform the gambles into final outcomes or calculate subjective moments" (p. 519). An earlier pair of studies by Slovic and Lichtenstein (1968) and Payne and Braunstein (1971) also provides evidence that explicit or surface information, and not the underlying probability distributions, dominates risky choice behavior. In the Slovic and Lichtenstein study, people expressed little or no preference between two gambles with the same apparent (explicit) probabilities and payoffs, but different underlying probability distributions. In the Payne and Braunstein study, people had significant preferences between gambles with different stated probabilities and payoffs, but identical underlying distributions.

Important display effects related to concreteness have also been found in several other studies. Bettman and Kakkar (1977) found that information acquisition will proceed in a fashion that is consistent with the display format. For example, with a display that encouraged alternative-based processing (e.g., the typical supermarket displays), more alternative-based processing was observed. Jarvenpaa (1989, 1990) extended the Bettman and Kakkar result to the problem of designing graphical displays to be used in computer-based decision support systems. She found that graphical format differences accounted for a large proportion of the variance in information acquisition and evaluation. Like Bettman and Kakkar, she found that processing tended to be consistent with how the graphical display was organized, for example, by alternative or by attribute. The findings by Bettman and Kakkar and by Jarvenpaa, although perhaps not surprising, are important. They suggest, along with the Russo (1977) results discussed next, how decision behavior can be changed and improved by simple information display changes.

Available versus processable information. Information-processing considerations and the effects of alternative information displays were stressed by Russo (1977) in a classic study of the use of unit price information by supermarket shoppers. He found that the use of unit price information increased when the information was brought together for shoppers in the form of organized lists where the available brands were ranked by increasing unit price. Russo argued that standard presentations of unit price information, with unit prices posted on the shelf under each item, made prices hard to compare and thus were not fully used. Making information available is not sufficient; information must be easily processable. Russo's list makes the available unit price information easier to process and compare. Viscusi, Magat, and Huber (1986) have also shown that different formats for presenting information about risks from household chemicals (e.g., bleach) can affect consumers' intentions to take precautions. As noted by Einhorn and Hogarth (1981), an important aspect of the Russo study and other information format studies is that they represent a form of decision aiding based on the information acquisition stage as opposed to more traditional aids based on the evaluation stage of decision behavior.

Recent attempts to replicate the unit price success using nutritional information have met with mixed success (Muller, 1984; Russo, Staelin, Nolan, Russell, & Metcalf, 1986). Russo et al. (1986) found no effects of in-store listings if positive nutrients (e.g., vitamins) were presented, but did find effects if negative nutrients (e.g., sugar) were disclosed. They argue that this is a motivational effect, in that individuals did not feel they were deprived of the positive nutrients but were motivated to avoid the negative ones.

Completeness of information displays. Another important issue concerned with the display of information is the problem of partially described options. That is, what happens when a subject is asked to evaluate alternatives on a set of dimensions but is not given complete information about the values for each alternative on various subsets of the dimensions? There are a number of ways in which decision makers may respond to such a situation. For example, the missing values may be inferred by the subject. The inferred value might be the average value or might depend on the values of the alternative on other dimensions. G. Ford and Smith (1987) find that consumers' inferences about a missing value for a given brand are influenced more by information about other attributes of that brand than by information about the same attribute for other competing brands.

A related idea is that subjects recognize the uncertainty of an inference and consequently discount partially described alternatives as a form of uncertainty avoidance (Yates, Jagacinski, & Faber, 1978; Meyer, 1981; R. Johnson & Levin, 1985; Jagacinski, 1991). Other possibilities include the idea that subjects will weight common dimensions more heavily than unique dimensions because of cognitive ease of comparison (Slovic & MacPhillamy, 1974), or the somewhat contrary idea that dimensions that are occasionally unique (i.e., have missing values) may draw more attention (Yates et al., 1978).

In discussing these results, Yates et al. (1978) raised two important issues. First, they noted that a given effect may be a function of several response tendencies. Second, Yates et al. pointed out that events affecting attention in the real world are likely to be numerous and powerful. Consequently, if one wants to represent accurately how people make real judgments, naturally occurring events influencing attention – such as incomplete displays – should not be dismissed as just experimental nuisance factors.

Further studies dealing with the completeness of information displays have been conducted by Dube-Rioux and Russo (1988), Fischhoff, Slovic, and Lichtenstein (1978), Hirt and Castellan (1988), and M. Weber, Eisenführ, and von Winterfeldt (1988). In the context of a fault-tree analysis of why a car might not start, Fischhoff et al. showed how the apparent completeness of the display can blind a decision maker to the possibility of information that is missing from a problem description. This basic effect was replicated by Hirt and Castellan (1988) and Dube-Rioux and Russo (1988). M. Weber et al. (1988) showed a similar effect in the context of varying structures for value trees and judgments of preference. Finally, Phelps and Shanteau (1978) showed that the number of cues used to make a judgment depends on the degree to which a stimulus display is decomposed for the decision maker.

Effects of different formats for attribute values. Another important issue in the design of information environments for decision makers concerns the format in which attribute values are presented, for example, numerically versus linguistically (i.e., words). O. Huber (1980) has shown, for example, that there are more direct within-attribute comparisons with numerical information and less use of comparisons against some criterion. More recently, Stone and Schkade (1991b) found that representing attribute values with words, relative to numbers, led to more alternative-based information searches and less use of cognitive operations associated with compensatory processing. A related series of experiments testing differences between the numerical and verbal representation of probability information can be found in the work of Wallsten and his colleagues (e.g., Wallsten, 1990; Wallsten, Budescu, Rapoport, Zwick, & Forsyth, 1986).

Thus, whether information is presented in a numerical or verbal form seems to affect decision behavior. Further, even within the same general form (e.g., numerical), information display also matters. For instance, E. Johnson et al. (1988) found a lower rate of preference reversals when probabilities were displayed in a simple form (e.g., .88 or 7/8) than when they were displayed in a more complex form (399/456). The argument advanced was that the simple form reduced the effort required to execute normative strategies such as expected value calculation.

The fact that information display can affect decision behavior is now clearly established. However, the relative magnitudes of all the effects and how they may interact when placed in conflict are not known. Such knowledge is clearly needed. Information on display effects not only provides insight into basic decision processes but also should be considered in the design of decision aids such as computer-based decision support systems (see Keen & Scott-Morton, 1978; D. Kleinmuntz & Schkade, 1990), in the design of messages to inform people about risks they face in their daily lives (Slovic, Fischhoff, & Lichtenstein, 1981), and in presenting information to professional decision makers (Politser, 1989).

Agenda effects

Tversky and Sattath (1979) explored the effects on choice of placing constraints on the order in which elements of a choice set are considered by an individual. As an example, they consider a decision about a faculty appointment in psychology. There are four candidates, x, y, v, w. Two of the candidates would be senior appointments, x and y, and two would be junior appointments, v and w. Two are in one subfield of psychology, x and v, and two are in another subfield, y and w. Given that one of the four candidates is to be selected, the issue is how the probability of choice might be affected by the requirement first to choose between the pairs $[x, y]$ and $[v, w]$ and then to choose from the selected pair versus choosing between the pairs $[x, v]$ and $[y, w]$ first and then choosing from the selected pair.

Tversky and Sattath (1979) demonstrated agenda effects on individual choices among sets of gambles consisting of two risky prospects (x and y) with similar probabilities and outcomes and one sure thing option, z. For example, gamble x might yield $40 with probability .75, otherwise nothing; gamble y might yield $50 with probability .70, otherwise nothing; option z would yield $25 for sure. Note that y is superior to x in terms of expected value. Two agenda constraints were considered. Under one agenda, the choice was first between the pair $[x, y]$ and z. Under the second agenda, the choice was first between the pair $[x, z]$ and y. In both cases, if the pair was selected, the subject later had to choose the preferred element of the pair.

The hypothesis was that the first agenda reflected a natural hierarchical choice process involving a choice between risky options $[x, y]$ and a nonrisky option. If the decision maker decides to take a risk, y is likely to be selected because of a greater expected value. Note, however, that the agenda $[x, z]$ and y conflicts with such a hierarchical choice process. The prediction was that forcing the decision maker to choose under the latter agenda would increase the probability that x would be selected. The results supported that prediction.

It is not clear from Tversky and Sattath's data to what extent the evaluation rules may have been changed under the two agendas. The implicit assumption seems to be that a hierarchical elimination process was used under both agendas, in which case the agenda effect would have to be interpreted as involving a change in the features (i.e., aspects) considered in the elimination process. Plott and Levine (1978) discussed how agendas might influence committee decisions, and Kahn, Moore, and Glazer (1987) report further results demonstrating the effects constrained agendas exert on choice.

Recently, Hauser (1986) has suggested that even if no constraints are imposed externally, a decision maker might self-impose an agenda on the order of selecting or eliminating choice alternatives. The idea is that self-imposed agendas may be a method for simplifying cognitive processing.

Decision problem characteristics: Context effects

The previous sections of this chapter have identified a number of task variables that have been shown to impact decision behavior. The influences of general characteristics of the decision problem, such as complexity and response mode, have received much of the attention in decision research. In addition, as we shall see, there is also a growing literature demonstrating contingent decision behavior as a function of context variables. As defined earlier, context variables reflect the particular values of the objects in particular decision sets.

Similarity of alternatives

Perhaps the most studied context variable has been the similarity of objects in a decision set. The classic examples of the influence of similarity structures on choice involve violations of the constant ratio model (CRM) or Luce's choice model. The model developed by Luce (1959) states that the probability of choosing an alternative X from some set of alternatives A is given by the following equation:

$$P(X, A) = \frac{U(X)}{\sum U(A_i)}, \tag{2}$$

where $U(X)$ reflects the utility of alternative X and $U(A_i)$ reflects the utility of each of the alternatives A_i contained in set A. Note that the ratio $P(X, A)/P(Y, A)$ would be a constant if X and Y are two alternatives in A. This means that the relative choice probabilities of two alternatives, X and Y, would depend on the utilities of X and Y but not on the values of other alternatives in the offered set A.

Evidence that the values of the other alternatives in A do make a difference on the ratio $P(X, A)/P(Y, A)$ has been provided by a number of researchers (Debreu, 1960; Restle, 1961; Rumelhart & Greeno, 1971; Tversky, 1972). It appears, in the words of Tversky (1972), "that the addition of an alternative to an offered set hurts alternatives that are similar to the added alternative more than those that are dissimilar to it" (p. 283). It should also be noted that the effect of similarity on choice probabilities violates not only the CRM but also a more general principle of choice referred to as independence from irrelevant alternatives. (See Luce, 1977, for a review of the CRM, other probabilistic choice models, and relevant experimental studies.)

The elimination-by-aspects model described earlier was developed by Tversky (1972) to account for the effect of similarity of choice. He showed how an EBA rule would account in particular for the observed violations of CRM because of similarity. One reason for the continued interest in issues of similarity and choice is the role that such concepts may play in such applied problems as new product introduction strategies and the problem of "cannibalization" in product lines (e.g., Batsell & Polking, 1985).

The foregoing discussion has focused on the effects of similarity on choice probabilities; however, similarity has also been hypo-thesized to affect the information-processing strategies leading to choice. For instance, similarity may affect the ease of comparison between alternatives (Shugan, 1980; Tversky & Sattath, 1979). Of particular relevance to this review is Shugan's (1980) idea that the cost of thinking associated with the use of various decision strategies is based, in part, on the perceptual similarity between alternatives. Specifically, he argues that the cost of thinking is inversely related to perceptual similarity. If the Shugan hypothesis is true, it suggests that the use of compensatory versus noncompensatory decision strategies may vary as a function of the perceived similarity among alternatives. The more similar the alternatives, the more a com-pensatory rule will be used, because the cost of thinking will be relatively low as a result of the relatively few distinct dimensions that will have to be considered. In support of the hypothesis that similarity leads to more compensatory processing, Biggs et al. (1985) found that the amount of information acquired in making a deci-sion increased as similarity increased. Similarity was defined in terms of the size of the differences between options on the attributes;

the smaller the differences, the more similar the options. Further, Biggs et al. found that the variability in search across alternatives decreased as similarity increased. Both information search measures are consistent with the use of compensatory decision strategies. In addition, an analysis of verbal protocols also suggested that compensatory strategies were more frequent in problems with similar options. Additional evidence that information acquisition is greater when the differences between alternatives are smaller is provided by Bockenholt et al. (1991). Finally, Stone and Schkade (1991b) found that the total time to make a decision was greater for decision sets with more similar options.

Although there does seem to be an effect of similarity on choice strategy use, there is some confusion in the literature regarding how similarity is operationally defined. The empirical studies already cited generally operationalize similarity in terms of the size of attribute differences. Shugan (1980), on the other hand, defines similarity in terms of the covariance structure across attributes. Although related, the two measures are not the same. More research is needed to clarify the varying impact on decision strategies of differences in differences and differences in covariance structures.

The asymmetric dominance effect. Rules like EBA handle a number of important context effects due to similarity. However, it is not always true that "if x has more in common with y than with z, for example, then the addition of x to the set (z, y) tends to hurt the similar alternative y more than the less similar one z" (Tversky & Sattath, 1979, p. 548), as the EBA model would suggest. J. Huber, Payne, and Puto (1982) have shown that this hypothesis about the effects of similarity is violated by the addition of an asymmetrically dominated alternative. An alternative is "asymmetrically dominated" if it is dominated by at least one alternative in the set but is not dominated by at least one other. The addition of an asymmetrically dominated alternative increases the choice of the alternative that dominates it. Because the new alternative is typically closest to the item that dominates it, this implies that the new alternative "helps" rather than "hurts" the items that are closest.

The asymmetric dominance effect also violates the principle of regularity, which states that the addition of a new alternative cannot increase the probability of choosing a member of the original set. Regularity is a necessary condition for most probabilistic choice models, and had generally been supported empirically (Luce, 1977). J. Huber and Puto (1983) and J. Huber (1983) extend the asymmetric dominance findings to nondominated alternatives and document the existence of an attraction effect (i.e., a new item can lead to increased choice of similar items) as well as the normal substitution effects (i.e., a new item takes choice from those items to which it is most similar). Simonson and Tversky (1992) have demonstrated these context effects with stimuli reflecting real consumer products, (e.g., paper towels).

J. Huber et al. (1982) suggest several explanations for the effect of asymmetrically dominated alternatives on choice. One explanation views the choice process in terms of a series of paired comparisons, with each pair evaluated on an attribute-by-attribute basis (Russo & Rosen, 1975). If that is the choice process actually used, then one might see an effect of the dominated alternative for several reasons. For example, an initial pairing of the dominated alternative (called the decoy) with the nondominating alternative (called the competitor) results in some probability that the competitor is eliminated early. Thus, the probability that the dominating alternative (called the target) is chosen is increased. Notice that this explanation depends on an agenda for comparing pairs of alternatives. Another possibility is that the choice process involves a complete round-robin tournament in which each alternative is compared with all other alternatives in the set and the item with the most wins is chosen. If a subject just counts the number of pairwise attribute wins (a variation of the majority of confirming dimensions strategy), then it is easy to show that addition of the decoy helps the target.

Another process explanation is that people initially search for dominating alternatives (Montgomery, 1983) as a way of making a simple decision. If some subjects satisfice and take the first dominating alternative, then that would lead to a decoy helping the target.

Ratneshwar, Shocker, and Stewart (1987) offered an alternative interpretation of the asymmetric dominance and attraction effects, suggesting that the effects are the result of lack of meaningfulness of the stimulus materials for the subjects. They showed that the attraction effect is moderated, though not eliminated, when more detailed explanations of attribute values are given. However, more recent research (Payne, Bettman, & Simonson, in progress; Simonson & Tversky, 1992; Wedell, 1991) has shown the attraction effect for stimuli that are more familiar, are more easily understood, and have real consequences for the decision maker. For example, Payne et al. and Wedell used gambles as stimuli, with cash values and probabilities as attribute values, both of which are likely to be meaningful to subjects. In addition, in the Payne et al. study, subjects actually played one of the gambles they selected, and in the Simonson and Tversky studies, the respondents were able to keep the items they chose (e.g., cash, pens, or paper towels). All these studies found that an option was more likely to be selected when it dominated another option in the set than when it did not.

Another explanation of the asymmetric dominance effect that has recently gained some support is that the effect reflects an individual's use of the relations among considered options to justify a choice to themselves and to others (Simonson, 1989). That is, one could justify the choice of the target by pointing out that it is clearly better than the decoy. Consistent with that explanation, Simonson found that the asymmetric dominance effect tended to be stronger among subjects who expected to justify their decisions to others, although the effect still existed even when subjects were assured of total confidentiality. Wedell (1991), in an attempt to distinguish among explanations of the asymmetric dominence effect, also found that his results supported an account directly linked to the dominance structure of the choice alternatives, such as that proposed by Simonson.

At a more general level, Tversky and Simonson (1992; Simonson & Tversky, 1992) have proposed a model to account for context effects such as the asymmetric dominance effect. Their model of choice has two components. The first component is a measure of the value of each alternative in the choice set considered separately. This value for each alternative is assumed to be represented adequately by an additive model. The second component of the Tversky and Simonson model is a measure of the *relative advantage* of each alternative as compared with all other alternatives in the choice set. It is this latter component that is seen as the basis for explaining effects such as asymmetric dominance. The dominating alternative, for example, has a clear relative advantage over the asymmetrically dominated alternative, while the relative advantages of the nondominated alternative over the dominating and dominated alternative are less clear-cut.

The context-dependent model of choice proposed by Tversky and Simonson does not involve the concept of choice among different decision strategies that is emphasized in this book. It has a contingent aspect, however, in that the relative advantage component of their model is only applied to choice sets with more than two alternatives. Their approach also shares with this book a focus on how elements of decision tasks and contexts affect the construction of preferences.

Attribute range effects. As alternatives become less similar, the variance in the values on the attributes across alternatives increases. Researchers have examined whether the importance weight given an attribute depends on this variation in scores. The results are mixed. Meyer and Eagle (1982) report that weights did shift as a function of variance: Attributes with greater variance received more weight. Goldstein (1990) also found that ratings of attribute importance and preferences were a function of attribute ranges. In contrast, other studies have found that weights do not depend on the variation in scores (Beattie & Baron, 1991; Curry & Menasco, 1983; Gabrielli & von Winterfeldt, 1978; Stewart & Ely, 1984). Finally, Fischer (1991) reports range sensitivity for two response modes and range insensitivity for a third response mode. He suggests that different response modes evoke different strategies and that these strategies vary in their sensitivity to the range of values on an attribute. More research on range or variance effects is needed.

Correlated attributes. A concept closely related to similarity is the correlation of the attribute scores across alternatives. In general, if the alternatives are similar, the attributes will be positively correlated; if they are very dissimilar, the attributes are negatively correlated. Interattribute correlation is also related to dominance, because when the number of attributes is small, removing dominated alternatives from a choice set results in a more negative correlation between the attributes for the remaining alternatives (Curry & Faulds, 1986; Krieger & Green, 1988). Several normative models assume that people make choices from such sets in which dominated alternatives are removed (e.g., Hauser & Gaskin, 1984; Shugan, 1987). Several descriptive models of choice also assume that dominated alternatives are removed (e.g., Coombs & Avrunin, 1977; Kahneman & Tversky, 1979b) prior to the complete evaluation of alternatives.

With a negatively correlated attribute structure, many simplified heuristics become relatively less accurate compared with a weighted additive model (Newman, 1977; McClelland, 1978; Einhorn, Kleinmuntz, & Kleinmuntz, 1979). A cost–benefit perspective would therefore suggest that decision makers might shift away from heuristics toward more normative models when faced with such negatively correlated choice sets. On the other hand, J. Huber and Klein (1991) point out that a general effect of negative correlation is to reduce the difference among the alternatives in terms of overall value. Thus, negative correlation structures have the effect of making the difference in value achieved from a choice of the first- versus the second-best alternative generally smaller. Therefore, one could argue that under negative correlation the use of heuristics (effort-saving strategies) becomes more attractive because the size of an error is smaller even though the chance of an error is greater. It appears, however, that people process more information, not less, when the attractiveness difference between alternatives is small (Bockenholt et al., 1991).

Research in this area is just beginning. E. Johnson, Meyer, and Ghose (1989) report that their subjects did not appear to shift strategies when faced with negatively correlated attributes. One possible reason for this result is that the perception of correlation is often inaccurate (Crocker, 1981), suggesting that this may be one important context effect that is difficult for decision makers to detect. On the other hand , Klein and Yadav (1989) found that the accuracy and effort associated with a decision were a function of the proportion of dominated options in a choice set; the larger the proportion, the more accurate and less effortful the decision. More recently, we have also found that correlational structures impact the amount of processing, the selectivity in processing, and the extent of alternative versus attribute-based processing (Bettman, Johnson, Luce, & Payne, 1992). The amount of processing is greater, the selectivity is less, and the processing is more alternative-based in the case of negatively correlated attribute structures (see chapter 6 for further details). More research is needed to clarify the effects of this important context variable on choice.

Comparable versus noncomparable choices. Until recently, choice research has concentrated almost exclusively on examining decision processes for comparable alternatives, such as selecting among several brands of microwave ovens. M. Johnson (1984, 1986, 1988) for the first time examined how people may evaluate and choose among noncomparable alternatives (e.g., things to buy with a bonus). For example, the decision maker might try to decide among taking a vacation trip, buying a new television set, or buying several new outfits of clothing. M. Johnson (1984) shows that as alternatives become more noncomparable, consumers represent attributes at higher levels of abstraction (e.g., necessity or enjoyment) so as to allow comparisons within attributes. At some point, however, people shift to a strategy where they form overall evaluations for each alternative and then compare the overall evaluations. Bettman and Sujan (1987) further showed that one fundamental distinction between noncomparable and comparable alternatives is knowledge of goals and goal-relevant attributes for making choices, rather than any inherent difference in the types of choices. When a goal was provided, decision processes for noncomparable alternatives more closely resembled how consumers made decisions between comparable alternatives. Thus, one aspect of knowledge – knowledge of goals – explained differences in decision processes between the two types of alternative sets.

Quality of the option set

The quality or nature of the options available in the choice set has been suggested as another context variable affecting the information processing involved in risky decisions. Williams (1966), for example, suggested that a distinction be made between "pure risk" and "speculative risk" situations. In both there is doubt or uncertainty concerning the outcomes, but in the pure risk situation there is no chance of gain. The person faces only a loss of the status quo. In the speculative risk situation there is a chance of gain. On the basis of a small pilot study, Williams concluded that, "people react differently to pure risks and speculative risks" (p. 585).

The idea that choice processes would differ depending on whether the outcomes of the gambles were primarily losses or primarily gains has been extensively investigated by Payne, Laughhunn, and Crum (1980, 1981, 1984). In a series of experiments involving both students and business managers as subjects, the relationship of a pair of gambles to an assumed reference point, target, or aspiration level was varied by adding or subtracting a constant amount from all outcomes. It was shown that such a translation of outcomes could result in a reversal of preference within the pair. The key determinant of the effect of the translation was whether the size of the translation was sufficient to result in one gamble having outcome values either all above or all below a reference point, while the other gamble had outcome values that were both above and below the reference point. A model of the effects of aspiration levels on risky choice is presented in Payne et al. (1980). The heart of the model is the idea that the preference function that is used to choose among gambles is contingent on whether the choice problem is one involving mainly positive outcomes, a mixture of positive and negative outcomes, or mainly negative outcomes. Interestingly, Keren (1991) has recently suggested that one potential explanation for the different patterns of choice observed for unique versus repeated gambles is that repeating a given gamble *n* times can result in that gamble's being viewed as having a negligible probability of either not winning or not losing. Thus, a particular gamble might be viewed as involving a mixture of positive and negative outcomes for a single play and be viewed as having either mainly positive or mainly negative outcomes for repeated plays.

A related theory to that of Payne et al. was proposed by Coombs and Avrunin (1977), who viewed choice as a form of conflict resolution. Three types of conflict situations were identified: approach–avoidance, approach–approach, and avoidance–avoidance. Both Coombs and Avrunin and Payne et al. emphasize the importance of the nature of the decision conflict and how behavior will be contingent on the perceived conflict.

Additional empirical support for the role of choice set quality is provided by experiments reported in Payne (1975), Payne and Braunstein (1971), and Ranyard (1976). Those studies suggest that individuals will often make an initial judgment about whether they are faced with an attractive set of gambles (where the probability of winning exceeds the probability of losing) or an unattractive set (where the probability of losing exceeds the probability of winning) before deciding on the choice rule to be used. Payne and Braunstein suggested that such a contingent processing strategy may provide a mechanism for reducing the information that needs to be processed in making a choice.

Reference point effects

The concepts of gains–losses, winning–losing, and so forth imply the existence of a neutral reference point that can be used to code outcomes. Such a coding process is a central component of prospect theory (Kahneman & Tversky, 1979b; Tversky & Kahneman, 1981, 1990). The need for a reference point concept in the analysis of risky choice behavior is supported by showing that the preference ordering between gambles involving negative amounts of money is often the reverse (reflection) of the preferences between gambles involving positive amounts of money (see Kahneman & Tversky, 1979b). Some possible limits on the reflection affect are discussed by Hershey and Schoemaker (1980) and S. Schneider and Lopes (1986).

Tversky and Kahneman (1991) have recently extended the concept of reference point from an analysis of risky choice to an analysis of riskless choice. They show how a change in reference point can lead to reversals in preference. For example, consider the following question taken from Tversky and Kahneman:

Imagine that as part of your professional training you were assigned to a part-time job. The training is now ending and you must look for employment. You consider two possibilities. They are like your training job in most respects except for the amount of social contact and the convenience of commuting to and from work. To compare the two jobs to each other and to the present one you have made up the following table:

	Social Contact	*Daily Travel Time*
Present job	isolated for long stretches	10 min.
Job x	limited contact with others	20 min.
Job y	moderately sociable	60 min.

The majority of respondents choose job x over job y. Tversky and Kahneman argued that such a preference was consistent with a focus by the subjects on the attribute of daily travel time, which represented a loss in comparison to the reference job, whereas the social contact attribute would be seen as a gain. A hypothesis of both prospect theory (Kahneman & Tversky, 1979b) and reference theory (Tversky & Kahneman, 1991) is that losses loom larger than corresponding gains. This concept of *loss aversion* is emerging as an important general principle of value and preferences.

In a second version of the problem just given the reference job was changed. The new reference job was described by the following attributes: "much pleasant social interaction and 80 minutes of daily commuting time." In this version, the social contact attribute was expected to be coded as a loss and the travel time attribute as a gain. Again, the results supported a focus on the loss attribute; 67% of the participants given the second version preferred job y to job x, a reversal in preferences.

This reference point effect may also be related to the asymmetric dominance effect described earlier (J. Huber et al. 1982). Note that compared with the asymmetrically dominated alternative, the dominating option has gains on all dimensions, while the non-dominating option has at least one loss. If one assumes the two undominated options were equal in preference to begin with, the addition of the asymmetrically dominated option could cause the nondominating option to be perceived as less desirable through loss aversion. It would be interesting to see how the asymmetric dominance effect would work if the asymmetric dominance were defined in terms of a superior option that could not be chosen (e.g., because it was sold out).

Finally, another important form of reference level effect is the status quo bias (Samuelson & Zeckhauser, 1988). In this bias, the retention of the status quo option is favored over other options. The status quo bias, and the related concept of loss aversion, have also been offered as explanations for the discrepancy between willingness-to-pay and willingness-to-sell (also called willingness-to-accept) prices mentioned earlier in the section on response mode effects.

Framing effects

Tversky and Kahneman (1981) have shown how simple changes in the wording of a decision problem can reverse preferences because of differences in response to gains and losses. For example, suppose you are asked to imagine that the United States is faced with the outbreak of a certain Asian disease that is expected to kill 600 people. You are asked to indicate your preference between two alternative programs to combat the disease. In one wording of this problem, the first alternative is said to result in 200 people being saved. The second alternative is said to save 600 people with a one-third probability and no people with a two-thirds probability. Most people prefer the first alternative. In a rewording of the problem, the first alternative is said to result in the death of 400 people. The second alternative gives a one-third probability that none will die and a two-thirds chance that 600 people will die. Most people prefer the second alternative in this case. Why the reversal in preference? Tversky and Kahneman argue that the first wording causes people to code the possible outcomes as gains and the second wording causes the outcomes to be coded as losses. Furthermore, because people are often risk-averse for gains and risk-seeking for losses, there is a reversal in choice between two problems that are *effectively identical*.

The framing effect just illustrated has been replicated in several contexts and by several researchers (V. Huber, Neale, & Northcraft, 1987; Kramer, 1989; Levin & Gaeth, 1988; Maule, 1989; McNeil, Pauker, Sox, & Tversky, 1982; Puto, 1987). As noted by Tversky and Kahneman (1986), such framing effects violate the normative principle of descriptive invariance. That principle states that different representations of the same choice problem should yield the same preference. Together with the earlier research on information display effects, the framing studies of Kahneman and Tversky and others make clear that descriptive invariance does not always hold.

An important feature of the studies showing that decisions are contingent upon frames is that it is hard to see how a simple change in wording could change either cognitive costs or the desire for accuracy, although one could make the argument that choice in the loss domain is somehow more important and thus the decision process might change. Such an argument is related to the assumption of prospect theory that losses loom larger than equivalent gains. We have also collected data showing that subjects take longer to make decisions framed as losses rather than gains. Nonetheless, contingencies in behavior due to framing appear different in kind than decision contingencies such as the effect of the number of alternatives available; the latter have clear accuracy–effort explanations. We discuss explanations for such framing effects in chapter 3.

One difficulty in fully understanding framing effects is that it has proved hard to predict when certain frames will be used (Fischhoff, 1983). Further, Fischhoff found no relationship between subjects' frame preferences and their choices. On the other hand, Puto (1987) was able to relate the selection of reference point to expectations and objectives in an industrial buying context. Payne et al. (1981) were also able to manipulate the reference values used by managers to evaluate risky capital investment projects. Clearly, the development of a theory of framing is badly needed.

Contingent usage of strategies for probabilistic reasoning

As stated at the beginning of this chapter, the focus of our review has been on studies involving the expression of preferences. It should be made clear, however, that there is substantial evidence of contingent processing in the domain of probability judgments as well as in the domain of preference judgments. Three recent illustrations of such contingency are provided by Gigerenzer, Hell, and Blank (1988), Ginossar and Trope (1987), and Grether (1992). Both the Gigerenzer et al. and Ginossar and Trope studies were concerned with the extent to which people use base rate information in the making of probabilistic judgments. Prior research has shown that base rate information is often neglected in assessing the probability of an event. What Gigerenzer et al. (1988) and Ginossar and Trope (1987) show is that the use of base rate information is highly sensitive to a variety of task and context variables such as the order and content of the problem statement. For example, Gigerenzer et al. changed the problem content from the standard guessing of the profession of a person, given a brief personality description (i.e., the engineer–lawyer problem, Kahneman & Tversky, 1973), to the prediction of the outcome of a soccer game, given the half-time score of the game and base rate information on the target team's total number (proportion) of games won in that season. They found that use of base rates was greater with the soccer problem and argued that "the content of the problem strongly influenced both subjects' performance and their *reported strategies*" (p. 523) (emphasis added).

Grether (1992) tested the extent to which either Bayes rule or the representativeness heuristic is used in probabilistic tasks (use of the representativeness heuristic is one reason why people have been hypothesized to ignore base rate information). Although Grether found ample evidence of the use of the representativeness heuristic, he also reported that its use was not consistent across all experiments. Grether concluded that "this suggests that in making judgments under uncertainty individuals use different decision rules in different decision situations" (p. 56).

At a more general level, Ginossar and Trope (1987) also argue that people have a variety of rules for making probabilistic judgments. Further, they propose that which rule is used to solve a particular judgment task will be contingent upon a number of task factors, such as the recency and frequency of the prior activation of the rules, the relation of the rules to task goals, and their applicability to the givens of the problem. More generally, Ginossar and Trope view strategies for thinking under uncertainty as sequences of production rules whose application depends on the same general cognitive factors that determine production rule application in other task domains (Anderson, 1982). They conclude that instead of asking whether people are inherently good or bad statisticians, attention should be directed to understanding the cognitive factors that determine when different inferential rules, statistical or nonstatistical, will be applied. The Ginossar and Trope viewpoint is one we share completely.

The idea that the same person will use a variety of approaches to solving probabilistic reasoning tasks also arises in discussions of the conjunction fallacy. Tversky and Kahneman (1983) distinguish intuitive (holistic) reasoning about the probabilities of events from more extensional (decomposed) reasoning, where events are analyzed into exhaustive lists of possibilities or compound probabilities are evaluated by aggregating elementary ones. A fundamental law of probability derived from extensional logic is the conjunction rule: The probability of a conjunction of events, $P(A \& B)$, cannot exceed the probability of any one of its constituents, $P(A)$ and $P(B)$. Intuitive reasoning, on the other hand, is seen by Tversky and Kahneman as being based on "natural assessments" such as representativeness and availability, which "are often neither deliberate nor conscious" (p. 295). Consistent with the hypothesis that probabilistic reasoning is often intuitive, Tversky and Kahneman demonstrate numerous instances where people state that the probability of $A \& B$ is greater than the probability of B, violating the conjunction rule. Additional evidence of violations of the conjunction rule can be found in several studies (Crandall & Greenfield, 1986; Thuring & Jungermann, 1990; Wells, 1985; Yates & Carlson, 1986). Einhorn and Hogarth (1986b) relate causal reasoning to the conjunction fallacy and suggest that there is a link between the need for multiple causes of an event and the conjunction fallacy.

Tversky and Kahneman argue that violations of the conjunction rule are both systematic and sizable; however, they also note that "probability judgments are not always dominated by nonextensional heuristics...judgments of probability vary in the degree which they follow a decompositional or holistic approach" (p. 310). Thus, understanding when the decision maker will use one approach or another in solving problems under uncertainty is of the same crucial importance as understanding the use of different strategies in the assessment of preferences. A related argument is offered by Beach, Barnes, and Christensen-Szalanski (1986), who propose that a person has a repertoire of strategies for making forecasts that includes both strategies utilizing aleatory reasoning (extensional) and explicit reasoning (unique characteristics). They suggest that the selection of a forecasting strategy will depend on a variety of task factors. Beach et al. also make a useful distinction between task factors that determine which strategy will be used and environmental factors that determine the vigor with which a strategy will be applied.

Summary

The present review strongly supports the conclusion that decision making is a highly contingent form of information processing. Decision behavior is sensitive to such task factors as number of alternatives and attributes, time pressure, response mode, and information format. Decision behavior is also highly sensitive to such context factors as the similarity of the options in a choice, the quality of the choice set, and reference points and framing. The pervasiveness of such task and context effects may create a view of decision behavior as chaotic, to paraphrase Hogarth and Einhorn (1992). However, we believe that generalizations about decision behavior have emerged, and will continue to emerge, as we ask questions about the conditions under which different types of information and different decision processes are more likely to be used. For example, the effects of task complexity on strategy use provide an example of a generalization about decision behavior that has emerged. Phenomena like loss aversion also suggest that there are general principles of value to be discovered.

Continued research to identify task and context effects is needed. However, the existence of such widespread contingencies implies that it is extremely important to try to identify principles that would help explain *why* contingent processing occurs and help predict *what form* of contingent processing would occur for a given task. It is also important to be able to predict which features of the decision environment we would expect to have greater or lesser impact on judgment and choice behavior. In the next chapter we offer one possible theoretical framework for understanding contingent processing and guiding questions about task and context effects. That framework emphasizes the role played by cognitive effort considerations in the contingent responses of individuals to decision problems.

3

Deciding how to decide:
An effort–accuracy framework

Introduction

Multiple strategies and contingent processing

In the preceding chapter, we developed two themes, the first concerning strategies themselves and the second their application. Our first theme was that different decision strategies have different characteristics. For example, some strategies, such as elimination by aspects, simplify the acquisition and evaluation of information, bringing the processing demands within the constraints of human information processing; others, such as additive utility, do not provide such simplifications. In addition, some strategies, such as additive utility, deal directly with conflict, whereas others do not.

Our second theme was that many different task and context variables affect which decision strategies will be employed. Our review of the literature clearly shows that decision behavior is highly contingent. Not only do different people use different strategies for the same task, but a given individual may apply different strategies to subtly different tasks.

This chapter offers a theoretical framework for understanding how people decide which decision strategy to use in solving a particular judgment or choice problem. Underlying that framework is the belief that the use of multiple strategies by a decision maker is an adaptive response to decision problems by a limited information-processing system with multiple goals for the decision process.

Theoretical assumptions

The proposed framework (model) is based on five major assumptions: First, we assume that people have available a repertoire of strategies or heuristics for solving decision problems of any complexity. The different strategies may have been acquired through formal training (e.g., Larrick et al., 1990) as well as through natural acquisition, or experience (Kruglanski, 1989). The strategies that are most available will also be a function of the frequency and recency of prior use (Ginossar & Trope, 1987). Thus, a decision maker can be thought of as having an "evoked set" of strategies that might be applied to solving the current decision problem.

Second, the available strategies are assumed to have differing advantages (benefits) and disadvantages (costs) with respect to the individuals' goals and the constraints associated with the structure and content of any specific decision problem. Third, different environments (tasks) are assumed to have properties that affect the relative advantages and disadvantages of the various strategies. The second assumption implies that the structure of a *particular* decision environment can determine the likelihoods that various strategies will yield a good solution to the decision problem. That structure can also interact with the cognitive capabilities of a decision maker to determine how much cognitive effort various strategies require to be executed in that environment. The third assumption implies that the *relative* advantages and disadvantages of decision strategies will vary across decision environments. In conjunction, the second and third assumptions imply that a given strategy may look relatively more attractive than other strategies in some environments and relatively less attractive than those same strategies in other environments.

Fourth, it is assumed that an individual selects the strategy that he or she anticipates as "best" for the task. In that regard, strategy selection itself may be viewed as a form of multiattribute choice where the options are the strategies and the attributes are the advantages and disadvantages of each strategy (Einhorn & Hogarth, 1981).[1]

A fifth assumption, implicit in the first four, is a top-down view

---

[1] As noted in chapter 1, we believe that such selections are sometimes conscious; however, individuals often may have already learned the contingencies between elements of a choice task and the accuracy and effort characterizing different strategies for that task. In such cases, contingent strategy use might simply reflect pattern recognition regarding elements of the task followed by computations of the strategy previously learned to be appropriate for such conditions. Hence, strategy selection often may not involve a conscious and effortful decision on how to decide. This issue is discussed in more detail later in this chapter.

of strategy selection. That is, for the moment we assume that information about the task is used by the decision maker to assess the advantages and disadvantages of the available strategies, and then the best strategy is selected and applied to solving the decision problem. In the top-down view, a priori perceptions of the task and strategies determine subsequent behavior. The initial formulation of our strategy selection framework includes this fifth assumption. Later in the book (see chapter 5), we explore the implications for strategy selection of relaxing this assumption and allowing for a more bottom-up or opportunistic (Hayes-Roth & Hayes-Roth, 1979) view of the selection of decision processes. According to bottom-up approaches, subsequent actions are more influenced by the data encountered than by a priori notions. We explore the possibility that strategies may be developed "on the fly," and that strategy selection may depend as much on knowledge developed during the course of solving the decision problem as on information extracted from the initial problem definition.

In the rest of this chapter, we first present an overview of our framework. As presented, the framework leads to a number of questions about the measurement of a strategy's advantages and disadvantages, which we try to answer. Next, we consider making tradeoffs between accuracy and effort. Finally, we relate our framework to other frameworks that have been proposed for understanding contingent decision behavior.

Costs and benefits in decision making

Effort and accuracy

We start with a decision maker faced with a particular decision task, for example, making a choice from a set of options defined on multiple attributes. We also assume that the decision maker has a set of strategies available for solving that choice problem. Given a set of strategies, our first question is what are the key considerations that underlie strategy selection? Two factors seem preeminent: the accuracy of a strategy in yielding a "good" decision, and the cognitive effort required of a strategy in making a decision. For instance, in deciding how to decide, a decision maker may consider (explicitly or implicitly) the likelihood that the use of a particular strategy will lead to the identification of the best alternative in a choice set. In addition to the accuracy of the decision, the decision maker might also consider how much effort it would take to use a particular strategy for a particular problem. Our focus on effort follows from the belief that cognitive effort (attention) is the *scarce* resource in decision making (Simon, 1978). We also believe that in many environments, feedback on effort expenditures will be more available than feedback on accuracy of choice.

All else being equal, decision makers prefer more accurate choices and less effortful choices. Unfortunately, strategies yielding more accurate choices are often more effortful, and easy strategies can sometimes yield lower levels of accuracy. We view strategy selection, therefore, to be the result of a compromise between the desire to make the most correct decision and the desire to minimize effort.

The idea that strategy selection is the result of a compromise between the desire to make a correct decision and the desire to minimize effort is not unique to us. In fact it is the most frequently invoked explanation of contingent strategy use in decision making (Beach & Mitchell, 1978; Johnson & Payne, 1985; Klayman, 1983; Russo & Dosher, 1983; Shugan, 1980; see also Lipman, 1991, and the references therein). It is also an idea that fits directly into the concept of decision making as bounded rationality (Simon 1955, 1981a).

The general view that strategy selection involves benefits and costs has several appealing aspects. It is easy to see, for example, how the advantages and disadvantages of strategies would be affected by a variety of changes in task environments – for example, the number of alternatives to be considered should impact the effort required to make a decision. In addition, the assumption of calculated rationality on the part of the decision maker (March, 1978) can be maintained once the costs of the decision process itself are included in the assessment of rationality. Even errors, such as intransitive preferences, may be seen as the outcome of a rational process (Tversky, 1969).

It is also worth noting that the concepts of strategy choice, effort, and task performance have been applied to a variety of problem domains. Wickens (1986), for example, discusses the relationship between the concepts of effort and accuracy in decision making and the concept of a performance–resource function in such domains as the diagnostic troubleshooting of complex electronic systems. He argues that when there are two or more strategies that may be employed to perform a task, the strategy used will be the one that attains the desired criterion level of performance at the minimum resource effort level.

After a brief consideration of other possible costs and benefits in decision making, we focus on the components of our view of strategy selection: cognitive effort, accuracy, and tradeoffs between accuracy and effort.

Other benefits and costs

Although the focus of our research is on accuracy and effort, other benefits and costs may also influence strategy selection. For example, the need to justify a decision may be an important factor in determining how a person decides how to decide (Tetlock, 1985; Simonson, 1989). Hence, one benefit of a choice strategy is the ease with which it can be justified. For example, Tversky (1972) suggests that an advantage of the elimination-by-aspects process is that it is easy to explain and defend.

Another cost that may influence strategy selection is the emotional cost of dealing with conflicts among values. Shepard (1964), in a classic paper on the selection among multiattribute alternatives, noted that "at the moment when a decision is required the fact that each alternative has both advantages and disadvantages poses an impediment to the attainment of the most immediate subgoal – namely, *escape from the unpleasant state of conflict induced by the decision problem itself*" (p. 277, emphasis added). More recently, Hogarth (1987) has stated that, whenever possible, people will avoid strategies such as additive utility that require the explicit resolution of difficult value tradeoffs.[2] Finally, Tversky and Shafir (1991) analyze the tendency to delay making any decision (choice aversion) by combining the notions of avoidance of conflict and the need to justify decisions to oneself and others. Thus, a list of benefits

---

[2] Beattie and Baron (1991) note that pairs of dimensions vary in terms of how difficult people find it to trade off the value of one dimension against the value of a second dimension. As an example, they argue that trading off "lives saved" with "$ saved" in highway maintenance may seem more difficult *in principle* than trading off "size" and "rent" when selecting an apartment (p. 571). Together with Hogarth's argument, this suggests the hypothesis that the use of compensatory strategies will be more common for certain types of tradeoff problems (size vs. rent) in comparison to other types (lives vs. $).

associated with a decision strategy might include ease of justification as well as accuracy, and a list of costs might include the emotional cost of conflict as well as the cost of mental effort. In this chapter, however, we focus on the strategy selection problem in terms of one benefit (accuracy) and one cost (effort).

Despite the intuitive appeal of cost–benefit (effort–accuracy) framework for explaining strategy selection, this perspective has been difficult to examine directly. A conceptually appropriate and easily calculable measure of effort and a generally accepted measure of accuracy have been elusive. One major goal of the research described in this book has been the development of measures of effort and accuracy for decision strategies. We consider such measures in the following sections.

Cognitive effort and decision strategies

A decomposition approach to measuring effort

Mental effort has a long and venerable history as a theoretical construct in psychology (Kahneman, 1973; Navon & Gopher, 1979; Thomas, 1983; Hockey, Gaillard, & Coles, 1986). In addition, as noted previously, the idea that decision making is influenced by considerations of cognitive effort is an old one (e.g., Simon, 1955; Marschak, 1968). It seems obvious, for example, that different strategies require different amounts of computational effort. Expected utility maximization, for instance, requires a person to process all relevant problem information and to trade off values and beliefs. In contrast, the lexicographic rule chooses the alternative that is best on just one (the most important) attribute, ignoring much of the potentially relevant problem information.

At a more precise level of analysis, however, a comparison among decision strategies in terms of cognitive effort is more difficult. In part this reflects the fact that some comparisons of strategies have been at a fairly general level, such as comparisons of analytic versus nonanalytic (Beach & Mitchell, 1978) or analytic versus intuitive strategies (Hammond, 1986). It has also been difficult to compare the cognitive effort of various decision strategies due to the fact that strategies have been proposed in the literature with widely differing levels of formalism. Some have been proposed as formal mathematical models (e.g., elimination-by-aspects, Tversky, 1972), whereas others have been proposed as verbal process descriptions (e.g., the majority of confirming dimensions rule, Russo & Dosher, 1983). What has been needed is a metric that could allow a diverse set of decision strategies to be evaluated in terms of cognitive effort.

Elementary information processes in decisions. In the late 1970s and early 1980s, three researchers independently suggested ways in which decision strategies could be compared in terms of such an effort metric. Shugan (1980, p. 100) suggested that effort or "the cost of thinking" could be captured by "a measurable (i.e., well-defined and calculable) unit of thought." He proposed the binary comparison of two alternatives on an attribute as that basic unit. The more comparisons made, the more effortful the choice. He postulated that the number of comparisons used to make a binary choice was a function of three variables: (1) the difference in the mean utilities of the two options, (2) the confidence level at which the decision must be made (probability of not making an error), and (3) the perceptual complexity in comparing the two options. The last-named factor is, in part, a function of the perceptual similarity of the two options.

The basic idea behind Shugan's cost-of-thinking model is that people will continue to sample binary differences until the confidence that one option is best reaches α, the desired level of confidence. The parameter α is meant to capture the effect of all outside choices on the need to make a good decision for the choice at hand.

Shugan's use of the binary comparison as the fundamental unit of effort, unfortunately, restricted his analysis to those decision rules in which binary comparisons are the primary operation. For example, Shugan analyzes the conjunctive, disjunctive, and maximin strategies. However, his approach cannot deal with strategies utilizing arithmetic operations as well as comparisons, such as the weighted adding or equal weight strategies. In addition, Shugan's approach requires some questionable assumptions when dealing with multiple alternative choice problems (e.g., he assumes that the average cost of a comparison remains constant as the number of alternatives increases). Two important contributions of Shugan's work, however, are (1) the notion that decomposing decision strategies into components can provide estimates of their relative costs, and (2) the observation that the effort required by a choice rule can be affected by task characteristics such as the covariance between attributes (see also P. Wright, 1977).

Table 3.1. *Elementary EIPS used in decision strategies*

READ	Read an alternative's value on an attribute into STM
COMPARE	Compare two alternatives on an attribute
DIFFERENCE	Calculate the size of the difference of two alternatives for an attribute
ADD	Add the values of an attribute in STM
PRODUCT	Weight one value by another (multiply)
ELIMINATE	Remove an alternative or attribute from consideration
MOVE	Go to next element of external environment
CHOOSE	Announce preferred alternative and stop process

Source: Reprinted by permission from "A componential analysis of cognitive effort in choice," James R. Bettman, Eric J. Johnson, and John W. Payne, *Organizational Behavior and Human Decision Processes, 45,* (1990), p. 114. Copyright © 1990 by Academic Press, Inc.

Based upon the work of Newell and Simon (1972), O. Huber (1980) and E. Johnson (1979) offered decompositions of choice strategies using more extensive sets of components. Each study independently suggested that decision strategies be described by a set of elementary information processes (EIPs). An EIP could include such mental operations as reading a piece of information into STM (short-term-memory), comparing the values of two alternatives on an attribute to determine which is larger, and multiplying a probability and payoff.

A set of EIPs for decision making that we have used in our research is shown in Table 3.1. A particular decision strategy would be defined in terms of a specific collection and sequence of EIPs. For example, a lexicographic choice strategy would involve a number of reading processes and comparison processes but no adding or multiplying EIPs. In contrast, an expected utility maximization strategy would have reading processes, a number of adding and multiplying processes, and some (but fewer) comparison processes.

A particular set of EIPs, such as the one given in Table 3.1, represents a theoretical judgment regarding the appropriate level of decomposition for decision processes. For instance, the product operator might itself be decomposed into more elementary processes

EXTERNAL WORLD

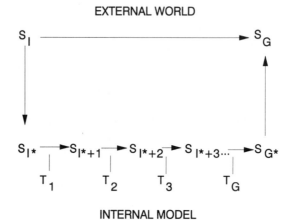

INTERNAL MODEL

Figure 3.1. Decision making as a sequence of operations. Adapted from Holland, Holyoak, Nisbett, and Thagard (1986, p. 40).

(e.g., Lopes, 1982). Decision processes could also be discussed at a more aggregate level; for instance, the detection of dominance relationships among alternatives, which would involve numerous reads and compares, has been suggested as an important subprocess in decision making (e.g., Coombs & Avrunin, 1977; Kahneman & Tversky, 1979b; Montgomery, 1983). We argue, however, that the level of decomposition shown in Table 3.1 provides the basis for meaningful comparisons among decision strategies in terms of effort. Later in this chapter we provide empirical evidence validating this hypothesis.

The EIPs for decision strategies described by O. Huber (1980) and E. Johnson (1979) and shown in Table 3.1 are similar to those postulated for other cognitive tasks, such as mental arithmetic (Dansereau, 1969) and problem solving (Newell & Simon, 1972). A hope of those advancing the concept of EIPs is that there exists a small set of elementary processes common to a variety of tasks. Chase (1978) provides a more general discussion about using the EIP concept in the analysis of information processing.

The set of EIPs can be thought of as the operations used to transform the initial state of problem knowledge into the final goal state of knowledge. Figure 3.1, adapted from Holland et al. (1986), provides a schematic view of how a particular set of EIPs might be used to transform an initial problem-specifying state of knowledge into a final goal state of knowledge. S_I refers to the initial problem information provided to the decision maker. S_G refers to the goal statement given as part of the initial problem information. S_G may be no more complex than "choose the most preferred alternative." S_{I*} is the decision maker's internal representation of the initial problem state. The S_{I*+j} are intermediate states of knowledge; S_{G*} is the final internal goal state of knowledge, which represents an elaboration of S_G, which evolves as the problem is solved. The T_j's represent the application of EIPs to transform a decision maker's knowledge state. This view of decision processing is essentially the same as the view of problem solving, mental models, and rules offered by Holland et al. (1986).

Cognitive effort as total EIP workload. Newell and Simon (1972) have suggested that cognitive processing effort be measured in terms of the number of EIPs needed to complete a task. Empirical support for this approach in areas other than decision making has been provided by showing a relationship between the predicted number of EIPs used and response times for a variety of cognitive tasks (Card, Moran, & Newell, 1983; Carpenter & Just, 1975). We adopt the Newell and Simon (1972) suggestion and propose that a measure of the cognitive effort required to make a decision in a given environment using a specific strategy is the number of EIPs required to execute that particular strategy in that particular task environment. Russo and Dosher's (1983) definition of decision effort as the total use of cognitive resources to complete the task is similar to ours. However, the decomposition of strategies into sequences of EIPs allows us to examine effort in terms of the specific mix of EIPs utilized as well the total number of EIPs used (see O. Huber, 1989 for a similar view).

To provide a better feel for the EIP approach to measuring effort, we next show examples of how EIP counts would be determined for the weighted adding and EBA rules applied to a particular decision problem. Before doing this, however, some general comments are in order. First, the number of EIPs required for a particular decision is a function of the specific rule used, the size of the problem (the number of alternatives and attributes), and the specific values of the data. Rules that examine all of the data for each alternative, such as the weighted adding rule, need more EIPs than rules that process only part of the data, such as the EBA rule. Larger problems

Table 3.2a. *Example of a four-alternative, three-attribute decision problem*

	Attributes		
	Leadership	Creativity	Experience
Weights	6(1)	4(2)	2(3)
Alternatives			
A	4(4)	7(5)	4(6)
B	2(7)	7(8)	2(9)
C	6(10)	6(11)	3(12)
D	5(13)	7(14)	2(15)

also tend to require more EIPs. Problems with more values that surpass cutoffs will also generally require more EIPs. Second, we assume that the rules are applied in these examples so as to take advantage of the left-to-right, top-to-bottom natural reading order. Third, because MOVES and READS are perfectly linked for these problems, only READS are considered; also, because CHOOSE occurs once for every rule, we do not mention it explicitly.

For the weighted adding rule, consider the four-alternative, three-attribute decision problem shown in Table 3.2a. The numbers in parentheses are labels that will be used for convenience in identifying the sequence of acquisitions in the following. An individual might acquire the first weight (1) and then the rating on the first attribute (4). He or she would then multiply these two numbers and retain the score. This process would be repeated – sequence (2), (5), (3), and (6) – until alternative A was finished. For the first alternative, the total score of 60 would then simply be retained as the current best. After processing the first alternative, there would be 6 READS, 3 PRODUCTS, 2 ADDS, and no COMPARISONS, DIFFERENCES, or ELIMINATIONS. For alternative B, the sequence would be (1), (7), (2), (8), (3), and (9). Then the total score for alternative B, 44, would be compared with the current best, and the current best of 60 would be retained. We assume in this example that the losing alternative is not explicitly eliminated when comparing total scores. Rather, the subject merely stores the alternative that was retained. With this assumption, after two alternatives we would

Table 3.2b. *Example of a three-alternative, four-attribute decision problem*

	Attributes			
	Leadership	Motivation	Creativity	Experience
Weights	4(1)	5(2)	3(3)	6(4)
Cutoffs	7(5)	4(6)	6(7)	6(8)
Alternatives				
A	6(9)	5(10)	7(11)	7(12)
B	7(13)	4(14)	3(15)	6(16)
C	4(17)	3(18)	4(19)	4(20)

Note: The numbers in parentheses refer to the sequence of acquisitions discussed in the text.

Source: Reprinted by permission from "A componential analysis of cognitive effort in choice," James R. Bettman, Eric J. Johnson, and John W. Payne, *Organizational Behavior and Human Decision Processes, 45* (1990), pp. 118–119. Copyright © 1990 by Academic Press, Inc.

have 12 READS, 6 PRODUCTS, 4 ADDS, 1 COMPARISON, no DIFFERENCES, and no ELIMINATIONS. This process would be repeated for the remaining two alternatives – sequence (1), (10), (2), (11), (3), (12), (1), (13), (2), (14), (3), and (15). Hence, the EIP model predicts that in total this problem would require 24 READS, 8 ADDITIONS, 12 PRODUCTS, 3 COMPARISONS, no DIFFERENCES, and no ELIMINATIONS.

The three-alternative, four-attribute problem shown in Table 3.2b is used to examine the EIP counts for the EBA rule. The individual would have to first find the most important attribute. This might be done by starting with the first weight and comparing it with the second, and retaining the larger (the second). The second would then be compared with the third, and the second retained. Then the second would be compared with the fourth, and the fourth (experience) retained as the most important attribute. The sequence of acquisitions would thus be (1), (2), (3), and (4). There would be 4 READS and 3 COMPARISONS. Then the individual would acquire the cutoff for experience and examine the value for all alternatives on experience, comparing each value with the cutoff and eliminating any alternative not passing the cutoff. In this case, the sequence would be (8), (12), (16), and (20), with alternative C eliminated. The total EIPs thus far would be 8 READS, 6 COMPARISONS, and 1 ELIMINATION. Then the experience attribute would be eliminated, and the weights for the remaining three criteria would be acquired and compared, resulting in motivation's being selected as the second most important attribute – sequence (1), (2), (3). Then the cutoff for motivation would be acquired and the values for the retained alternatives, A and B, compared to the cutoff – sequence (6), (10), (14). At this point, there would be a total of 14 READS, 10 COMPARISONS, and 2 ELIMINATIONS. Both alternatives A and B pass the cutoff, so the individual would then eliminate the motivation attribute and return to the weights to determine the third most important remaining attribute, leadership – sequence (1), (3). Then the cutoff for leadership would be examined, A and B would be compared with the cutoff, and A eliminated. Alternative B would then be chosen – sequence (5), (9), (13). In total, there would be 19 READS, 13 COMPARISONS, and 4 ELIMINATIONS (2 attributes and 2 alternatives).

These examples illustrate two principles: the number of EIPs varies with problem size and with the particular values used, and different rules use different subsets of the EIPs. With regard to the second point, the weighted adding rule uses READS, ADDITIONS, PRODUCTS, and COMPARISONS; the equal weighted adding rule uses READS, ADDITIONS, and COMPARISONS; the lexicographic rule uses READS, COMPARISONS, and ELIMINATIONS; the EBA rule uses READS, COMPARISONS, and ELIMINATIONS; the satisficing rule uses READS, COMPARISONS, and ELIMINATIONS; and the MCD rule uses READS, ADDITIONS, COMPARISONS, ELIMINATIONS, and DIFFERENCES (recall that we are not including MOVES and CHOOSE for convenience; these would occur in all rules).

It should also be noted that certain rules (weighted adding, equal weighted adding, MCD) have the same EIP counts for any problems of the same size (i.e., with the same number of alternatives and attributes). On the other hand, the other rules (lexicographic, EBA, satisficing) can have different EIP counts even for problems of the same size, depending upon the particular values of the data and the cutoffs.

Validation of an EIP approach to decision effort

As noted, the concept of effort plays a fundamental role in our attempts to understand the contingent use of strategies in decision making. It is crucial, therefore, to provide empirical evidence supporting this EIP (componential) approach to measuring decision effort. More details on the validation study reported below can be found in Bettman, Johnson, and Payne (1990).

To validate the idea that EIPs are a measure of effort, we need to (1) know which EIPs are being used, and (2) be able to vary the number of EIPs used in a given decision. To accomplish this, we asked decision makers to use different prescribed decision strategies on choice sets that varied in size. Both decision latencies (response times) and self-reports of decision difficulty were obtained as measures of strategy execution effort. The crucial question is whether models based on EIP counts predict these two indicators of cognitive effort in choice. In addition, we briefly consider how the effort required by subjects to use different decision strategies varies as task size (number of alternatives and number of attributes) varies.

Overview of method. Seven subjects were trained to use six different decision strategies: weighted additive, equal weighting, lexicographic, elimination-by-aspects, satisficing, and majority of confirming dimensions. Each strategy was used by each subject in a separate session to make 20 decisions ranging in problem size from two to six alternatives and from two to four attributes. Each subject, therefore, made 120 decisions in total using these six rules. The decision problems involved selection among job candidates. For each session, subjects were to use the prescribed rule exactly as given to them to make their selections.

Subjects used the Mouselab computer-based information acquisition system to acquire information and make their decisions (see the Appendix). Subjects used a mouse as a pointing device to move a cursor around a screen containing the information on the weights, cutoffs, and attribute values for the different alternatives in a matrix format. When the cursor pointed to a cell, the information in that cell was displayed, with all other information remaining concealed. For an example of the display, see Figure 3.2. The computer-based acquisition system monitored the subjects' information sequences and recorded latencies for each acquisition, the

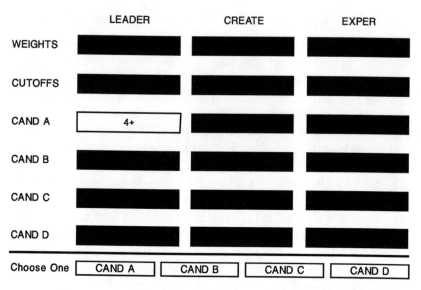

	LEADER	CREATE	EXPER
WEIGHTS	■	■	■
CUTOFFS	■	■	■
CAND A	4+	■	■
CAND B	■	■	■
CAND C	■	■	■
CAND D	■	■	■

Choose One | CAND A | CAND B | CAND C | CAND D |

Figure 3.2. Example of a stimulus display using the Mouselab system. *Source*: Reprinted by permission from "A componential analysis of cognitive effort in choice," James R. Bettman, Eric J. Johnson, and John W. Payne, *Organizational Behavior and Human Decision Processes*, 45 (1990), p. 122. Copyright © 1990 by Academic Press, Inc.

overall time for each problem, any errors made by the subject (i.e., departures from the prescribed search pattern or choice), and the choice. In addition, subjects rated the difficulty of each choice and the effort each choice required on two 0–10 response scales presented at the end of each decision problem.[3] Subjects also provided data in a seventh session for 12 choice problems of various sizes where the subject was free to use any strategy desired.

A crucial feature of Mouselab for this research is the ability to *monitor the sequence of acquisitions* made by a subject. Because the EIP models of effort we propose shortly require EIP counts for each problem, it is crucial that subjects use the strategy exactly as it is specified, so that the EIP counts are accurate. For example, to ensure that the EIP counts for the weighted adding and EBA examples given above are correct, we must monitor that subjects

---

[3] We argue in this chapter that judgments of anticipated effort, rather than experienced effort, are the important factors in strategy selection. In the present study, however, subjects made 120 choices, so judgments of experienced effort and anticipated effort are highly likely to be consistent.

Table 3.3. *Response times and self-reports of effort by strategy for three problem sizes*

Problem size (alternatives by attributes)	WADD	EOW	SAT	MCD	LEX	EBA
2 × 3						
RT	24.6	11.5	12.8	18.2	12.5	15.7
SR	3.8	1.7	1.8	2.6	1.4	2.4
4 × 3						
RT	47.8	29.7	22.3	32.2	18.7	17.6
SR	7.6	3.0	3.2	4.7	3.2	3.4
6 × 4						
RT	154.5	71.7	62.5	46.9	46.7	31.0
SR	11.0	9.7	7.2	6.0	6.2	5.4

Note: RT = average response time, in seconds; SR = average self-reported effort, summed over two 0 (low) to 10 (high) scales.

follow the exact acquisition sequence for each rule. Mouselab includes a move monitoring feature, which allows the correct sequence of cells to be specified for each decision problem. If the subject enters a "wrong" cell, the cell will not open, and after 2 seconds the computer will emit an audible buzz. The attempt to enter an incorrect cell is also recorded in the output information about the subject's move sequence. Hence, trials where a specified number of incorrect moves has occurred can later be discarded or analyzed as error trials if desired.

Results. As expected, decision problems of increasing complexity – that is, more alternatives and/or more attributes – took longer and were viewed as more effortful. Table 3.3 provides the average response times and self-reports of effort for the six strategies for three different problem sizes representing 6, 12, and 24 different alternative-attribute values. Of greater interest, the effects of task complexity varied by strategy. Compared with other strategies, the weighted additive rule (WADD) generally showed much more rapid increases in response time and somewhat more rapid increases in self-reports of effort as a function of increased task complexity. Thus, there was evidence of a strategy by task interaction in terms of these two indicators of cognitive effort.

The central question of interest, however, was whether the EIP framework could predict the effort required by each strategy for the various decision problems. To answer this question, we used regression analyses to assess the degree to which four alternative models of effort based on EIPs fit the observed response times and self-reports of effort. The simplest model treated each EIP as equally effortful and summed the numbers of each component EIP to get an overall measure of effort (the *equal-weighted EIP* model). The second model allowed the effort required by each individual EIP to vary (the *weighted EIP* model) by using counts for each of the individual EIPs as separate independent variables. A third model allowed the effortfulness of the individual EIPs to vary across rules (the *weighted EIP by rule* model). Although such a variation is possible, of course, the goal of developing a unifying framework for describing the effort of decision strategies would be much more difficult if the sequence of operations or the rule used affected the effort required for individual EIPs. The fourth model allowed the required effort for each EIP to vary across individuals, but not rules (the *weighted EIP by individual* model), based on the expectation that some individuals would find certain EIPs relatively more effortful than other individuals. A fifth model, based simply on the amount of information processed (i.e., the number of READS – the *information acquisitions* model), was also assessed as a baseline model of decision effort. This last model implies that the specific type of processing done on the information acquired makes no difference in determining decision effort.

Overall, the results yielded strong support for the EIP approach to strategy effort. A model of effort based upon weighted EIP counts provided good fits for response times ($R^2 = .84$) and self-reports of effort ($R^2 = .59$). In addition, the fit of the weighted EIP model to the data was statistically superior to the baseline information acquisitions model and to the equal-weighted EIP model. Thus, it appears that a model of cognitive effort in choice requires not only concern for the amount of information processed, but also differential weighting of the particular processes (EIPs) applied to that information.

Interestingly, the estimates of the time taken for each EIP were mostly in line with prior cognitive research. For example, the READ EIP combines encoding information with the motor activity of moving the mouse. Its estimated latency is 1.19 seconds. This estimate is plausible, since it might consist of the movement of the mouse, estimated to be in range of 0.2–0.8 seconds (see the Appendix), and an eye fixation, estimated to require a minimum of 0.2 seconds (Russo, 1978). ADDITIONS and SUBTRACTIONS both take less than 1 second, with estimates of 0.84 and 0.32, respectively. These values are not significantly different and are consistent with those provided by Dansereau (1969), Groen and Parkman (1972), and others (see Chase, 1978, Table 3, p. 76). Our estimate for the PRODUCT EIP, 2.23 seconds, is larger than that commonly reported in the literature. The time for COMPARES is very short, 0.08 seconds, and that for ELIMINATIONS, 1.80 seconds, is relatively long. This may reflect the collinearity of COMPARES and ELIMINATIONS in our data.[4]

The weights for the various EIPs were essentially the same regardless of the decision strategy used. That is, the fits for the more complex weighted EIP by rule model were essentially the same as the fits for the weighted EIP model. This supports the assumption of independence of EIPs across rules.

However, the results showed significant individual differences in the effort associated with individual EIPs, suggesting that individuals may choose different decision strategies in part because component EIPs may be relatively more or less effortful across individuals. In fact, Bettman et al. (1990) show that the processing patterns used by subjects in an unconstrained choice environment were related to the relative costs of certain EIPs, although the limited number of subjects in that study precluded any strong conclusions. Subjects for whom arithmetic operators were relatively more difficult, as indicated by the coefficients for the various EIPs, showed greater selectivity in processing.

We should also caution that our estimates of the effort associated with individual EIPs reflect the particular task environment from which they were derived. We would expect the effort associated with EIPs to vary as a function of such task variables as information

---

[4] This collinearity occurs because strategies with small numbers of ELIMINA-TIONS, like weighted adding, also tend to have few COMPARES; strategies requiring many COMPARES, such as EBA, also have many ELIMINATIONS.

format. For example, the effort associated with EIPs like ADDI-
TION and PRODUCT would certainly be expected to vary as a
function of how the scale values were represented – easy versus
hard fractions (E. Johnson et al., 1988) or numbers versus words
(Stone & Schkade, 1991b).[5]

To summarize, we found strong support for the EIP approach
to conceptualizing and measuring the effort of executing a particular
choice strategy in a specific task environment.

The accuracy of decisions

The accuracy of a judgment or choice, the other major component
of our approach in addition to cognitive effort, can be defined in
many ways. Quality of choice can be defined by basic principles of
coherence, such as not selecting dominated alternatives or not
displaying intransitive patterns of preferences. Grether and Wilde
(1983), for example, use the frequency of selection of dominated
alternatives as a measure of decision quality. When considering
several choices or judgments, one can also define quality of a
decision in terms of consistency: Does the decision maker make the
same judgment or choice when faced with the same stimuli at
different points in time? Consistency in judgments over time is
frequently used by social judgment theorists in their work on
decision behavior (e.g., Rothstein, 1986). One form of inconsistency
in judgment that has been of much interest is preference reversals,
for example (see chapter 2).

There is little argument that choosing a dominated alternative
or being intransitive are errors of decision making (however, see
Fishburn, 1991). Unfortunately, such measures of decision quality
are limited in their application. For example, the prevalence of choice
sets containing dominated alternatives is not readily apparent.
Truly inferior alternatives may be eliminated early or never
considered (see Hjorth-Andersen, 1984, 1986; Curry & Faulds, 1986;
and Sproles, 1986, for some discussion of dominated alternatives
in consumer markets, however). One might also desire a measure
of accuracy that distinguished not only that an error had occurred
but also the severity of the error.

---

[5] Todd and Benbasat (1991) have used the idea of varying the effort associated with
particular operations in designing computer-based decision support systems. We
discuss their approach to decision aiding in further detail in chapter 7.

Consequently, many researchers have suggested more specific criteria for decision quality in certain types of decision environments. For instance, the expected utility model (EU) is often suggested as a normative decision procedure for risky choice because it can be derived from more basic principles. A special case of the EU model, the maximization of expected value (EV), has been used as a criterion to investigate the accuracy of decision heuristics in risky environments (e.g., Thorngate, 1980). The main advantage of EV as an accuracy measure is that utility values from individual decision makers are not required to operationalize the rule. A similar model, the compensatory weighted additive rule, is often used as a criterion for decision effectiveness in multiattribute choice (e.g., Zakay & Wooler, 1984). The weighted additive model, like the EU model, can be derived from more basic principles. It is also normative in that it specifies how we can best reflect our preferences, if certain assumptions about those preferences are met (see Keeney & Raiffa, 1976). Both the EU and additive utility models also have the property that they utilize all the relevant information presented in the problem.

This last point, regarding the complete use of information by rules like EU, represents a "process" view of rationality: A good decision is seen as one that follows a good decision process. Alternatively, one could define a good decision solely on the basis of the outcome that is experienced. That is, a good decision is one that yields a good outcome. In the case of decisions involving risk or uncertainty, process and outcome measures of decision quality can differ. For any given decision episode, the alternative with the highest EV or EU may not yield the best outcome, given the chance event that actually occurs. To illustrate, paying $10 for a gamble that yields $20 with 1 chance in 100, otherwise nothing, is not a good decision according to the expected value criterion. However, one could pay the $10, win, and experience the good outcome of being $10 richer. Nevertheless, we adopt the view that a good decision requires the use of all relevant information. It is important that decision makers share, at least to a first approximation, the conception of accuracy adopted by the researcher. In that regard, we report in the next chapter an experiment involving risky choice in which subjects were asked what strategy they would advocate to identify the "best" choice. The use of all information, including weighting of the payoffs by the probabilities, was identified by many of the subjects.

Is normative accuracy the only criterion for a good decision?

There has been much recent debate about the adaptivity of certain biases or errors in judgment. Specifically, it has been argued that some biases in probabilistic reasoning may have adaptive value, such as the overconfidence phenomenon, in which one expresses more confidence in one's judgment than is warranted by the facts. Overconfidence may allow one to cope better with the challenges of life by increasing one's willingness to engage in activities that one would not otherwise choose to do, leading to better mental health (Taylor & Brown, 1988). From a societal perspective, there may also be a benefit from overconfidence on the part of individuals, in that more risks and innovative activities will be undertaken. On the other hand, Griffin and Tversky (1991) argue forcefully that the benefits of overconfidence may be purchased at a high price. In their words, "Overconfidence in the diagnosis of a patient, the outcome of a trial, or the projected interest rate could lead to inappropriate medical treatment, bad legal advice, and regrettable financial investments. It can be argued that people's willingness to engage in military, legal and other costly battles would be reduced if they had a more realistic assessment of their chances of success. We doubt that the benefits of overconfidence outweigh its costs" (pp. 31–32).

The debate about the adaptivity of certain decision biases is of interest; for the purposes of this book, however, the key assumptions are that it is possible to distinguish between more accurate and less accurate decisions and that accuracy does constitute a sufficient measure of decision quality.

After weighing such considerations as those we have addressed, many researchers have emphasized measures of accuracy that are based on comparing the choices of an individual (or of a particular heuristic strategy) against the standard of a normative model like expected value (utility). For example, in risky choice environments, Thorngate (1980) adopted a measure of accuracy based on the proportion of decisions for which several heuristics selected the alternative with the highest expected value.

In our research program, we generally have emphasized a measure of accuracy that compares the performance of heuristic strategies (or an individual's choice) *relative* both to the upper limit on performance expected if one followed a strict expected value rule and to the lower baseline of performance, in terms of EV, represented by a random choice rule. Our measure of relative accuracy considers where performance falls between these two extremes. In particular, we often use a measure defined as

$$\text{Relative Accuracy} = \frac{EV_{\text{heuristic rule choice}} - EV_{\text{random rule choice}}}{EV_{\text{expected value choice}} - EV_{\text{random rule choice}}}$$

More details on this particular measure of relative accuracy are presented in chapter 4.

Anticipated accuracy and effort

As noted earlier, the fifth assumption of our model of strategy selection is the top-down view: The decision maker assesses the various benefits and costs of the different strategies that are available and then chooses the strategy that is best for the problem. In the previous two sections, we have discussed some of the measurement issues associated with the concepts of decision effort and decision accuracy. In the following section of this chapter, we will discuss issues dealing with trading accuracy for effort savings in choosing the most appropriate decision strategy. Before proceeding, however, it is important to make clear the distinction between *anticipated* and *experienced* accuracy and effort (D. Kleinmuntz & Schkade, 1990). Our top-down perspective on strategy selection implies that it is anticipated accuracy and effort that will guide strategy selection. That is, a decision maker is assumed to make judgments a priori, without attempting to carry out the strategy, about the benefits (accuracy) that a strategy will yield if applied to a problem and about the effort that will be required to use the strategy for a problem. It is these judgments or perceptions of anticipated accuracy and effort that are crucial to strategy selection, although such judgments will likely be a function of the accuracy and effort that have been experienced when using a particular strategy in the past.

Judgments of anticipated accuracy and anticipated effort, like other types of judgments, can be understood in terms of a series of questions. For example, what cues are used to make the assessments of likely accuracy and likely effort? How are those cues combined into perceptions of anticipated accuracy and effort? What biases exist in such judgments? It is important to recognize that a decision maker's judgments of anticipated accuracy and/or effort may not always be veridical. All the right cues may not be utilized in forming perceptions of accuracy and effort, or these cues may be combined in inappropriate ways. To illustrate this point, consider the possibility of bias in the judgment of anticipated accuracy. As noted already, one of the most-established errors in judgment is the "overconfidence" trap; people think they know more than they really do know (Lichtenstein, Fischhoff, & Phillips, 1982).

Although the overconfidence bias has typically been shown with tests of declarative knowledge (facts), the same bias may also affect procedural knowledge (e.g., estimates of the likelihood that following a particular series of steps will lead to a problem solution). For example, memory for when a heuristic worked may be better than the memory for decision failures (see Einhorn, 1980). As a result, in judging the anticipated accuracy of a heuristic, people may overestimate the odds that the heuristic will lead to a good decision. Thus, a heuristic may seem to be an attractive strategy because people perceive that it will save effort and will provide good accuracy, with the latter perception biased. In any event, it is the perceptions of accuracy and effort that will be a major determinant of strategy selection. The other major determinant will be the tradeoff a decision maker is prepared to make between accuracy and effort.

Trading accuracy for effort savings

Characterizing strategies' effort and accuracy levels

The idea that one could trade off the accuracy of a decision against the effort of making that decision is central to a cost–benefit analysis of strategy selection. One way to conceptualize the tradeoff question is to think of the strategies available to the decision maker as points in a two-dimensional space, with one dimension representing the relative accuracy of the strategies and the other dimension representing the amount of effort (EIPs) necessary to complete the strategies. Figure 3.3a is an example of such a space for a sample set of six strategies available to solve a particular decision problem. Recall that the particular values of relative accuracy and effort associated with a strategy would be expected to differ as the nature of the problem were changed, for example, if the problem size were changed. The strategies shown in Figure 3.3a include a weighted additive rule (WADD), which represents the maximum accuracy and maximum effort rule, and several heuristic strategies – lexicographic (LEX), equal weighting (EQW), majority of confirming dimensions (MCD), and elimination-by-aspects (EBA) – that represent various combi-

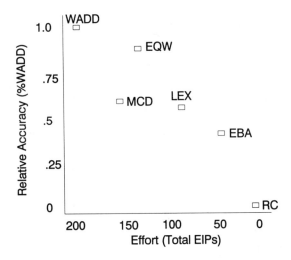

Figure 3.3a. Effort and accuracy levels for various strategies.

nations of accuracy and effort levels. A random choice rule (RC), which is used to represent a minimum effort and very low accuracy decision rule, is also included in Figure 3.3a.

The accuracy dimension in Figure 3.3a is defined in relative terms; that is, the quality of the choice expected from a rule is measured against the standard of accuracy provided by a normative model like the weighted additive rule (we also generally take into account the relative improvement over the accuracy provided by random choice, but in this example the accuracy of random choice is essentially zero). In general, we feel that accuracy is best defined as a relative measure. An expected outcome of $10 for a particular strategy, for example, would mean different things if the other available strategies all had expected results that were greater than $10 or all had expected results that were less than $10. However, one can imagine situations where a more absolute measure of decision quality would make sense. For example, knowledge that a particular strategy is expected to yield an outcome of $10 is important if all you need from the decision is an outcome greater than $9.

The effort dimension in Figure 3.3a, on the other hand, is measured using an absolute scale, a count of the number of EIPs[6]

---

[6] For purposes of discussion, in this chapter we assume that every EIP contributes equally to mental effort. In later chapters we relax this assumption and let the EIPs differ in the extent to which they contribute to feelings of mental effort. For example, a PRODUCT operation may be more effortful than a COMPARISON.

needed to execute that strategy for that decision problem. We postulate that most individuals think of effort and its indicators in absolute terms (e.g., time taken rather than relative time). One advantage of thinking of effort in absolute terms is that it makes a discussion of the concept of a constraint on processing load easier. One can, for instance, think of the subset of available strategies that all have processing demands less than some number of EIPs. Although we focus on effort as an absolute measure in this chapter, we also discuss the concept of the relative effort of strategies against the standard of a normative model in later chapters.

In examining the accuracy–effort tradeoffs characterizing the strategies shown in Figure 3.3a, first note that heuristic strategies may exist that provide a high level of accuracy with a substantial savings in effort – for example, EQW for the hypothetical example shown. Thorngate (1980) has called such heuristics "efficient." The fact that efficient heuristics can exist for certain decision environments supports the position that the use of heuristic strategies by decision makers is not necessarily a sign of "irrational" behavior.

A second point to note from Figure 3.3a is that one of the strategies is dominated. Specifically, the MCD rule provides less accuracy and requires more effort than the EQW rule. Thus, for the decision environment represented in Figure 3.3a, one would seldom, if ever, expect to see MCD selected as a decision strategy.

Choosing a strategy based upon effort–accuracy tradeoffs

Figure 3.3a shows several heuristic strategies that offer nondominated combinations of accuracy and effort. Which strategy will be selected from that set? Obviously, that depends on the relative weight (importance) a decision maker places on the goal of making an accurate decision versus saving cognitive effort. In Figure 3.3b we have drawn two preference functions (lines), one of which reflects a goal that emphasizes accuracy more than effort savings and a second that reflects a goal that emphasizes accuracy less than effort savings.[7] In either case, the decision maker receives more overall satisfaction the farther the line is from the origin. Therefore, the

---

[7] Although these preference functions are depicted as linear for the sake of simplicity, nonlinear monotonic functions could certainly be used.

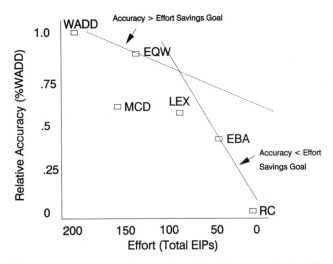

Figure 3.3b. Selection of strategies with different goals for effort savings and accuracy.

optimal strategy for each preference function is the one that is intersected last by the function as it is moved outward. In the first case (accuracy > effort savings), the indicated strategy is EQW; in the second case (accuracy < effort savings), the appropriate strategy would be EBA.

The relative weight placed on maximizing accuracy versus achieving effort savings depends on a variety of factors. For example, one clear implication of an accuracy–effort framework for strategy selection is the hypothesis that the more important a decision problem, the more accuracy is desired and the more effort a decision maker will be willing to expend (leading to choice of strategies in the upper left part of the accuracy–effort space). Although we strongly believe that increased importance of the decision will motivate more work on the decision, it does not necessarily follow that we always will see more normative decision rules used for important decisions; people may work harder, not smarter (see chapter 1 and the discussion on incentives later in this chapter). Other factors that might lead to greater emphasis upon accuracy include the degree to which the decision is irreversible, the degree of personal responsibility for the decision, and the degree to which accuracy concerns are made more salient (e.g., by providing feedback on accuracy and not on effort).

*Strategy selection with constraints on effort
and accuracy*

Another reason why increased decision importance may not lead
to shifts in strategies is the presence of constraints on the cognitive
resources that may be expended or the accuracy levels that are
tolerable. In Figure 3.3c we have added lines representing possible
constraints on effort and accuracy to the accuracy–effort space of
decision strategies. The effort constraint implies, for example, that
no strategy to the left of that line would be used by the decision
maker.[8]

For the types of problems typically studied by decision researchers – that is, a few alternatives and a few attributes or outcomes –
a constraint on effort might be the result of some form of time
pressure. For much larger decision problems, there may be a constraint simply due to the complexity of the problem. A more normative decision strategy like expected utility maximization, for instance,
may exceed the information-processing capabilities of a decision
maker, given any "reasonable" time limit. Deciding how to choose
then becomes a selection of the "best" of the available heuristics, not
a choice between using some heuristic or the more normative rule.

In Figure 3.3c, the effort constraint implies selecting from the
strategies LEX, EBA, and random choice. For the preference function emphasizing accuracy more than effort savings, LEX would be
selected; EBA would be selected for the preference function where
effort savings is emphasized more than accuracy. We shall have more
to say about the effects of incentives and constraints like time
pressure on the use of decision strategies later in the book.

Figure 3.3c also includes a constraint on accuracy.[9] This particular constraint represents the idea that for this decision problem
one might rule out any decision strategy that does not offer accuracy
at least half that of the normative rule. The choice of strategies in

---

[8] The constraint is defined in terms of the total number of EIPs necessary to
complete a strategy. We assume at this point that a decision maker will not use
a strategy he or she expects cannot be completed. Later, we explore the effects of
allowing strategies to be used until a constraint is reached, and then selecting the
best option available to date.

[9] Shugan (1980), in his model of the cost of thinking, uses the related notion of a
cutoff on the probability of making an error. See also Bockenholt et al. (1991).

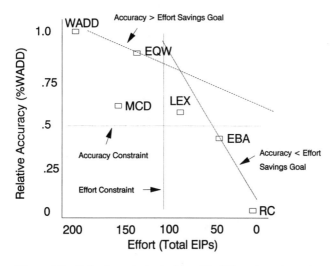

Figure 3.3c. Selection of strategies with different goals and constraints on effort and accuracy.

that case would be limited to LEX, EQW, MCD, and WADD (see Figure 3.3c). In this case, for the preference function emphasizing accuracy more than effort savings, EQW would be selected. For the function emphasizing effort savings more than accuracy, LEX would be chosen. Note that in the presence of constraints, different strategies may be selected. Also, it is interesting that in this example, LEX was selected with *different* tradeoffs depending upon the constraints. We expect that constraints on accuracy are much less common influences on strategy selection than constraints on effort.

Effects of different environments on strategy selection

Finally, in Figure 3.3d, we have plotted a second set of accuracy and effort values for the decision strategies in a second decision environment. Environment B might differ from environment A, for example, in terms of how differentially important the attributes of the problem were. In environment A one might have a problem with many attributes that are approximately equally important. Environment B, on the other hand, might have a few very important attributes and a number of attributes of lesser importance. A line

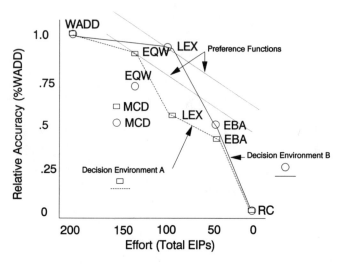

Figure 3.3d. Effort and accuracy levels for various strategies for different decision environments.

is used to connect the strategies for each environment that offer nondominated combinations of accuracy and effort.[10]

The pattern of strategies in Figure 3.3d emphasizes the fact that the accuracy and effort associated with a given decision strategy may be highly situation dependent. The most efficient decision heuristic for a given set of accuracy–effort tradeoffs generally will vary across decision task environments. For example, for the preference function shown, the LEX rule is a very attractive decision heuristic in the case of decision environment B (see Figure 3.3d). It provides almost as much accuracy of choice as the more normative rule while using just about half the effort. In decision environment A, the EQW rule would be selected, given the preference function shown. Note also that the EQW rule is dominated by the LEX rule in decision environment B. Thus, one would not expect to see the EQW rule used in decision environment B, while it is the most attractive rule for environment A, given the tradeoffs implied by the preference function shown. This suggests that a decision maker who wanted to

[10] Our analysis is based on the concept of discrete strategies; we do not consider all possible combinations of strategies as necessarily available to the decision maker (e.g., randomized strategies). Thus, the lines connecting the "efficient" strategies in Figure 3.3d are not formally efficient frontiers.

achieve both a reasonably high level of accuracy and low effort would have to use a repertoire of strategies, with selection contingent upon properties of the decision environment.

To summarize, Figures 3.3a–d suggest the following hypotheses about trading accuracy for effort. First, there exist decision heuristics that approximate the accuracy of normative decision rules with substantial savings of effort in particular decision environments. Second, the selection of a heuristic will be a function of the emphasis placed on maximizing accuracy versus saving effort. Third, there exist constraints on decision behavior that will make the selection of decision strategies a choice among heuristics rather than a choice between a heuristic and a normative strategy. Fourth, a decision maker concerned with both accuracy and effort will be likely to use decision heuristics in a highly contingent fashion. In chapter 4 we use Monte Carlo simulation techniques to make these, and other, hypotheses about contingent decision behavior more precise. We also present empirical data that test some of the derived predictions. However, the most important point for now is the idea that a consideration of the accuracy and effort levels of strategies in different decision environments provides a basis for understanding the contingent use of decision strategies. In the next section of this chapter we discuss in more depth the relationships of our framework for contingent decision behavior to the frameworks offered by other researchers.

Relationships to other frameworks

Awareness of the highly contingent nature of decision behavior has led a number of researchers to propose frameworks or models within which contingent decision behavior could be understood. Those frameworks fall into two broad categories: cost–benefit, and perceptual (Payne, 1982). The cost–benefit models emphasize the contingent use of strategies for the acquisition and evaluation of information. The perceptual perspective, in contrast, places the emphasis on the earlier processes of problem framing, problem formulation, or problem representation. In this part of the book, we present examples of cost–benefit and perceptual perspectives on contingent decision behavior. The similarities and contrasts among various cost–benefit models (including our own accuracy–effort approach) and the perceptual perspective will be discussed. Finally, we will offer a few thoughts on how the different frameworks can be seen as complementary, rather than as conflicting.

Cost–benefit frameworks

As noted earlier, a cost–benefit perspective is the most frequently used framework for explaining contingent decision behavior. Many researchers, in addition to ourselves, have found the idea that strategy selection involves the consideration of the benefits and costs of different strategies appealing.

The Beach and Mitchell model. Beach and Mitchell and their colleagues offer one version of a cost–benefit framework (Beach & Mitchell, 1978; Beach et al. , 1986; Christensen-Szalanski, 1978, 1980; McAllister, Mitchell, & Beach, 1979; J. Smith, Mitchell, & Beach, 1982; Waller & Mitchell, 1984). Beach and Mitchell assume that we all possess repertoires of decision strategies. They identify three broad categories of strategies: "aided-analytic," "unaided-analytic," and "nonanalytic." Aided-analytic strategies involve the use of some form of decision aid (e.g., paper and pencil or a computer) and the use of a normative or prescriptive decision model. An example of this strategy is the use of a computer-based decision tree program to calculate the expected values of various risky options. Unaided-analytic strategies can include approximations to subjective expected utility calculations; however, the decision maker processes only in his or her own mind. Also included in this second category of strategies are the various noncompensatory choice processes, such as elimination-by-aspects. The third category, nonanalytic strategies, includes such procedures as flipping a coin or just repeating a previous response. More generally, Beach and Mitchell distinguish among decision strategies on two dimensions: the amount of resources required to use each strategy, and the ability of each strategy to produce an accurate response.

The costs of applying various decision strategies and the value of a correct decision are assumed to be functions of the following eight variables: unfamilarity or novelty of the decision task, ambiguity of goals, complexity, instability in task structure, irreversibility of response, significance of outcomes, accountability, and time and money constraints. The influence of these task characteristics on strategy selection is assumed to be mediated by the decision maker's perceptions of the variables. It is further assumed that the strategy selected will be the one that maximizes the expected benefits of a correct decision against the cost of using the process. The combination of benefit and cost considerations is assumed to follow an additive rule. According to Christensen-Szalanski (1978), one should not assume that decision makers consciously make all the computations implied by the formal Beach and Mitchell model, although he argues that decision makers do consciously "consider the potential payoffs and costs of engaging in various acts" (p. 322).

As noted in chapter 2, Beach et al. (1986) extend the original Beach and Mitchell model to the question of how a person selects from a repertoire of strategies for making forecasts. One important addition discussed in that article is the distinction between factors that determine which strategy will be used and factors that determine the rigor with which a strategy will be applied. They suggest that variables like the extrinsic benefit of making an accurate forecast and the irrevisability of the forecast (decision environment characteristics) will be more likely to determine *how rigorously* a strategy is applied than to determine *which* strategy is applied.

The work of Christensen-Szalanski (1978) illustrates how the Beach and Mitchell model has been tested. In that study, subjects were required to select a strategy to use in estimating the expected profits someone might realize from a hypothetical investment. Information was provided on the probabilities of various states of the world and on the expected payoffs for each state of the world. The subjects were given a set of possible strategies for solving the estimation problem and asked to select one strategy. The strategies ranged from a complete analysis of the problem information (i.e., accurately calculate all three possible states of the world) through various simplifications (e.g., round and calculate the two most likely states of the world) to a guessing strategy. In the Christensen-Szalanski study, and others like it, the results showed that the selection of a strategy generally was influenced in the expected direction by such factors as the size of the payoff associated with a correct answer.

Recently, Beach and Mitchell have argued that their original model is too limited and have proposed a new model called "image theory" that stresses the intuitive and automatic aspects of decision making (Beach, 1990; Mitchell & Beach, 1990). The emphasis in image theory is on noncompensatory tests of the acceptability or compatibility of a single alternative (candidate option) with the decision maker's values or goals (images). The image(s) reflects relevant standards or criteria, each weighted according to its importance to the task and to the decision maker. An option is rejected if the weighted violation of the criteria exceeds some critical threshold. The focus of image theory is thus on the criteria that an option fails to meet. Beach and Mitchell stress that making judgments about the compatibility of an option with one's image is a rapid, smooth process that can be called "intuitive" decision making. The more analytical processes specified in the original Beach and Mitchell model are assumed to be evoked only if there is more than one acceptable alternative.

The Beach and Mitchell model of strategy selection relates in many ways to the framework we have proposed for understanding contingent decision processes. For example, we both seek to explain contingent decision behavior as the result of the decision maker's concern for both the benefits and costs of various decision strategies. We also emphasize some of the same variables as keys to strategy use (e.g., task complexity and time constraints), although Beach and Mitchell consider some factors we have not examined explicitly (e.g., irreversibility of response). However, the Beach and Mitchell model and our approach also differ in several ways. It seems clear, for example, that we focus on strategy selection at a somewhat more detailed information-processing level than Beach and Mitchell. We are interested in understanding when a *particular* type of simplifying strategy will be used (e.g., EBA vs. equal weight) as well as the more general question of analytic versus nonanalytic strategy use. We also emphasize to a greater extent the measurement of cognitive effort and its role as a key determinant of strategy use. Finally, we also differ from Beach and Mitchell in the types of methods we use to investigate decision behavior; we tend to emphasize a combination of simulation and process-tracing techniques (see chapter 4). Nonetheless, our framework for strategy selection and the Beach and Mitchell approach clearly share many elements.

Criterion-dependent models. Our framework and that of Beach and Mitchell view contingent decision behavior as reflecting a choice among decision strategies. An alternative cost–benefit viewpoint has been expressed by Bockenholt et al. (1991). They argue that choice can be modeled in terms of the following additive difference type model: Let $v(x_i)$ and $v(y_i)$ represent the subjective valuations of two alternatives x and y, respectively, on attribute i. The decision maker is assumed to compare alternatives one attribute at a time and to generate a difference in value score, $[v(x_i) - v(y_i)]$, for each attribute. They assume that attributes are processed in an order that reflects their importance to the decision (Aschenbrenner et al., 1986). In addition, it is assumed that the attributes are processed only once.

These differences are added over the selected attributes until the absolute value of the sum equals or exceeds a critical value K, and the alternative with the higher score at that time is then chosen.[11] Bockenholt et al. argue that the critical value K reflects the effort–quality tradeoff intended by the decision maker. The more important the decision, for example, the higher the value of K, and the more processing of attribute differences will be done. Bockenholt et al. (1991) note that a criterion-dependent choice process can "mimic" a variety of decision rules, such as the lexicographic strategy (a low value of K) and the additive strategy (a high value of K).

Although Bockenholt et al. offer some interesting evidence in support of the idea of criterion adjustment in binary choice, it is not clear how their model would be generalized to multiple alternative choice problems. One possibility is to use a "tournament" comparing the winner from one paired comparison with the next option in the set (see the discussion of the MCD heuristic in chapter 2). More important, as is discussed in chapters 2 and 4, there is clear evidence for both alternative-based and attribute-based processing in choice. The criterion-dependent framework emphasizes attribute-based processing. Further, process-tracing data show evidence for comparisons of attribute values against standards or cutoffs, not just against the values of another alternative. In addition, processing sometimes involves comparisons across more than just two alternatives at a time. Thus, it seems necessary to distinguish multiple decision strategies; one generic strategy with a variation in a parameter is not sufficient.

The idea of using adjustments in the parameters of different decision rules to reflect accuracy–effort tradeoffs, however, is a reasonable one. Grether and Wilde (1984), Klein and Bither (1987),

---

[11] This idea of sampling attribute differences and the concept of a confidence criterion for choice are similar to Shugan's (1980) model of the cost of thinking discussed earlier.

and J. Huber and Klein (1991), for example, have investigated how the cutoffs used in rules like the satisficing strategy might reflect accuracy–effort tradeoffs. In chapter 4 we explore the impact of different cutoffs on the performance of strategies like EBA and SAT.

Hammond's intuitive versus analytical framework. Hammond and his associates have long emphasized the important effects of task variables on judgment (Hammond, Stewart, Brehmer, & Steinman, 1975). Recently, Hammond, Hamm, Grassia, and Pearson (1987) have proposed a general theory relating properties of the judgment task to the mode of cognition used to solve the task. The cognitive processes available to the judge are seen as falling on a continuum that runs from intuition to analysis. Intuition is said to be characterized by rapid data processing, low cognitive control,[12] and low awareness of processing. Analysis, on the other hand, is said to be characterized by slow data processing, high cognitive control, and high awareness of processing. The comparison between analytical and intuitive decision making is also stressed by Beach (1990).

To the extent that time to make a judgment is a first approximation of decision effort, intuition, which is characterized by rapid data processing, represents a low effort mode of thinking. In contrast, analysis is seen as slow and therefore potentially more effortful. Hammond et al. also distinguish intuition from analysis in terms of errors in judgment. In particular, intuition is seen as leading to errors that are more frequent and normally distributed in terms of the size of the errors, whereas analysis is viewed as leading to fewer but larger errors. Consequently, Hammond and his associates do not believe that intuition is necessarily a less accurate decision process than analytical thinking. This is a distinction between the Hammond et al. framework and the Beach and Mitchell model.

We believe, as noted previously, that analytical approaches are generally more accurate; we also believe that careful selection of heuristics can often lead to performance that is nearly as accurate in a given situation. However, our belief in the relative effectiveness of certain decision strategies (e.g., WADD) versus others (e.g., EBA) is based on the assumption that the strategies are all executed without error. It may be, as suggested by Hammond and his associates, that

---

[12] Cognitive control refers to the consistency with which a judgmental policy is applied.

certain decision strategies can generate very large errors if not implemented correctly. For example, the more quantitative decision processes may be more susceptible to either simple errors of calculation (e.g., $7 \times 9 = 72$) or errors in the assessment of the information needed to operationalize a rule (e.g., 6.0 read as 60). Hammond et al. (1987) provide an example of a computational error in decision making involving an engineer who wrote down a weight of 0.8 for a cue instead of the .08 that he intended, thus reducing his judgmental accuracy to little better than chance.[13]

Hammond et al. have specified combinations of task conditions that are expected to induce intuitive and analytical modes of thinking. Table 3.4 provides a listing of the values for the task features that are said to induce each mode of thought. Note that the features listed in Table 3.4 contain "surface only" as well as "depth" characteristics of tasks. An important aspect of the Hammond et al. framework is the distinction between task variables that are overtly part of the display (surface) and task variables that refer to the covert relationships among the variables within the task (depth). Surface and depth characteristics may be congruent (both implying the same form of thought) or incongruent (each implying a different form of thought).

Although there has not been much direct testing of the Hammond et al. framework, evidence in Hammond et al. (1987) supports a relationship between the location of a task on their task index (an index based on an equal weighting of the features in Table 3.4) and the mode of thinking employed by subjects. A finding of particular interest is the important influence exerted by display features (e.g., pictures vs. bar graphs) on judgment performance.

The framework for strategy selection proposed in this book and the Hammond et al. framework share an emphasis on the role of task characteristics in determining judgment and choice behavior. Another idea that is shared is the concept that tasks may induce a "compromise" or tradeoff between intuition and analysis. However, our framework and that of Hammond et al. do seem to differ on several dimensions. For instance, we focus more on the alternative information processing strategies (e.g., EBA and weighted adding)

---

[13] Of course, any decision strategy will lose something when it is performed on flawed data. However, Hammond's argument is that certain classes of decision strategies are more susceptible to execution or input errors, and/or that the effects of such errors will be relatively severer for some classes of strategies.

Table 3.4. *Inducement of intuition and analysis by task conditions*

Task characteristic	Intuition-inducing state of task characteristic	Analysis-inducing state of task characteristic
1. Number of cues	Large (> 5)	Small
2. Measurement of cues	Perceptual measurement	Objective reliable measurement
3. Distribution of cue values	Continuous highly variable distribution	Unknown distribution; cues are dichotomous; values are discrete
4. Redundancy among cues	High redundancy	Low redundancy
5. Decomposition of task	Low	High
6. Degree of certainty in task	Low certainty	High certainty
7. Relation between cues and criterion	Linear	Nonlinear
8. Weighting of cues in environmental model	Equal	Unequal
9. Availability of organizing principal	Unavailable	Available
10. Display of cues[a]	Simultaneous display	Sequential display
11. Time period	Brief	Long

[a]Applicable to surface conditions only.
Source: Reprinted by permission from "Direct comparison of the efficacy of intuitive and analytical cognition in expert judgment," Kenneth R. Hammond, Robert M. Hamm, Janet Grassia, and Tamra Pearson, *IEEE Transactions on Systems, Man, and Cybernetics*, 17 (1987), p. 756. Copyright © 1987 IEEE.

that are induced by tasks rather than on the general intuition versus analysis question. We also place a great deal of emphasis on cognitive effort as a prime determinant of strategy use. The Hammond et al. framework is less clear on why certain task features induce certain modes of thinking. Nevertheless, the Hammond et al. framework, like ours, implies that different modes of thinking have different costs and benefits that vary with tasks.

The infinite regress issue. One difficulty shared by the various cost–benefit approaches to strategy selection is the potential for infinite regress. One decides on the basis of costs and benefits how to choose to decide how to choose... As noted earlier in this chapter and in chapter 1, we believe that the control of decision processing sometimes occurs at a conscious level and that people sometimes do plan how to solve problems (Anderson, 1983). More generally, one can easily imagine a set of metacognitive productions that have as their actions the explicit (conscious) consideration of accuracy and error conditions and the setting of goals and subgoals for the decision process. For example, one such production might be "If the number of alternatives is greater than six, then conclude weighted adding is too effortful and set the goal of finding a less effortful heuristic." Further, as is discussed in chapter 7, some educators have suggested that higher-level cognitive skills like reading may be improved by teaching conscious metacognitive procedures for making better decisions about how to read a particular text. That is, one decides how to read based on considerations of the nature of the text and the goals for the task.

Over time, metacognitive processes (productions) may be invoked directly by task features such as complexity. In fact, it is our view that conscious decisions on how to decide are not made that often; instead, the relationships between task and context factors and the effectiveness and efficiency of various decision strategies are learned over time. For example, a decision maker may learn over time that a screening process will substantially reduce effort in large choice sets without much loss in accuracy. Such metaknowledge could be instantiated in a production of the form "If the number of alternatives is greater than six, then screen on the most important attribute." In the simulation work reported in chapter 4, we analyze the performance of a heuristic related to such a metacognitive production for the control of processing. The application of metaknowledge could also involve a more general pattern-matching or categorization procedure than the one suggested here. Thus, we believe that people sometimes explicitly control their mode of cognition; however, we also feel that individuals learn metacognitive rules for such control and apply them often. The latter belief differs markedly from the notion of calculated rationality (March, 1978); we assume that adaptation can occur over time, but it is not necessarily immediate.[14]

Perceptual frameworks

The framing of decisions. As reviewed in chapter 2, some of the most dramatic demonstrations of the lack of invariance in human decision behavior across tasks have been offered by Kahneman and Tversky (1979b; Tversky & Kahneman, 1981, 1988). Although Tversky and Kahneman acknowledge that contingent processing in decision making can sometimes be explained in terms of mental effort, they prefer to trace such behavior to more basic perceptual principles governing the formulation or framing of decision problems. Consider, for example, how Kahneman and Tversky (1979b) explain why people appear to code outcomes as gains or losses as opposed to final wealth positions. An economic analysis argues for treating outcomes in terms of final wealth. Kahneman and Tversky, however, suggest that an early stage of the choice process involves the coding of outcomes as either gains or losses relative to some neutral reference point, because our perceptual apparatus is attuned to evaluate changes or differences rather than absolute magnitudes (Kahneman & Tversky, 1979b). Furthermore, risk aversion for gains and risk seeking for losses are seen as consequences of the fact that monetary changes, like sensory and perceptual dimensions, "share the property that the psychological response is a concave function of the magnitude of physical change" (Kahneman & Tversky, 1979b, p. 278).

In their work on the framing of decisions, Tversky and Kahneman (1981) continue their use of perceptual metaphors, comparing the

---

[14] Lipman (1991) has proposed another "solution" to the infinite regress problem of deciding how to decide. His proposal rests on characterizing the decision problem perceived by the decision maker by two aspects: presented options, about which the decision maker has some preference uncertainty; and computational procedures for resolving this subjective uncertainty. Lipman argues that under some plausible assumptions, the sequence of decisions on deciding how to decide converges to a fixed point. Lipman also notes the analogy between the infinite regress problem in deciding how to decide and the potentional infinite regress problem in game theory regarding one's beliefs about the beliefs of others, who have beliefs about one's beliefs about the beliefs of others...

effects of frames on preferences to the effects of perspectives on perceptual appearances. An important implication of their perceptual metaphor is that subjects "are normally unaware of alternative frames and of their potential effects on the relative attractiveness of options" (Tversky & Kahneman, 1981, p. 457). This represents a major difference between the perceptual framework of Tversky and Kahneman and the error–effort ideas of our approach and others.

The theory of choice discussed in Kahneman and Tversky (1979b) and Tversky and Kahneman (1981, 1990), called *prospect theory*, distinguishes two phases in the choice process: an initial phase in which the problem is edited into a simpler representation and a subsequent phase of evaluation. The purpose of editing is to make the evaluation phase easier (see the discussion of Coupey's work, 1990, in chapter 5 for more details on this notion). An example of an editing operation is the coding of outcomes as gains or losses. Other editing operations include the detection and removal of dominated alternatives, the cancellation of identical outcomes across two alternatives, the combination of identical outcomes within an option into a single compound outcome, and the rounding off of some numerical information. The evaluation phase consists of a generalized expected utility process.

The editing phase is the primary source of context effects in decision making; the same set of options might be edited in different ways depending upon the context in which it appears. Once the editing phase is completed, however, the basic evaluation process is assumed to be invariant across representations. Thus, one does not really have a selection among choice strategies; different outputs result from a single evaluation process depending on the edited representation that is the input.

Note, however, that prospect theory does include two methods by which an option might be chosen. First, a dominance relationship might be detected in the editing phase and the dominating option chosen. Second, the evaluation rule might be applied and the option with the largest value chosen. In a recent paper on framing, Tversky and Kahneman (1988) argue that use of the dominance process to make a choice instead of the more general evaluation process is sensitive to information display effects. To illustrate, consider the lotteries described here, taken from Tversky and Kahneman (1988):

Color of ball in urn	Lottery A %	Lottery A Payoff	Lottery B %	Lottery B Payoff	Lottery C %	Lottery C Payoff	Lottery D %	Lottery D Payoff
White	90%	0	90%	0	90%	0	90%	0
Red	6%	+45	6%	+45	6%	+45	7%	+45
Green	1%	+30	1%	+45	1%	+30	—	—
Blue	1%	−15	1%	−10	—	—	1%	−10
Yellow	2%	−15	2%	−15	3%	−15	2%	−15

Given a choice between lotteries A and B, everyone chooses B, since it is easy to see ("transparent") that B dominates A. When given a choice between C and D, 58% of Tversky and Kahneman's subjects chose C. However, lottery C is a version of A with the common outcomes of losing $15 combined, and lottery D is a similarly edited version of B. Thus, a choice rule like dominance will be used in some situations when its application is transparent and not be used in nontransparent situations. The perceptual framework of Tversky and Kahneman therefore allows for the contingent use of a limited set of decision rules (i.e., dominance or expected utility), depending on how a decision problem is represented.

The perceptual framework raises an important question concerning how the perceptual–decision responses have developed: To what extent are the responses we observe due to basic processes that may be "hardwired" into the human organism by evolutionary processes? The statements by Tversky and Kahneman that people are normally unaware of framing effects and, further, often do not know how to resolve inconsistencies in judgment when they are made aware of them suggest that the responses are to some extent hardwired into the system.

An implication of this view is that task effects, like perceptual illusions, will tend to be more universal across subjects, although Tversky and Kahneman (1988) note that framing is controlled by the norms, habits, and expectancies of the decision maker as well as by the manner in which the choice problem is presented. Thus, individual differences in framing effects due to such factors as experience are clearly possible.

Another implication of the perceptual framework is that incentives are not as likely to influence task or context effects as they are within a cost–benefit framework. Tversky and Kahneman (1988) stress that "in the persistence of their appeal, framing effects resemble visual illusion more than computational errors" (p. 175). They argue that there is no obvious mechanism by which the mere introduction of incentives would reduce visual illusions like the famous Muller-Lyer illusion, and by extension, the decision framing effects they have shown.

If the only factors influencing decision behavior were a concern with accuracy and a concern for decision effort, however, then one might expect that violations of rational decision principles could be eliminated by proper incentives. For example, many economists continue to argue that the lack of incentives may cause suboptimal behaviors on the part of individuals (e.g., Harrison, 1989). Further, as we report in chapter 4, the processes used in decision making sometimes become more consistent with normative models as incentives are increased. However, errors in preferential choice and probabilistic reasoning persist even in the presence of monetary payoffs (Grether & Plott, 1979; Tversky & Kahneman, 1983). Even a casual view of decision making in the real world suggests that reasoning errors sometimes occur in very important decisions. Consequently, much recent research has examined the effects of incentives on decision behavior, leading to a view that incentives can both help and hinder decision performance (Ashton, 1990; Berg & Dickhaut, 1990; Hogarth, Gibbs, McKenzie, & Marquis, 1991).

As noted by Tversky and Kahneman (1986), incentives do not work by magic. Generally, what incentives do is prolong deliberation or attention to a problem; people generally work harder on more important problems. More effort is generally believed to lead to better performance. However, as reported in Paese and Sniezek (1991), increased effort may lead to increased confidence in judgment without accompanying increases in accuracy. Devoting more effort to using a flawed decision strategy can lead to poorer performance (Arkes, Dawes, & Christensen, 1986).

For incentives to change decision strategies and increase performance, several conditions seem necessary. First, one must believe that one's current decision strategy is insufficient in terms of desired accuracy (i.e., if you don't think it's broken, you won't fix it). Failure to adapt may result from overconfidence in assessing the likelihood that a current strategy will lead to a successful outcome. In many decision environments, feedback is often not sufficient to sway such assessments (Einhorn, 1980). Second, for incentives to lead to a strategy shift, a better strategy must be available. If one does not know what else to do, a belief that one is stuck with a flawed strategy may lead to a panic response under very high incentives (Janis, 1989). There is evidence that better strategies are sometimes unavailable (e.g., John & Cole, 1986; Kaplan & Simon, 1990). Thus, it is certainly possible that better decision strategies for some situations are not known by most decision makers.

Third, one must believe that one is capable of executing the new, hopefully more optimal strategy. For complex problems there may be a constraint on which strategies are believed to be feasible. In the words of Simon (1981a), "what a person cannot do he will not do, no matter how much he wants to do it" (p. 36). More detailed discussion of factors that may cause failure to adapt to incentives and other task and context variables is provided in chapter 6.

The Kahneman and Tversky approach to dealing with contingent decision behavior differs from ours in several ways. First, they emphasize the role of problem representation in determining choices to a greater degree than our approach does. Whereas Kahneman and Tversky emphasize the role of incentives in determining decision behavior to a lesser extent, both Kahneman and Tversky and we argue that the greatest impact of incentives is on how hard a decision maker will work, not necessarily on how smart he or she will work. Finally, we clearly emphasize the role of cognitive effort much more in our framework than do Kahneman and Tversky, although Kahneman and Tversky do not totally ignore the importance of cognitive effort considerations. As noted earlier, Kahneman and Tversky argue that the function of the editing stage is to "simplify subsequent evaluation and choice" (Kahneman & Tversky, 1979b, p. 274).

Later in this book (see chapter 5), we explore one approach to integrating the concern with the problem representation of Kahneman and Tversky and our concern with the selection of strategies that minimize effort and maximize accuracy. That integration stresses the ability of a decision maker to reduce decision effort either through the restructuring of a problem (e.g., editing operations) or through the use of simple decision rules like LEX or EBA. We also consider more general ideas for integrating perceptual and cost–benefit approaches.

Searching for a dominance structure. Another perceptually based model that deals with the use of multiple decision rules is that of Montgomery (1983; Montgomery & Svenson, 1983). Like the work by Kahneman and Tversky, the emphasis in Montgomery's model is on problem representation in the decision process. Montgomery sees decision making as a series of structuring and restructuring activities (see chapter 5 for related views). The various compensatory and noncompensatory decision rules are seen as operators that are used to restructure the decision problem. For any given decision problem, a variety of operations corresponding to rules like LEX, MCD, EBA, and WADD might be applied. That is, within a single decision episode one might observe the elimination of alternatives, a count of the number of advantages possessed by an alternative, a comparison of the most important attribute, and trading off a good value on one attribute against a bad value on another attribute. The purpose of the restructuring activities is to arrive at a representation of the decision problem in which the simple decision rule of dominance is applicable. Montgomery argues that by constructing a problem representation in which one alternative dominates the others, the decision maker will be able to reach a solution to the decision problem that is easily justified to oneself and to others.

Montgomery (1983), like our view and that of Beach and Mitchell, sees specific decision rules as having advantages (ease of use) and disadvantages (neglect of important information). Recently, he has also suggested that the rules used in dominance structuring may depend on such factors as the perceived importance of the decision (Lindberg, Garling, & Montgomery, 1989). Thus, there are similarities between the Montgomery model of multiple decision rule use and the general cost–benefit framework. The difference between Montgomery's and most other models lies in the emphasis he places on problem restructuring. Note also that Montgomery sees restructuring as an active search process, which differs from the more passive view of framing processes expressed by Kahneman and Tversky. Montgomery's model also emphasizes justifiability of the decision as a goal of the decision process more than the other approaches. Finally, Montgomery argues that a single decision episode will involve the use of multiple decision rules, so that the Montgomery model is concerned not with what decision rule is used but rather with what collection of rules will be used. As we discuss in the next chapter, a combination of decision strategies can sometimes offer a good compromise between effort and accuracy in decision making.

Integrating the cost–benefit and perceptual frameworks

The perceptual framework clearly complements the cost–benefit framework, because it is difficult to see how simple wording changes alone (e.g., as seen in "lives saved" versus "lives lost" in Tversky & Kahneman, 1981) change either cognitive effort or the desire for accuracy. On the other hand, it is not clear how the perceptual framework would handle contingent behavior due to the number of alternatives, for example, yet that phenomenon fits nicely into a cost–benefit framework.

There are opportunities to integrate the cost–benefit and perceptual frameworks. For example, Tversky and Kahneman (1986) note that several of the ideas of prospect theory, particularly those involved in the editing and framing of decisions, are consistent with Simon's conceptions of bounded rationality. In addition, Tversky and Kahneman (1990) suggest that the framing process is governed by such rules of mental economy (effort saving) as the general tendency to accept the problem as given and the segregation of the decision problem at hand from its broader context. In addition, during the course of constructing a heuristic (see chapter 5), decision makers may cycle between noticing aspects or characteristics of the choice set (e.g., extreme values across alternatives) and deciding how to exploit those aspects. Perceptual frameworks may be most relevant for the noticing process, whereas cost–benefit notions may be more relevant for determining what to do to take advantage of what has been noticed. A third opportunity for integrating the two frameworks would be to consider that individuals' assessments of costs and benefits for any heuristic may be greatly influenced by perceptual concerns, such as how information is presented or how the problem is framed. See Hammond (1990) for another perspective on integrating cost–benefit and perceptual notions.

Summary

This chapter has offered a theoretical framework for understanding how people decide which decision strategy to use in solving a particular judgment or choice problem. The heart of that framework is the view that strategy selection is the result of a compromise between the desire to make the most accurate decision and the desire to minimize effort. This chapter also reviews the perspectives offered

Table 3.5. *Summary of major points from chapter 3*

People have available a repertoire of strategies for solving decision problems, acquired through prior experience or formal training.

Different strategies have differing advantages and disadvantages for any particular decision problem.

Different decision tasks have properties that affect strategies' relative advantages and disadvantages.

Individuals select among strategies by trading off their relative advantages and disadvantages.

Strategy selection is sometimes a top-down process in which information about the current task is used to assess the advantages and disadvantages of the available strategies; the strategy offering the best tradeoff of advantages and disadvantages is then selected.

Strategy selection also can sometimes be bottom-up, with strategies developed on the fly and strategy selection influenced by information encountered during the decision process.

The major advantage considered by decision makers for a strategy is that strategy's anticipated accuracy; the major disadvantage is the anticipated cognitive effort required. Hence, strategy selection is often a compromise between accuracy and effort concerns. Other factors sometimes affecting strategy selection are the need to justify and conflict.

Judgments of the anticipated accuracy and effort associated with various strategies may be biased through such mechanisms as overconfidence in one's knowledge or abilities.

The cognitive effort associated with a decision strategy for a particular task can be usefully measured in terms of the number of elementary information processes (EIPs) (e.g., READS, COMPARISONS, ADDITIONS, and ELIMINATIONS) needed by that strategy to complete that task.

Different EIPs require different amounts of cognitive effort, and this varies across individuals and tasks. However, the effort required for a given EIP remains essentially constant regardless of the strategy in which that EIP is used.

The accuracy of a particular decision strategy can be usefully measured by comparing the performance of that strategy relative to that of the weighted adding rule (expected value or expected utility for risky choice) and that of random choice.

Decision heuristics exist that approximate the accuracy of more normative decision rules with substantial savings of effort for many decision problems;

Table 3.5. (*Cont.*)

which heuristic best approximates the accuracy of a more normative rule and saves the most effort will be highly situation-dependent.

The selection of a decision strategy will be a function of the emphasis placed on maximizing accuracy versus saving effort.

Constraints on decision behavior can make the selection of decision strategies a choice among simplifying heuristics rather than a choice between a heuristic and a normative strategy.

by a number of other researchers on the problem of understanding contingent decision behavior. Our framework clearly builds upon the ideas of other researchers; however, it does have its own emphases. In particular, we focus on strategy selection at a more detailed information-processing level than most other researchers. We also stress the role that cognitive effort plays in strategy selection. In that regard, this chapter describes a method for measuring decision effort based on the total number of elementary information processes needed to solve a problem. Evidence in support of that method of measurement is also provided. Table 3.5 summarizes the major theoretical and empirical points presented in this chapter.

Our concern with a process level explanation of contingent decision making has implications for both the level at which theoretical predictions are made and the nature of the data needed to test those predictions. In the next chapter we illustrate how our general accuracy–effort framework can be explored. In particular, we use computer simulation to generate specific predictions regarding adaptive decision behavior and use process-tracing methodology to generate detailed data. These data then allow us to characterize the extent to which actual decision behavior adapts in ways predicted by the simulation.

4

Studying contingent decisions:
An integrated methodology

Introduction

The preceding chapter offered a theoretical framework for under-standing how people decide which decision strategy to use in solving a particular judgment or choice problem. We hypothesized that the use of multiple strategies by a decision maker was an adaptive response to decision problems, given that the decision maker had goals for both the accuracy of the decision and for the effort required.

A major distinction between our framework and that of several other researchers is the emphasis we place on understanding con-tingent decision behavior at a detailed information-processing level of explanation. This emphasis on understanding process requires an integrated methodology with two features: the capability to derive specific process level predictions regarding adaptivity in decision processes; and tests of those predictions on detailed, process-tracing data from individuals facing decision problems. We propose and illustrate such an approach in this chapter. Our approach combines the use of simulation of decision processes to make detailed predictions with the use of a computerized system for collecting process-tracing data on information acquisition behavior, which can then be used to test those predictions. This integrated method-ology is unique to our work and is at a more detailed level than is typical in most research on decision making.

In the next sections we present the components of our method-ology. First, we examine how to simulate decision strategies using production systems, discuss some computer simulation results, and consider the predictions for process data that these results imply. Next, we outline various approaches to collecting process-tracing data. Finally, we present several applications of our integrated methodology in an attempt to validate our approach to understanding contingent decision behavior.

Production systems as models of decision strategies

In chapter 3 we have suggested ways in which the cognitive effort and accuracy associated with the use of a particular strategy in a particular decision environment might be measured. The proposed measure of cognitive effort is based on a decomposition of decision strategies into sets of elementary information processes (EIPs). We have also demonstrated in that chapter how one could derive counts of the number of EIPs necessary to execute a strategy in order to solve a particular decision problem.

Of the several measures of decision accuracy discussed in chapter 3, we have proposed a relative measure based on a comparison of the performance of heuristic strategies (or an individual's choice) with the performance expected if one followed a normative decision strategy as an upper limit and the performance expected from random choice behavior as a lower limit. Therefore, we have measures that allow us to describe both the effort and accuracy associated with a decision strategy for a particular task.

Approaches to modeling decision strategies

Ideally, one would like to derive closed-form equations describing how the effort and accuracy associated with decision strategies vary with changes in specified task and context variables. Such closed-form expressions are indeed possible for some decision rules in some tasks, such as for weighted adding as a function of the number of alternatives and number of attributes.[1] Yet such purely analytic methods fall short in several respects. First, many task and context variables would be quite difficult to model in any analytic framework. For example, the effects on effort and accuracy of time pressure or the presence or absence of dominated alternatives depend critically upon the interaction between particular choice heuristics and the values of the specific choice alternatives. Second, the problem becomes worse when we look at combinations of and

---

[1] For example, if there are m alternatives and n attributes, then there will be $2mn$ READS, mn PRODUCTS, $m(n-1)$ ADDS, $(m-1)$ COMPARISONS, and so on.

interactions between factors, such as the effects of time pressure in choice sets where dominance is absent. Finally, we would like to be able easily to compare and contrast the effects of task and context changes on a variety of measures of accuracy and/or effort, not just those which are most analytically tractable.

The approach we adopt is to use production system modeling of decision strategies and Monte Carlo computer simulation techniques to estimate how the effort and accuracy of various strategies vary with changes in decision environments. Computer simulation offers a fairly easy way to study strategy accuracy and effort across populations of choice problems. Computer simulation also makes it easy to examine multiple measures of accuracy and/or effort.

A production system (Newell & Simon, 1972) consists of a set of productions, a task environment, and a working memory. The productions specify a set of actions (EIPs) and the conditions under which they occur. As noted in chapter 1, the productions are expressed as (condition)–(action) pairs, and the actions specified in a production are performed (fired) only when the condition side is satisfied by matching the contents of working (active) memory. Working memory is a set of symbols, both those read from the external environment and those deposited by the actions performed by previous productions. In our simulations, we limit the size of working memory to eight or fewer symbols at any one time. The set of productions possessed by an individual is part of long-term memory.

As noted in chapter 1, the condition side of a production rule can include goals and subgoals. A subgoal for a decision might be, for example, reducing task complexity by elimination of some of the alternatives. Such a subgoal could result from a production that is fired if certain problem characteristics are noticed – for example, "we have a whole bunch of alternatives here." More specifically, there is evidence to be discussed later for a production of the form "If the number of alternatives is greater than three, then set current goal equal to the elimination of alternatives."

Production systems are partially data-driven, in that conditions will be matched against the contents of working memory, and those contents are, in part, the results of perceptual input. The presence of goals in the condition side, however, allows for the inclusion of more top-down aspects of decision processing.

Production systems have a number of advantages for studying

behavior. One of the foremost is that production systems, in combination with the notion of EIPs, provide a common language for describing all the decision strategies we examine. Production systems also are a congenial metaphor for studying the adaptation of strategies with experience (J. Anderson, 1983) and the introduction of new strategies (Langley et al., 1987). Additional arguments for the value of production systems as representations of human cognitive processes can be found in Newell (1980).

Implementation of decision strategies as production systems

In the previous chapter we proposed a set of elementary information processes (EIPs) that could be used to describe decision strategies (see Table 3.1). Table 4.1 contains a production system representation based on the proposed set of EIPs for the expected value maximization strategy for choice among gambles. The production system contains three productions, each of which performs the actions listed on the right-hand side of the table only when the condition on the left-hand side is true. Thus, at the beginning of the decision, only the third production would be true, and the production system would then READ the payoff for the first alternative into working memory, MOVE its attention to the probability of that outcome, READ it, and use the PRODUCT operator to weight the payoff by its probability.[2] This result is then ADDed to a running sum for the alternative, and attention is then MOVEd to the next payoff. This production continues to be applied until all outcomes have been examined. Now the second production fires, COMPARES this alternative to the best found until now, and marks the winner as the current best alternative found. This process repeats until all alternatives have been examined, and the condition side of the first production in the list becomes true, announcing that the alternative that is the current best alternative has been chosen.

Although expectation-based decision rules are generally thought to be very effortful, it is worth noting that the rule can be implemented without making large demands on working memory. This is

---

[2] The adjustment of values by the probabilities may not involve a literal multiplication of two numbers; rather, they may be combined by some analogical process that adjusts the value of one quantity given another (Lopes, 1982).

Table 4.1. *A production system representation of the expected value strategy*

(if at the end of alternatives)	then (CHOOSE alternative that is currently the best)
(if at the end of the outcomes)	then (COMPARE the current alternative to the current best; winner becomes current best)
(if not at the end of the outcomes)	then (READ the outcome's payoff; MOVE to the probability; READ the outcome's probability; PRODUCT the probability times the payoff; ADD the result to the current alternative; MOVE to the next outcome's payoff)

Source: Reprinted by permission, "Effort and accuracy in choice," Eric J. Johnson and John W. Payne, *Management Science, 31* (4), April 1985, p. 399. Copyright © 1985, The Institute of Management Sciences, 290 Westminster Street, Providence, RI 02903.

accomplished by combining the partial results as soon as possible (note the ADD operation in Table 4.1). All the decision rules we discuss operate similarly and do not store results in long-term memory.[3] Additionally, all are designed to minimize the number of operations. Because human decision makers may not necessarily adopt this technique, our implementations represent minimum estimates of the effort required to use each strategy. For example, variations of the strategies that would use long-term memory operations would lead to greater estimates of effort.

Several conflict resolution mechanisms could be proposed to select a production to execute if more than one is true. For example, Holland et al. (1986) suggest a general procedure in which a matching process is used to screen out those productions that do not match the current state of knowledge. Selection among the matched production rules is based on a "bid" representing such factors as the

---

[3] The computer program that implements the production system models short-term working memory as an array with eight cells, one of which is used to hold the name of the alternative that has been chosen.

history of past usefulness of the rule and the degree of specificity of the production's condition (the more specific the condition side of a matched production, the more likely the production will be selected). The greater the bid value of a production, the greater the probability of its execution. One could also select among productions based upon the degree to which their conditions are matched (J. Anderson, 1983). However, our implementations simply assume that the first production in the list whose condition side is matched fires.

We also assume that the decision processes are implemented without error. As noted by Weber, Goldstein, and Busemeyer (1991), decay, distortion, or confusion of intermediate computations is possible in the execution of a decision strategy. Similarly, J. Anderson (1983) has noted that failures in working memory regarding goals can make behavior appear less structured and apparently more data-driven than it may really be. Nevertheless, as a first approximation we do not allow for errors in the execution of the production system representing a decision strategy.[4]

Once production system representations of decision strategies have been constructed, it is fairly straightforward to implement the production systems as computer programs. Using Monte Carlo simulation techniques, it then becomes possible to count the number of elementary information processes (EIPs) used by each strategy for a given decision task over many trials, while simultaneously observing the accuracy of the choices that are made. Such estimates of the effort and accuracy of various strategies in a variety of decision environments can yield insights into how the performance of decision strategies interacts with changes in tasks. These insights can be used to generate predictions about how *aspects of processing*, as exemplified by the individual strategies, might change across different task environments if employed by an *idealized* adaptive decision maker attending to both effort and accuracy in selecting a decision strategy. The simulation results can be used to help us better understand existing empirical findings regarding contingent decision behavior or can help to generate hypotheses for new experiments.

---

[4] Every model of behavior makes various simplifying assumptions. We have identified some of the assumptions that may limit the generalizability of our production system models. Nevertheless, as will be illustrated later in this chapter, we believe that even the simple production system models of decision strategies we propose are useful in providing insights into adaptive decision behavior. In chapter 5 and 8 we discuss how our models might be extended.

In the following sections of the chapter we describe a simulation study that we have conducted, discuss the accuracy–effort tradeoffs implied by the results of that simulation, relate the simulation results to prior empirical findings, and describe the results of experiments that directly test some of the predictions generated by the simulation.

A Monte Carlo study of effort and accuracy in choice

The decision environment

The decision task used in the simulation study described here (taken from Payne et al., 1988) was a special type of risky choice problem, with alternatives with outcomes that have different payoffs but a constant probability for each outcome across all the alternatives. In other words, each of the alternatives may have a different value for a given outcome, but the probability of receiving that outcome is the same for all the alternatives. We used such choice problems for two main reasons: first, this particular type of risky choice problem is structurally similar to a riskless multiattribute choice problem (Keeney & Raiffa, 1976). In the riskless interpretation, the probabilities function as attribute weights that apply across alternatives. One can look at a probability of .20, for example, as the weight given to a particular attribute across all alternatives. Second, we could easily relate consequences to choice among gambles in our later experimental work (i.e., people can play selected gambles for money).

Decision strategies

In solving choice problems of the kind just described, the decision maker must search among the probabilities (weights) for each outcome and the values associated with the outcomes for each alternative. Different decision strategies can be thought of as different rules for conducting that search. In the simulation we examined six heuristic search and evaluation strategies (equal weight, elimination-by-aspects, satisficing, lexicographic, lexicographic semiorder, and majority of confirming dimensions) as well as the normative strategy of weighted additive value (expected value maximization) and the simple random choice rule. These heuristics were selected because they vary substantially in the amount of information used and in the way that the available information is used to make a choice (see chapter 2). Further, these heuristics were selected for study because they had been observed in previous studies of judgment and choice (see chapter 2) and/or had been suggested on theoretical grounds as useful simplification procedures for decisions (Einhorn & Hogarth, 1975).

Finally, we examined two combined strategies. The first was an elimination-by-aspects plus weighted additive (EBA + WADD) rule. This rule used an EBA process until the number of available alternatives remaining was three or less, and then used a weighted additive rule to select among the remaining alternatives. The other combined strategy, elimination-by-aspects plus majority of confirming dimensions (EBA + MCD), used an EBA process to reduce the problem size to three remaining alternatives or less and then used a majority of confirming dimensions heuristic to select from the reduced set. In this rule, as in the straight MCD procedure, if an equal number of winning attributes existed for the two alternatives, the alternative winning the comparison on the last attribute was retained. These particular combined strategies were used because they had been observed in several previous choice process studies (e.g., Bettman & Park, 1980).

Task and context variables

In order to generate predictions about strategy usage, one must manipulate features of the decision environment. We manipulated both task and context variables in the simulations. Three task variables were examined. The first two variables, number of alternatives and number of attributes, were each varied at three levels (2, 5, and 8) in order to manipulate problem size. Size was included because variations in choice problem size have produced some of the clearest examples of contingent decision behavior (see chapter 2).

The third task variable included was time pressure. Time pressure is a very significant task variable, which has been hypothesized to lead to task simplifications (P. Wright, 1974). Furthermore, under time constraints, heuristics might be even more accurate than a "normative" strategy such as maximization of expected value, because the heuristic's accuracy may degrade under increasing time pressure at a slower rate than a more comprehensive processing rule (e.g., EV) degrades. One reason for this is that heuristics require fewer operations and will generally be "further along" when time runs out.

Furthermore, people may use heuristics under time pressure because they have no other choice (Simon, 1981a). A more normative decision strategy like expected utility maximization may exceed the information-processing capabilities of a decision maker, given any "reasonable" time limit. Deciding how to choose then becomes a selection of the "best" of the available heuristics, not a choice between using some heuristic or the more normative rule.

Time pressure was varied at four levels: (1) no time pressure, with each rule using as many operations as needed; or a maximum of (2) 50 EIPs (severe time pressure); (3) 100 EIPs (moderate pressure); and (4) 150 EIPs (low pressure). These time (EIP) constraint values were selected on the basis of an analysis of the maximum number of EIPs associated with the most effortful rule, weighted additive. The average number of EIPs required for the weighted additive rule to run to completion ranged from 28 for the two-alternative, two-attribute case to 400 for the eight-alternative, eight-attribute case. Comparable figures for the lexicographic strategy are 21.3 (2 x 2) and 172.5 (8 × 8).

Note that the total number of EIPs was used to operationalize time pressure. This implicitly assumes that each EIP takes a similar amount of time. The sensitivity of the analyses to this assumption is examined later using the results on EIP times reported in chapter 3.

A key issue in dealing with the time constraints is how rules should select among alternatives if they run out of time. Several rules identify one alternative as the best seen so far (i.e., the WADD, EQW, and MCD rules) and select that alternative when they run out of time. The EBA, lexicographic, and satisficing rules all pick an option randomly from those alternatives not yet eliminated. Because the EBA and lexicographic rules were able to process all alternatives on at least one attribute, even for the largest problem size under the severest time constraint, the choice came from the set already processed but not eliminated. For the satisficing rule in this severest case, if the first alternative was not acceptable, then random choice among the remaining alternatives seems to be the most reasonable option. For the two combined strategies, the selection was either made at random from the alternatives not yet eliminated if the combined strategy was still in the EBA phase, or the best so far if in the WADD or MCD phase.

Finally, two context variables were included. One context variable was the presence or absence of dominated alternatives. Removing dominated alternatives produces efficient or Pareto-optimal choice sets. McClelland (1978) suggests that the success of the equal weight simplification strategy is dependent upon the presence of dominated alternatives. The second context variable was the degree of dispersion of probabilities (weights) within each alternative. To illustrate, a four-outcome gamble (alternative) with a low degree of dispersion might have probabilities of .30, .20, .22, and .28 for the four outcomes respectively. On the other hand, a gamble with a high degree of dispersion might have probabilities such as .68, .12, .05, and .15 for the four outcomes. This variable was chosen because Thorngate (1980) suggested that probability information may be relatively unimportant in making accurate risky choices (see also Beach, 1983). Obviously, if all of the outcome probabilities were identical, probability information would not matter. On the other hand, if one outcome is certain, then examining the probability information to find that outcome is crucial. What is unclear is how sensitive heuristics are to the dispersion in probabilities, and how adaptive actual behavior is to such a context variable. We therefore examined decision sets with either low or high dispersion.

Parameters of choice rules: JNDs and cutoff values

The simulation requires us to make choices about the values of two particular parameters, cutoffs, and just noticeable differences (JNDs), which potentially affect the effort and accuracy of certain rules. In the EBA and SAT rules, the cutoff value determines the elimination of alternatives. For LEXSEMI, the JND determines such eliminations. Some researchers (Grether & Wilde, 1984; Klein, 1983; Klein & Bither, 1987; J. Huber & Klein, 1991) have suggested that the process of generating cutoffs may itself be adaptive. More generally, as we discuss later, one may be able to trade accuracy for effort savings through changes in a strategy's parameters, as well as through a change in strategies. Although this is an intriguing possibility, we desired single cutoff and JND values across all conditions to facilitate comparisons across strategies. The values were obtained from a pilot simulation, without time pressure, in which all attributes were drawn from a uniform distribution bounded by 0 and 1,000. From the initially manipulated set of cutoffs (100, 300, and 500) and JNDs (1, 50, 100), we found that cutoffs of 500 for EBA and 300 for SAT were most efficient. A JND of 50 performed best for the LEXSEMI rule.

Procedure

The 10 decision rules were individually applied to 200 randomly generated decision problems in each of the 288 conditions defined by a 3 (number of alternatives) by 3 (number of attributes) by 2 (low or high dispersion of probabilities or weights) by 2 (possibility or absence of dominated alternatives) by 2 (cutoff values) by 4 (time constraints) factorial. After each trial, the alternative selected was recorded, along with a tally for each elementary operation used by the rule.

Payoffs were randomly selected from a uniform distribution bounded by 0 and 1,000 by the multiplicative congruence method using the IMSL subroutine RNUN (IMSL, 1987, pp. 963–964). Probabilities (weights) were generated by one of two methods: The low-dispersion condition replicates the procedure used by Thorngate (1980). The required number of deviates, m, was generated from a uniform distribution and divided by the sum, normalizing the sum to 1.0. In contrast, the high-dispersion method first selected a deviate from the range $(0, 1)$. Each subsequent deviate was randomly selected from the interval

$$(0, 1 - \sum_{j}^{i-1} p_j),$$

where the p_j are the previously generated deviates. When $m - 1$ probabilities had been generated, the procedure halted and the mth probability was set to

$$1 - \sum_{j}^{m-1} p_j.$$

The presence or absence of dominated alternatives was manipulated by testing for the presence of first-order stochastic dominance and rejecting, in the dominance-absent condition, choice sets containing dominated alternatives. First-order stochastic dominance describes a relation between two risky alternatives A and B that ensures that A will always produce a higher utility than B for a decision maker with a finite, monotonically increasing utility function. It is analogous to simple dominance for riskless choice.

Note that despite the widely differing characteristics of the four cells created by the two types of context effects, all cells will have the *same* mean payoff and probability, and that the correlation between payoffs and probabilities will be close to 0. The differences due to context effects are reflected in the dispersion of the probabilities and in the presence or absence of dominated alternatives.

Results

As discussed in chapter 3, we measured effort in terms of the total number of EIPs used by a specific decision rule to make a selection from a set of alternatives. The results will first be presented using a measure of effort without any differential weighting of the individual EIPs. That is, our counts of EIPs will first assume that each EIP requires the same level of time or mental effort. Later we report results that relax that assumption using the data on EIPs and decision effort presented in chapter 3.

The measure of accuracy used compared the relative performance of the heuristic and combined strategies to the two baseline strategies, the maximization of weighted additive value (expected value) and random choice. The measure was defined by the following equation, as given in chapter 3:

$$\text{Relative Accuracy} = \frac{EV_{\text{heuristic rule choice}} - EV_{\text{random rule choice}}}{EV_{\text{expected value choice}} - EV_{\text{random rule choice}}}$$

The maximum expected value possible in a particular choice set and the expected value associated with a random selection were determined. The expected value of the alternative selected by a decision heuristic was then compared with these two baseline values. This measure is bounded by a value of 1.00 for the EV rule, and an expected value of 0.0 for random selection. It provides a measure of the relative improvement of a heuristic strategy over random choice.

We present first the results for the conditions without time pressure. We initially discuss the effects of the two context variables, dispersion in probabilities (weights) and dominance present or absent, followed by a discussion of the effects of the task complexity variables, number of alternatives and number of attributes. Next, we will compare the results for the conditions without time pressure to those with time pressure.

Performance of heuristics in different contexts. Table 4.2 presents the relative accuracy and effort scores for each of the 10 decision strategies in the 4 decision environments defined by crossing the context factors dispersion in weights (low or high) and dominance (possible or absent). The results are averaged over number of alternatives and number of attributes.

The simulation results shown in Table 4.2 indicate that in some environments the use of a nonnormative strategy may not only reduce the effort needed to reach a decision but can also provide a level of accuracy comparable with that obtained by a strategy in which all information is used. The most impressive example of this is the LEX rule, which achieves 90% relative accuracy with only 40% of the effort of the weighted adding rule in high-dispersion environments. Also, the EQW model provides 89% of the normative model's performance with a little more than 50% of the effort in the low-dispersion, dominance-possible case.

It is clear from Table 4.2 that the most efficient heuristic varies across task environments. In the low-dispersion, dominance-possible environment, for example, the processing simplification of ignoring probability (weight) information (i.e., the equal weight strategy) appears quite accurate. In contrast, when the dispersion in probabilities is higher, the lexicographic rule, which ignores all the payoff information except that associated with the single most likely outcome, is the most accurate heuristic and is substantially better than the equal weight rule. It is also clear that some heuristics (e.g., MCD and satisficing) perform reasonably in the dominance-possible environments, but their accuracy drops substantially when dominated alternatives are removed.

It may be that the accuracy of some of the heuristics in the presence of dominated options is due to their ability to screen truly inferior options. E. Johnson and Payne (1985) report that all the choice strategies they investigated, with the exception of the random and elimination-by-aspects rules, almost always avoided dominated alternatives. When dominated options are removed, some of the heuristics do not improve much on random selection.

Note that in the low-dispersion, dominance-absent environment, the best simple heuristic, LEX, has an accuracy score of .67. That accuracy score is .22 less than the accuracy score for the "best" heuristic in the other three environments. This suggests that a decision maker in such an environment would not be able to reduce effort much without suffering a substantial loss in accuracy. Decision problems involving low-dispersion, dominance-absent environments may therefore be particularly difficult.[5]

---

[5] We have asked subjects to rate the difficulty of choices representing the four context combinations. They reported that decisions in the low-dispersion, dominance-absent environments were more difficult, and they also took longer to make such decisions.

Table 4.2. *Simulation results for accuracy and effort of heuristics in the no time pressure decision problems across four task environments*

	Dominance possible		Dominance not possible	
Strategy	Low dispersion	High dispersion	Low dispersion	High dispersion
WADD				
RA	1.0	1.0	1.0	1.0
UOC	160	160	160	160
EQW				
RA	.89	.67	.41	.27
UOC	85	85	85	85
SAT				
RA	.32	.31	.03	.07
UOC	49	49	61	61
MCD				
RA	.62	.48	.07	.09
UOC	148	148	141	140
LEX				
RA	.69	.90	.67	.90
UOC	60	60	60	60
LEXSEMI				
RA	.71	.87	.64	.77
UOC	87	78	79	81
EBA				
RA	.67	.66	.54	.56
UOC	87	88	82	82
EBA + WADD				
RA	.84	.79	.69	.66
UOC	104	106	102	102
EBA + MCD				
RA	.69	.59	.29	.31
UOC	89	89	86	86

Note: RA = relative accuracy (95% confidence interval width = ±029). UOC = unweighted operations count (95% confidence interval width = 2.75). WADD = weighted additive strategy. EQW = equal weight strategy. LEX = lexicographic strategy. LEXSEMI = lexicographic semiorder strategy. EBA = elimination by aspects strategy. EBA + WADD = combined elimination by aspects plus weighted additive strategy. EBA + MCD = combined elimination by aspects plus majority of confining dimensions strategy.

The performance of the two combined decision strategies is also interesting. The combination of an elimination process with a weighted adding model (EBA + WADD) performed well across all task conditions. The rule offers a good combination of expected accuracy and reasonable levels of expected effort. The EBA + MCD rule, on the other hand, seems to be an inefficient combination strategy.

In summary, heuristic strategies can be highly accurate in some environments, but no single heuristic does well across all contexts. This suggests that if a decision maker wanted to achieve both a reasonably high level of accuracy and low effort, he or she would have to use a repertoire of strategies, with selection contingent upon situational demands.

The potential tradeoffs between accuracy and effort for the various strategies are highlighted in Figure 4.1. That figure, which is similar to the hypothetical strategy tradeoff figures discussed in the preceding chapter, shows the actual simulation results from two contexts – low dispersion in probabilities, dominance possible versus high dispersion, dominance possible – averaged over number of alternatives and outcomes. We highlight the two contexts shown in Figure 4.1 because they play a major role in several of the experimental studies described later. The measure of effort for each strategy has been turned into a relative measure based on the ratio of the number of EIPs required by a heuristic to the number of EIPs required by the most effortful strategy, WADD. A line that indicates an efficient set of pure strategies, considering both a desire for greater accuracy and a desire for lesser effort, is drawn for each context. Figure 4.1 illustrates the sensitivity of the accuracy and effort levels characterizing various strategies to relatively subtle changes in context, such as the dispersion in probabilities.

The simulation does not identify which particular strategy a decision maker will select in a given decision environment. That would depend on the degree to which a decision maker was willing to trade decreases in accuracy for savings in effort. However, note

Source to Table 4.2 (*cont.*)

Source: Adapted by permission of the publisher from "Adaptive strategy selection in decision making," John W. Payne, James R. Bettman, and Eric J. Johnson, *Journal of Experimental Psychology: Learning, Memory, and Cognition*, 14 (1988), p. 538. Copyright © 1988 by the American Psychological Association.

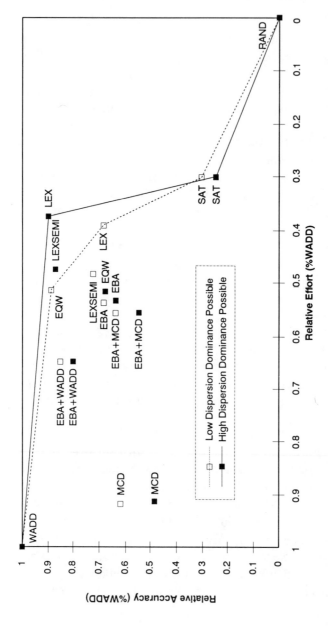

Note: Effort/Accuracy tradeoffs for various decision strategies in the low-dispersion (□) and high-dispersion (■) environments where dominance is possible. The lines join the most efficient pure strategies for each environment.

Figure 4.1. Effort–accuracy tradeoffs for various decision strategies. *Source:* Adapted by permission of the publisher from "Adaptive strategy selection in decision making," John W. Payne, James R. Bettman, and Eric J. Johnson, *Journal of Experimental Psychology: Learning, Memory, and Cognition, 14* (1988), p. 540. Copyright © 1988 by the American Psychological Association.

that if a decision maker desired relatively high levels of accuracy in an environment where dominance is possible, there are accurate strategies in each environment with substantial savings in effort: the lexicographic rule in the high-dispersion condition and the equal weight strategy in the low-dispersion condition. Thus, the simulation predicts that when dominance is possible, one should see more processing consistent with a lexicographic strategy (e.g., attribute-based processing, selective processing across attributes, and high proportions of processing on probabilities and the most important attribute) in environments with high dispersion in probabilities. In contrast, in low-dispersion, dominance-possible environments, one should observe more alternative-based processing, more consistent (i.e., less selective) processing, and a lower proportion of time spent processing the probabilities and the most important attribute, all of which are consistent with strategies like the equal weight rule. The prediction is based on the assumption that *people are sensitive to the relative accuracy of strategies in different contexts,* as well as being aware of differences in relative effort.

In addition to this prediction, a subtler prediction can also be made. Note from Table 4.2 and Figure 4.1 that if one uses the equal weight strategy in a low-dispersion environment and the lexicographic strategy under high dispersion, roughly equal accuracy can be attained. However, less effort is required in the high-dispersion environment. Thus, if subjects desire relatively high levels of accuracy, the simulation would predict that accuracy levels would not vary across dispersion conditions, but that effort levels would be lower for the high-dispersion condition. Further, the relative changes in processing that might be expected – for example, more attribute-based and more selective – are not sensitive to a particular tradeoff between effort and accuracy.

Effects of number of alternatives and number of attributes. Although not shown in Table 4.2, there were also systematic effects of the number of alternatives and number of attributes. Figure 4.2 shows the changes in relative accuracy for several common heuristics as the number of alternatives (panel a) or number of attributes (panel b) is increased, averaged over the four dispersion-dominance environments. Note that relative accuracy is fairly robust over changes in number of alternatives for the various heuristics. Relative accuracy is more sensitive to changes in number of attributes.

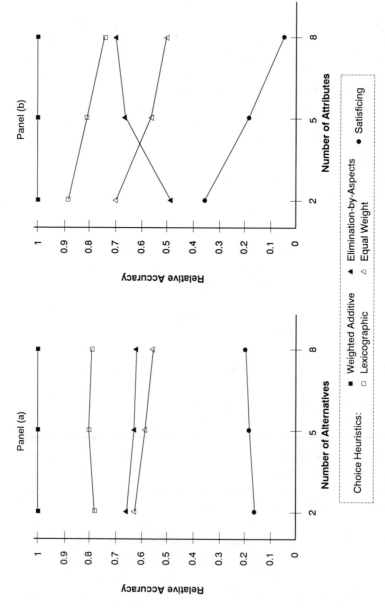

Figure 4.2. The effects of number of alternatives and number of attributes on the relative accuracy of choice heuristics. *Source:* Reprinted by permission from "Understanding contingent choice: A computer simulation approach," John W. Payne, Eric J. Johnson, James R. Bettman, and Eloise Coupey, *IEEE Transactions on Systems, Man, and Cybernetics, 20* (1990), p. 303. Copyright © 1990 IEEE.

Increasing the number of attributes leads to decreased performance for the equal weight, lexicographic, and satisficing rules; performance increases, however, with more attributes for the EBA heuristic. This latter effect occurs because the alternative finally selected by the EBA rule will tend to have surpassed cutoffs on more attributes as the number of attributes increases.

These results averaged over the four dispersion-dominance task environments reveal interesting differences between the effects of number of alternatives and number of attributes on accuracy. Further insights can be gained by examining the effects of number of alternatives and attributes in specific task environments. For example, the mean accuracy of the equal weight rule only decreased from .93 to .87 as the number of attributes increased from two to eight in the low-dispersion, dominance-possible environment. However, the mean accuracy of the lexicographic rule decreased substantially in that environment, from .86 to .55, as the number of attributes was increased. The decrease in accuracy for the lexicographic rule reflects the fact that a rule that uses only information associated with a single (although the most probable) outcome would be expected to perform worse as an increasing number of relatively important (probable) outcomes are ignored. In contrast, the impact of increases in number of attributes on the equal weight and lexicographic rules was reversed for the high-dispersion, dominance-possible environments. The mean accuracy for the equal weight rule decreased from .71 to .49 for the two-outcome and eight-outcome problems, respectively, reflecting the fact that the rule essentially overweights information from more and more outcomes with small probabilities as the number of outcomes is increased. The lexicographic rule only decreased from .93 to .87 for the same problems.

The number of alternatives also had effects on effort, as shown in Figure 4.3a. Of most interest, the effort required to use heuristics increased more slowly than the effort required to use a normative procedure like weighted adding as the number of alternatives was increased.

The effects of number of attributes on effort in the simulations are shown in Figure 4.3b. Again, the effort required for the weighted additive rule grows more rapidly than the effort needed by the various heuristics as the number of attributes increases.

A comparison of the data in Figures 4.2 and 4.3 leads to an

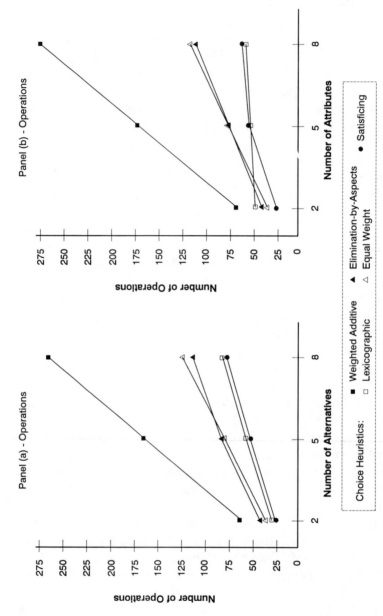

Figure 4.3. The effects of number of alternatives and number of attributes on the average number of operations of choice heuristics. *Source:* Reprinted by permission from "Understanding contingent choice: A computer simulation approach," John W. Payne, Eric J. Johnson, James R. Bettman, and Eloise Coupey, *IEEE Transactions on Systems, Man, and Cybernetics, 20* (1990), p. 304. Copyright © 1990 IEEE.

interesting conclusion. The accuracy of the heuristics is fairly robust as the number of alternatives increases, and the effort required for heuristics grows less rapidly than that required for the weighted adding rule. Thus, heuristics will appear relatively more efficient as the number of alternatives increases. For increases in the number of attributes, on the other hand, the relative accuracy of heuristics tends to decrease (except for EBA) and the effort required still increases. As the number of attributes increases, therefore, the relative efficiency of heuristics is not quite so clear.

Finally, note that for the set of variables studied in our simulation, task and context variables seem to differ in terms of their relative effects on the accuracy and effort of heuristics. In general, the effort levels associated with many of the heuristics are essentially the same across changes in the dispersion of probabilities and in the possible presence of dominated alternatives. In contrast, such context changes had substantial effects on the relative accuracy of heuristics. On the other hand, the effort of heuristics was generally impacted by task variables, whereas accuracy was less affected.

Overall, the simulation suggests that task variables tend to have greater influence on effort whereas context variables tend to have greater influence on accuracy. Interestingly, studies showing contingent processing due to changes in task variables are fairly common; studies showing changes due to context variables are much less common (see chapter 2).

Relaxing the assumption of equal effort for all EIPs. The simulation results so far are based on the assumption that all EIPs take an equal amount of time to execute. As mentioned in chapter 3, however, some EIPs may be more complex (e.g., PRODUCT). To examine the possible effects of the differential weighting of effort for the various EIPs, we ran the simulation with the following time estimates for the EIPs (taken from Bettman et al., 1990): 1.19s, READ and MOVE combined; 0.84s, ADDITION; 0.32s, DIFFERENCE; 2.23s, PRODUCT; 0.20s, COMPARE; and 0.39s, ELIMINATE. Although the results showed that all heuristics become relatively less effortful, relative to WADD, when EIPs are weighted individually, the key relationships between aspects of processing and context variables (e.g., dispersion, dominance) are largely unchanged.

Results under time pressure. We also present three sets of results

Table 4.3. *Simulation results for accuracy of heuristics under time pressure across various task environments*

Strategy	Dominance possible, low dispersion			Dominance possible, high dispersion			Dominance not possible, low dispersion			Dominance not possible, high dispersion		
	LTP	MTP	STP	LTP	MTP	STP	LTP	MTP	STP	LTP	MTP	STP
WADD	.91*	.80	.28	.91*	.80	.28	.90*	.77*	.12	.92*	.82	.24
EQW	.88	.82*	.72*	.66	.65	.55	.41	.34	.26	.24	.25	.18
SAT	.38	.34	.30	.32	.34	.23	.03	.04	.06	.07	.05	.04
MCD	.58	.49	.23	.44	.35	.17	.03	-.01	-.02	.04	.03	.02
LEX	.70	.69	.47	.90	.90*	.59	.69	.68	.48*	.90	.90*	.60
LEXSEMI	.71	.66	.40	.87	.83	.49	.63	.59	.43	.76	.75	.51
EBA	.70	.68	.49	.76	.73	.65*	.63	.60	.48*	.67	.67	.61*
EBA + WADD	.86	.79	.43	.86	.82	.48	.73	.66	.27	.75	.74	.43
EBA + MCD	.74	.65	.44	.67	.60	.49	.35	.32	.27	.40	.41	.36

Note: The 95% confidence interval width for the accuracy values is ±.029. LTP = low time pressure. MTP = moderate time pressure. STP = severe time pressure. WADD = weighted additive strategy. EQW = equal weight strategy. SAT = satisficing strategy. MCD = majority of confirming dimensions strategy. LEX = lexicographic strategy. LEXSEMI = lexicographic semiorder strategy. EBA = elimination by aspects strategy. EBA + WADD = combined elimination by aspects plus weighted additive strategy. EBA + MCD = combined elimination by aspects plus majority of confirming dimensions strategy. Figures marked by an asterisk represent the most accurate strategy for each task environment.

Source: Adapted by permission of the publisher from "Adaptive strategy selection in decision making," John W. Payne, James R. Bettman, and Eric J. Johnson, *Journal of Experimental Psychology: Learning, Memory, and Cognition, 14* (1988), p. 540. Copyright © 1988 by the American Psychological Association.

under time pressure. First, we examine the performance of various heuristics in the four different dispersion-dominance task environments. Then, results detailing the effects of the size of the choice task are considered. Finally, the effects of relaxing the assumption that EIPs take equal amounts of effort are detailed.

As shown by the results in Table 4.3, time constraints clearly have differential effects on the various rules. The WADD rule, for example, shows a marked reduction in accuracy from the baseline value of 1.0 under no time pressure to an average accuracy of only 0.12 under the severest time constraint in the no dominance, low-dispersion condition. In contrast, the EBA heuristic shows relatively little effect of time pressure. The EBA rule is actually the most accurate decision strategy in three of the four environments for severe time pressure. One general result from both the time pressure and no time pressure simulations is the robustness of the EBA strategy (Tversky, 1972) across a variety of task environments. Another rule that also usually holds up well under time pressure is the simple lexicographic strategy (as long as problem size is not large – see the discussion in the next section for further details). It appears that strategies like EBA and LEX, which involve an initial processing of all alternatives using a limited set of attributes, do well under severe time pressure. Based upon the simulations, it seems important under high time pressure to use a choice strategy that processes at least *some* information about *all* alternatives as soon as possible.[6] However, note that in one decision environment (dominance possible, low dispersion in weights), the alternative simplification strategy provided by the equal weight rule is superior for even the severest time constraint studied.

Effects of time pressure combined with task size. Both increased time pressure and larger problem size can be thought of as ways to increase the difficulty or complexity of a decision task (P. Wright, 1974). One way to examine how time pressure and choice task size interact is to consider how various heuristics perform under combinations of moderate and severe time pressure coupled with moderate and large problem sizes. Table 4.4 shows the relative

---

[6] Interestingly, Eisenhardt (1989) reports that firms in the computer industry operating in rapidly changing environments (time pressure) did better if they used a "breadth, not depth" strategy for evaluating options (i.e., considering many options rather than examining only one in great detail).

Table 4.4. *The effects of time pressure and choice task size on the average relative accuracy of choice heuristics*

Time Pressure	Choice task Size	Strategies				
		WADD	EQW	LEX	EBA	SAT
Moderate	Moderate[a]	.75	.51	.78	.75	.23
Moderate	Large[b]	.34	.21	.68	.67	.08
Severe	Moderate	−.05	.29	.77	.54	.15
Severe	Large	−.06	.13	.14	.35	.02

Note: The 95% confidence interval width for the accuracy scores is .013.
[a]Five alternatives and five outcomes.
[b]Eight alternatives and eight outcomes.
Source: Reprinted by permission from "Understanding contingent choice: A computer simulation approach," John W. Payne, Eric J. Johnson, James R. Bettman, and Eloise Coupey, *IEEE Transactions on Systems, Man, and Cybernetics, 20* (1990), p. 305. Copyright © 1990 IEEE.

accuracy scores for several decision methods for the four combinations of moderate and severe time pressure with moderate (five alternatives and five attributes) and large (eight alternatives and eight attributes) problem size. Only accuracy is considered, because the EIP counts are constrained by time pressure.

The accuracy scores show that time pressure and problem size differentially affect the performance of the various rules. Under moderate levels of both time pressure and problem size, the weighted adding, equal weight, lexicographic, and elimination-by-aspects rules perform reasonably well in terms of accuracy. As the task is made more difficult, either by combining a large-sized problem with moderate time pressure or a moderate-sized problem with severe time pressure, the performance of the weighted adding and equal weight rules falls off. The lexicographic and EBA heuristics continue to perform well, especially the lexicographic rule. In the severest environment studied, with severe time pressure and a large problem, EBA is the only heuristic that maintains a reasonable level of performance. Thus, EBA is the most robust procedure as task conditions grow more difficult. For all combinations other than the severest, the lexicographic heuristic also performs quite well.

The results under time pressure might be particularly sensitive

Table 4.5. *Time-weighted simulation results for accuracy of heuristics under severe time pressure for various task environments*

Strategy	Dominance possible, dispersion in possibilities		Dominance not possible, dispersion in possibilities	
	Low	High	Low	High
WADD	.27	.27	.15	.20
EQW	.81*	.62	.37	.27
SAT	.34	.32	.00	.03
MCD	.54	.39	.04	.01
LEX	.68	.89*	.68*	.90*
EBA	.70	.74	.60	.67

Note: The 95% confidence interval width for the accuracy scores is 0.41. Figures marked by an asterisk represent the most accurate strategy for each task environment.
Source: Reprinted by permission from "Understanding contingent choice: A computer simulation approach," John W. Payne, Eric J. Johnson, James R. Bettman, and Eloise Coupey, *IEEE Transactions on Systems, Man, and Cybernetics*, 20 (1990), p. 305. Copyright © 1990 IEEE.

to the assumption that all EIPs require equal amounts of effort. For example, we have discussed the drop in performance for the lexicographic heuristic for large problem sizes under severe time pressure. The lexicographic strategy uses many comparisons. Because we noted that comparisons require less effort (time) than several of the other operations, the performance of the lexicographic rule many improve if the individual EIPs are weighted in the simulation.

The results of running a simulation where the EIPs are time-weighted are presented in Table 4.5 for the severe time pressure condition. Many of the results mirror those of the unweighted simulation. However, there are some differences. Whereas the EBA rule remains robust, the performance of the LEX heuristic now exceeds that of EBA. LEX is now the most accurate strategy for three of the four environments. As before, the equal weight strategy is best for the dominance-possible, low-dispersion environment. In terms of the general conclusion just drawn, however, it is still the case that

Table 4.6. *The effects of time pressure and choice task size on the average relative accuracy of choice heuristics in the time-weighted simulation*

Time pressure	Choice task size	Strategies				
		WADD	EQW	LEX	EBA	SAT
Moderate	Moderate[a]	.72	.54	.80	.75	.21
Moderate	Large[b]	.39	.36	.71	.73	.14
Severe	Moderate	−.03	.52	.79	.73	.22
Severe	Large	.09	.24	.69	.66	.05

Note: The 95% confidence interval width for the accuracy scores is .041.
[a] Five alternatives and five outcomes.
[b] Eight alternatives and eight outcomes.
Source: Reprinted by permission from "Understanding contingent choice: A computer simulation approach," John W. Payne, Eric J. Johnson, James R. Bettman, and Eloise Coupey, *IEEE Transactions on Systems, Man, and Cybernetics*, 20 (1990), p. 306. Copyright © 1990 IEEE.

strategies that initially process all alternatives using a limited set of attributes (EBA and LEX) generally do well under severe time pressure.

The results presented in Table 4.6 provide further insight into the improved performance of the lexicographic rule. Whereas the LEX heuristic showed a large drop in performance for severe time pressure and large problem sizes in the unweighted simulation, the performance of the LEX rule in the time-weighted simulation remains high for this severest case. The LEX and EBA heuristics perform well for all four of the time pressure and problem size combinations, whereas the other heuristics show performance declines as either time pressure or problem size increases.

Conclusions from the simulations

The simulation results we have reported indicate what an idealized decision maker might do in the way of shifting strategies as task environments change. As such, the simulations are not meant to represent actual decision behavior, but rather to provide a "task analysis" of the problem of strategy selection in decision making.

The simulations indicate which strategies achieve fairly high accuracy with substantial effort savings, for example. Because the various strategies can be characterized in terms of such factors as the amount of information considered, the selectivity of processing, and whether processing is organized around alternatives or attributes (see Table 2.1), we can use the simulation results to derive hypotheses about these factors. For example, the simulation results for the context variable, dispersion in probabilities, suggest that when dominated alternatives are possible, more attribute-based processing, more selective processing across attributes and alternatives, and a higher proportion of processing on probabilities and the most important attribute should be observed in the high-dispersion rather than in the low-dispersion condition. Such aspects characterize rules, like the LEX rule, that are relatively accurate with substantial effort savings in the high-dispersion environment.

The simulation also suggests that strategies characterized by attribute-based processing and selectivity in processing, particularly across attributes, should be more effective under severe time pressure. Strategies such as LEX and EBA, which maintain accuracy relatively well under heavy time pressure, also are characterized by a greater proportion of processing on probabilities and the most important attribute.

Such predictions can be tested by collecting process-tracing data for different decision tasks and measuring aspects such as the amount, selectivity, and type of processing. These measures can then be used to test the simulations' predictions. Such comparisons between the simulations' predictions and actual behavior can be made both for previous empirical work and for new studies that have gathered the appropriate process-tracing data.

Validation of the simulation results

The results of the simulation can be validated in at least three ways. First, one can examine whether the results are compatible with existing findings from studies of contingent decision behavior (see chapter 2 for a review of such studies). Second, one can examine whether particular assumptions underlying the simulation are reflective of similar aspects of actual decision behavior. For example, in chapter 3 we report results showing that the total time taken by individuals to make a decision and their self-reports of decision effort are predicted by counts of EIPs that are functions of both tasks and strategies. Third, one can examine whether the efficient strategies for a given decision problem identified by the simulations are related to the actual strategies used by people in solving such decision problems.

In the next sections of the present chapter we will illustrate validation through a comparison of the simulation results with both prior empirical studies that were not directly designed to test the implications of the simulation and with studies that were designed as direct tests of the simulation predictions. In both cases, we emphasize studies that examined contingent decision behavior using various process-tracing techniques. In order to do so, we must first briefly discuss methods for process-tracing.

Process-tracing methods

As discussed in chapter 2, the various decision strategies like WADD and EBA can be characterized in terms of such processing features as the amount of information utilized, the selectivity of processing, and whether processing is alternative-based or attribute-based. In order to be able to characterize decision behavior in terms of such features, one needs to use more than standard input–output measures of analysis (Payne, Braunstein, & Carroll, 1978). What are needed are data collection methods that will yield data on predecisional behavior in order to identify what information a decision maker has and how it is being processed. Two process-tracing methods that have proved especially valuable in decision research are verbal protocol analysis and the analysis of information acquisition behavior. Brief descriptions of each method are provided below. For more details on each method, see Carroll and Johnson (1990). A review of decision research using process-tracing methods is provided by Ford, Schmitt, Schechtman, Hults, and Doherty (1989).

Collecting verbal protocols

The collection of verbal protocols is conceptually a straightforward method for obtaining process data. The subject is simply asked to give continuous verbal reports, "to think aloud," while performing the decision task. The verbal protocol is then treated as a record of the ongoing behavior of the subject, and what is said is interpreted as an indication of the subject's state of knowledge or the use of an operation (Newell & Simon, 1972). Note that verbal protocols are designed to provide information on the sequential (time-ordered) behavior of subjects.

As a method for obtaining psychological data, the collection of verbal reports is an old idea in experimental psychology. For researchers such as Wilhelm Wundt and Edward B. Titchener, introspection, the trained observation of the contents of consciousness under controlled conditions, was *the* method of investigation in psychology. The introspective method, however, was virtually abandoned in 20th-century America because of criticisms by John B. Watson and other behaviorists directed at the objectivity of the method as a basis for scientific psychology. It is interesting to note that Watson apparently was prepared to accept verbal reports as data ("verbal behavior") when they were verifiable and repeatable. See Marx and Hillix (1963) for an extensive historical discussion of the introspective method and the behaviorist criticisms.

More recently, the method of verbal protocols has been criticized on the basis that people have little or no ability to observe directly and report verbally upon higher-order mental operations (Nisbett & Wilson, 1977). As a consequence, it has been suggested that verbal data may reflect the norms for behavior in a task more than a veridical report of the underlying processes employed in the task. Another concern has been that the need to provide a verbal protocol, as a secondary task, may fundamentally alter the processes used in performing the primary task of interest, for example, making a choice. The reason is that the verbal protocol procedure will utilize at least some of the cognitive resources available to the respondent.

Ericsson and Simon (1984) have proposed a model of how people respond to instructions to think aloud that addresses these objections. Ericsson and Simon argue forcefully that verbal protocols are valid and provide a high density of observations of the intermediate stages of processing. They provide numerous examples of the successful use of verbal protocols in the study of cognitive processes. For a further discussion of issues associated with the validity of verbal protocols, see Russo, Johnson, and Stephens (1989).

Although we believe that verbal protocols can be a valuable source of data on the cognitive processes involved in the solution of complex tasks, verbal protocol methods can be difficult to use. They are usually quite labor-intensive, requiring considerable effort for transcription, coding, and analysis. The analysis itself also can be quite difficult. As Russo (1978) states in his critical comparison of process tracing techniques, "the most important point about verbal protocols is that they are difficult to analyze formally" (p. 564). Consequently, most verbal protocol studies of decision making use very few subjects.

Monitoring information acquisitions

The monitoring of information acquisition behavior has become a popular form of process tracing in decision research (J. Ford et al., 1989). The method is seen as a complement to verbal protocols. Essentially, this process-tracing technique involves setting up the decision task so that the subject must view or select information in a way that can be easily monitored. Data can be obtained on what information the subject seeks, in what order, and how much information is examined.

Several methods for monitoring information acquisition behavior have been used in studies of decision making. A number of studies have employed "information boards" (e.g., Jacoby, Chestnut, Weigl, & Fisher, 1976; Payne, 1976; Thorngate & Maki, 1976; Wilkins, 1967). In Payne (1976), for example, the information board consisted of a matrix of envelopes attached to a sheet of cardboard. To obtain the value on a particular dimension for a particular alternative, the subject had to pull a card out of the appropriate envelope, turn it around, and place it back into the envelope. The content, amount, and sequence of cards turned around provided the data on the information search process used in the decision episode. Since the mid-1970s, the information board approach has become more sophisticated by using a variety of computer-controlled information retrieval systems to present and record information acquisition behavior (e.g., Dahlstrand & Montgomery, 1984; Jacoby, Mazursky, Troutman, & Kuss, 1984; Payne & Braunstein, 1978). The newer information retrieval systems, such as our Mouselab system briefly discussed in chapter 3, have added the capability to monitor the time associated with the acquisition of particular pieces of information, to reduce the effort associated with the physical acquisition of the information through the use of pointing devices like a mouse, and even to provide information in a less structured format (Brucks, 1988).

The recording of eye fixations is a very sophisticated method for monitoring information acquisition behavior. Russo and his associates have been the primary users of eye movement recording to study decision behavior. Russo and Dosher (1983) used a photo-electric sensing device and a computer for recording and analyzing the fixations. One factor that has limited the use of eye movement recording is the complexity and expense of the equipment. As Russo (1978) acknowledges, to record eye movements precisely requires a "quite expensive" system. Just and Carpenter (1984), who have used eye fixations in a variety of cognitive tasks from reading to problem solving, also view the cost of instrumentation and cost of training personnel as major limitations of the eye movement methodology. Yet, despite these problems, monitoring eye fixations has proved informative.

Verbal protocol methods and information search techniques each have advantages and disadvantages. In general, verbal protocols provide the richest source of data; however, they are fairly difficult to analyze and have some validity problems. Monitoring information acquisition, on the other hand, is less informative regarding cognitive processes, but fairly straightforward in terms of data collection and analysis. In the next section of the chapter we illustrate the use of both forms of process data in the evaluation of the predictions of our simulation study.

Validation by relating the simulation results to prior studies of contingent processing

Much research has been concerned with the effects of task complexity on decision behavior (see chapter 2). The general hypothesis has been that increased task complexity will increase cognitive workload, which will in turn lead to the increased use of heuristics in decision making. Task complexity has typically been manipulated through changes in the number of alternatives available (the presence of more alternatives implies more complexity) and changes in the number of attributes on which the alternatives are described (the presence of more attributes implies more complexity). Many of the studies of task complexity and contingent decision making have used one or more process-tracing methods (J. Ford et al., 1989), and hence these studies can be compared with the results of our simulations.

As noted in chapter 2, the clear result from such studies is that decision processes are highly sensitive to the number of alternatives in the choice set. When faced with a choice problem involving only two or three alternatives, people generally use compensatory types of strategies. When faced with more complex (multialternative) decision tasks, people tend to use more heuristic choice processes. People appear to be less sensitive to changes in the number of attributes.

The simulation results presented earlier are consistent with such a shift in strategies as a function of the number of alternatives. As shown in Figure 4.2, the accuracy of the various choice strategies is relatively unaffected by increases in the number of alternatives. The elimination-by-aspects strategy, for example, shows a decrease in accuracy from about .65 in the case of two-alternative choice problems to an accuracy of about .60 in the case of eight-alternative choice tasks. Of course, the accuracy of the normative strategy, WADD (expected value) is constant across the number of alternatives. In contrast, the number of alternatives available impacts the relative effort of the various strategies to significantly different degrees, as shown in Figure 4.3. Although all the strategies require more effort to execute in the more complex decision environments, the increase in effort for the WADD strategy is much more rapid than for heuristic strategies like lexicographic and the elimination-by-aspects. Thus, the impact of increases in the number of alternatives is to leave the relative accuracy of heuristics like EBA fairly constant, while making the relative amount of effort saved in the use of such heuristics much greater. If one assumes that decision makers are sensitive to both effort and accuracy in the selection of decision strategies, this should make heuristics like EBA relatively more attractive. The existing data support that conclusion. In addition, we noted earlier that changes in the number of attributes had more ambiguous effects on the relative efficiencies of various heuristics.

Studies by Payne and Braunstein (1978) and Payne (1976) will be used to illustrate the consistency between the simulation results and empirical data. Payne and Braunstein (1978) examined the effects of number of alternatives on risky decisions (gambles), whereas Payne (1976) considered nonrisky choices (apartments). It is important to note, however, that the results reported in these studies have been replicated by many other investigators (see J. Ford et al., 1989, for a review).

Number of alternatives and risky decisions

Payne and Braunstein (1978) tested the effects of the number of alternatives available by using the process-tracing method of monitoring information acquisitions. In their study, subjects indicated preferences among three-outcome gambles, with one outcome always equal to a payoff of $0. The other two outcomes always included a gain (i.e., $x > 0$) and a loss (i.e., $x < 0$). Selected (preferred) gambles were actually played by the subjects for real money.[7]

The number of gambles available was either two, four, or eight. The gambles were displayed in matrix format on the screen of a computer terminal. The alternatives (gambles) were represented by the rows of the matrix for half the subjects, and by the columns for the other half. The corresponding columns (rows) of the matrix were used to represent available information on the probabilities of winning and losing, and the amounts to be won or lost. Subjects obtained information about a particular alternative on a particular risk dimension by pressing the key corresponding to the row and the key corresponding to the column of the cell that they wished to check and then pressing an "information" key. Upon selecting a new item of information, the previous item was erased, but an item could be rechecked if desired.

The information search data collected by Payne and Braunstein can easily be related to the processing characteristics associated with the various strategies explored in our simulation. For example, the amount of processing can be measured by the percentage of the available information searched; the selectivity of processing by the variation in the amount of search devoted to each alternative; and the degree of alternative-based versus attribute-based processing by the relationship between the $n + 1$st piece of information searched and the nth piece of information searched. If the $n + 1$st item

---

[7] In this study and in several studies that followed, the basic task for the subjects was choice among gambles. In part this selection of choice tasks was motivated by a general interest in risky decision making. However, as noted earlier, risky choice tasks also have the desirable feature of making it easy to relate real consequences to the choices made by subjects.

Table 4.7. *Means for amount, selectivity, and pattern of search*

Number of alternatives	Percent of information search	Variation in search per alternative	Pattern of search
2	.92	.01	.32
4	.83	.06	.14
8	.76	.08	.13

Source: Adapted from Payne and Braunstein (1978).

searched is within the same gamble but for a different risk dimension than the nth piece of information acquired, then that is an example of alternative-based processing. If the $n + 1$st item searched is within the same dimension (probability of winning) but for a different gamble, then that is an example of attribute-based search. A summary measure of search pattern developed by Payne (1976) and used by Payne and Braunstein (1978) is given by the number of search transitions within an alternative minus the number of search transitions within an attribute divided by the sum of the two numbers. The range of this measure is $+ 1.00$ (only alternative-based sequences) to $- 1.00$ (only attribute-based search).

The means for the amount, selectivity, and pattern measures of search found by Payne and Braunstein (1978) are given in Table 4.7. Overall, it is clear that the processing of information varied as a function of the number of alternatives available. Specifically, search was less complete, more selective, and more attribute-based as the number of alternatives increased. These three measures of search behavior are consistent with the increased use of attribute-based heuristics like EBA as the number of alternatives available becomes larger.

Another measure of search indicative of the use of a strategy like EBA is the length of the sequences of attribute-based processing. Payne and Braunstein report that for more subjects classified as having attribute-based and selective patterns of search, the average length of search within an attribute increased as the number of alternatives increased. Further, the average length of search for the sets of four and eight gambles was significantly greater than 1.0, indicating that the subjects were not using an additive difference process. These data are thus inconsistent with the criterion-dependent choice process proposed by Bockenholt et al. (1991).

Number of alternatives and nonrisky decisions

Similar effects of changes in the number of alternatives available on information search were found by Payne (1976) in a study of choices among apartments. In that study, all the subjects were also asked to "think aloud" as they made their choices. The verbal protocol data provided clear indications of the use of noncompensatory strategies and the sensitivity of processing to the number of alternatives available. Some excerpts from the protocols collected by Payne (1976) are given in Figures 4.4 and 4.5. Consistent with the procedure suggested by Newell and Simon (1972), the protocols are broken into short phrases corresponding to a single task assertion or reference by a subject. The phrases are numbered and labeled with a different letter for each subject.

The four panels (a–d) of Figure 4.4 provide excerpts from the protocols of two subjects (A and D) faced with two levels of task complexity: (1) two alternative choice problems (panels a and b), and (2) multialternative choice problems (panels c and d). The excerpts were selected to illustrate verbal protocol data indicative of variety of decision strategies. Thus, panels a and b suggest the consideration of tradeoffs among attributes. For example, subject D explicitly asks a tradeoff question dealing with the exchange of a higher rent for a lower level of noise in panel b. The difference between the excerpts in panels a and b is that the processing in panel a is more organized by alternative, whereas the processing indicated by the protocol in panel b seems more organized by attributes.

The excerpts in panels c and d, on the other hand, indicate more noncompensatory decision processing. For both subjects A and D, the presence of high noise level seems sufficient to "automatically eliminate" an alternative in the case of multialternative choice tasks. There is no apparent consideration of the possible tradeoffs against other attributes. Again, panel c is more alternative-based whereas the processing in panel d is more attribute-based.

It is important to note from Figure 4.4 that strategy differences are shown within the same subjects as well as across the two subjects. Thus, subject A seems to use both compensatory (additive) and

Figure 4.4 Verbal protocols of choice strategies. *Source*: Payne and Braunstein (1978).

(a)

C98: Well, with these many apartments (six) to choose from,

C99: I'm not going to work through all the characteristics

C100: Start eliminating them as soon as possible.

(b)

B1: With just two (gambles) to choose from,

B2: I'm going to go after all the information

B3: It won't be that much trouble.

Figure 4.5. Verbal protocol examples of task contingent processing. (a) Excerpt from Payne (1976). (b) Excerpt from Payne and Braunstein (1978).

noncompensatory (satisficing) strategies and subject D appears to use both an additive difference and elimination-by-aspects strategy.

A key assumption of our framework for strategy selection is that the use of a particular decision strategy will be contingent upon such task variables as the number of alternatives available. Panel d in Figure 4.4 and panels a and b in Figure 4.5 provide excerpts from verbal protocols collected by Payne (1976) and Payne and Braunstein (1978) that illustrate the selection of a decision strategy determined, at least in part, by the number of alternatives available. In panel a of Figure 4.5, the fact that there are many apartments to choose from appears to lead to a decision to employ an elimination strategy. In contrast, the verbal protocol excerpt given in panel b of Figure 4.5 suggests that a more comprehensive information processing strategy is to be employed, given that there are "just two" alternatives to choose from. As noted earlier, we do not believe that the contingent use of decision strategies is always "top-down" (see chapter 5); however, the verbal protocol data in Figure 4.4, panel d, and Figure 4.5, panels a and b, support the notion that decision makers sometimes explicitly consider task demands and the planning of processing.

To summarize, the information search data and the verbal protocols obtained by Payne (1976) and Payne and Braunstein (1978) are consistent with the predictions from our simulation study of the accuracy–effort tradeoffs across different task environments. However, the use of such studies as validation studies for the simulation is not as strong as it might be because they predate the simulation. We now turn to studies of actual decision behavior that were designed as direct tests of some of the predictions of the simulation study reported earlier.

Validation of the simulation results by direct tests

As discussed earlier, the current simulation results, and more generally the current framework, are compatible with prior studies of contingent decision behavior. Although suggestive, it would be more powerful support for the framework to use direct tests of the degree of correspondence between the efficient strategies for a given decision problem identified by our simulations and the actual strategies people use. In this section of the chapter we review two such tests. The first empirical study examined the sensitivity of decision behavior to variations in the goals for the task (emphasis on accuracy or emphasis on effort savings). The second series of empirical studies examined the sensitivity of decision processes to variations in time pressure (a task variable) and to variations in the dispersion of probabilities associated with the outcomes of the alternatives in a choice set (a context variable). More complete details on each series of studies can be found in Creyer, Bettman, and Payne (1990) and Payne et al. (1988). Before reviewing each study, however, we briefly consider the process-tracing methodology used in both studies and the relationship of the process-tracing data to aspects of strategies.

The Mouselab system and process-tracing measures used

Information acquisition, response times, and choices were monitored using the Mouselab system (see the Appendix). The stimuli were presented on a computer display in the form of a matrix of available information. For a four-alternative, four-outcome risky choice problem, the first row of boxes contained information about the probabilities of the four outcomes. The next four rows of boxes contained information about the payoffs associated with the different outcomes for each alternative, respectively. At the bottom of the screen were four boxes that were used to indicate which alternative was most preferred. Subjects use a mouse to open boxes in the matrix, and the Mouselab program records the order in which boxes are opened, the amount of time boxes are open, the chosen option, and the total elapsed time since the display first appeared on the screen. Response times are recorded to an accuracy of 1/60th of a second.

The data available from Mouselab can be used to characterize aspects of decision processing such as those described in chapter 2. One important aspect is the total amount of processing. One measure of amount is the total number of times information boxes were opened for a particular decision, denoted acquisitions (ACQ). A second measure is the total amount of time spent on the information in the boxes, called BOXTIME. A third measure related to the amount of processing effort is the average time spent per item of information acquired (TPERACQ).

The next several measures reflect the relative attention devoted to specific types of information and, hence, are relevant to characterizing selectivity in processing. One measure, denoted PTMI, is the proportion of the total time acquiring information that was spent in boxes involving the most important attribute of a particular decision problem. The attribute (outcome) with the largest weight (probability of occurrence) was defined to be the most important attribute. The other measure, denoted PTPROB, is the proportion of time spent on probability information as opposed to information about payoff values.

The next two measures are the variances in the proportions of time spent on each alternative (VAR-ALTER) and on each attribute (VAR-ATTRIB). Such variances are related to selectivity. As described earlier, more compensatory decision rules (e.g., WADD, EQW, and MCD) imply a pattern of information acquisition that is consistent (low in variance) across alternatives and attributes; in contrast, noncompensatory strategies, like EBA, LEX and SAT, imply more variance in processing.

A final measure of processing characterizes the sequence of information acquisitions. As noted earlier, a simple measure of the relative amount of alternative-based and attribute-based transitions is provided by calculating the number of alternative-based transitions minus the number of attribute-based transitions divided by the sum of these two types of transitions (Payne, 1976). This measure of the relative use of alternative-based versus attribute-based processing, denoted PATTERN, ranges from a value of -1.0 to $+1.0$. A more positive number indicates relatively more alternative-based processing, and a more negative number indicates relatively more attribute-based processing.

In addition to these seven measures of processing, a measure of relative accuracy, defined in the preceding simulation in terms of EV maximization and random choice, was developed and denoted by GAIN.

As we will indicate, the simulation results can be interpreted in terms of predictions about such aspects of processing. Thus, hypotheses about the process-tracing measures outlined earlier can then be derived from the simulation results.

Effects of accuracy and effort goals on the decision processes

A key assumption underlying any cost–benefit approach to strategy selection is that processing should be sensitive to the relative emphasis placed on the effectiveness of the decision (maximize accuracy) versus the efficiency of the decision process (minimize effort). It is generally assumed that people should utilize strategies that provide greater accuracy (often at the cost of greater effort) when the incentives associated with accuracy are increased. However, as pointed out by several authors (e.g., Ashton, 1990; Hogarth et al., 1991; Tversky & Kahneman, 1986; W. Wright & Aboul-Ezz, 1988), incentives sometimes enhance performance, sometimes have no effect on performance, and may at times actually decrease performance (see discussions in chapter 3 and 6).

One important concept relevant to understanding incentive effects is the distinction between working harder versus working smarter (see chapters 1 and 3). Working harder can be thought of as devoting more effort to the same strategy; working smarter, in contrast, refers to changing strategies appropriately to take advantage of the specific situation. We believe that a common response to general incentives is simply to work harder at the same strategy that one is already using. However, we believe that specific incentives that explicitly change the relative salience of effort and accuracy considerations in the decision environment can lead to changes in strategies.

Interestingly, although the role of incentives on decisions has been of long-standing concern, there has been surprisingly little research that has directly examined the impact of incentives at the process level of strategy differences (J. Ford et al., 1989). The purpose of the study to be reviewed was to examine directly how processing varies as the goals (incentives) in a decision environment are explicitly changed to shift the relative emphasis on accuracy and effort.

One direct and not surprising hypothesis of such a shift in emphasis is that a goal emphasizing accuracy should lead to greater accuracy than a goal emphasizing effort. By examining Figure 4.1, we can make further predictions, however. Note that a goal for effort savings will lead to greater use of heuristics. Such heuristics will clearly be characterized by less processing. *On average*, these heuristics will also be more selective and more attribute-based. However, note that, strictly speaking, these latter predictions depend upon the specific point where an individual is located on the tradeoff curve. In the low-dispersion, dominance-possible environment, for example, individuals might use either EQW or LEX to try to trade off accuracy for effort depending upon their particular weighting of accuracy and effort. EQW is nonselective and by alternative, whereas LEX is selective and by attribute.

In general, therefore, we hypothesize that a goal emphasizing accuracy to a greater extent will lead to more normative types of processing and improved accuracy. Such processing should include more processing of information, less selectivity in processing, and more alternative-based processing. A goal emphasizing effort minimization, on the other hand, is expected to lead to greater use of heuristics, less processing, greater selectivity, more attribute-based processing, and lower performance. As noted earlier, however, the simulation alone cannot make unambiguous predictions about all of these aspects.

Method. Subjects used Mouselab to acquire information and make decisions among 32 sets of multiattribute nonrisky alternatives.

The subjects' task was to select the alternative in each set that they thought was best overall. Each set contained four alternatives defined by six attributes. The sets varied within subjects with respect to the dispersion of the weights provided for the attributes (high or low) and the explicit goal of the decision maker for the set (minimize effort or maximize accuracy). Two between-subjects factors were the presence or absence of effort feedback and accuracy feedback. We discuss the results related to feedback in chapter 6.

Incentives were used to manipulate effort–accuracy tradeoffs by explicitly emphasizing either a goal of maximizing accuracy relative to effort or a goal of minimizing effort relative to accuracy. Subjects were told that an index of overall performance would be developed based upon the time taken and the accuracy achieved for each trial.[8] Subjects were instructed that for trials in which the goal was to minimize effort, time taken would be given a weight of three and accuracy a weight of one. On trials where the goal was to maximize accuracy, time taken would receive a weight of one and accuracy a weight of three. Thus, both accuracy and effort (time taken) mattered for all trials; we tried to manipulate the relative importance of those two issues.

Eight sets of low dispersion in weight options and 8 sets of high dispersion options were generated, with the possibility of dominated options allowed in all sets. Each of these 16 sets of options was presented to subjects twice. For one presentation, the subject was instructed that minimization of the effort used to decide among the alternatives was relatively more important. For the other presentation, subjects were told that the maximization of the accuracy of their choice was relatively more important. Thus, each subject received 32 decision problems (2 dispersion conditions × 2 goal conditions × 8 replications). A complete experimental session took from 40–60 minutes for each subject.

Results. Four main types of dependent measures were examined: amount of processing, selectivity in processing, pattern of processing, and accuracy of choice; several of the measures of these aspects described earlier were utilized and can be related directly to the hypotheses outlined earlier. A goal emphasizing accuracy should lead to higher values of PATTERN (more alternative-based proces-

---

[8] Accuracy was measured relative to the weighted additive rule.

Table 4.8. *Effects of weighting effort versus accuracy*

	Effort goal	Accuracy goal
ACQ	24.3	31.4
BOXTIME	11.3	18.1
PTMI	.41	.37
VAR-ALTER	.09	.08
VAR-ATTRIB	.17	.13
PATTERN	−.50	−.35
GAIN	.70	.76

Source: Adapted from Creyer et al. (1990).

sing); lower values of VAR-ALTER and VAR-ATTRIB (less selectivity); and lower values of PTMI (less focus on the most important attribute). In addition, there should be more acquisitions (ACQ) and greater BOXTIME (more processing effort). Finally, GAIN should be higher. Conditions leading to less normative processing would show the opposite pattern of results.

Table 4.8 provides the means for each of the seven dependent measures for each of the two goal conditions. As indicated by the results in Table 4.8, subjects did more processing when the goal was to maximize accuracy rather than to minimize effort. More information was acquired and more time was spent on the information in the boxes. In addition, information acquisition was less selective under a goal of maximizing accuracy. There was proportionally less time spent on the most important attribute, less variance in processing over attributes, and less variance in processing across alternatives. Finally, processing was relatively more alternative-based when the goal was to maximize accuracy. Note that the fact that there was greater processing by attribute when the goal was to minimize effort supports the suggestion by Russo and Dosher (1983) that attribute-based processing is cognitively easier.

Processing does become more extensive, less selective, and more alternative-based when the goal is to maximize accuracy, as hypothesized. Such processing, more consistent with normative strategies, also leads to better performance. When the goal is to maximize accuracy, subjects attain greater relative accuracy levels.

The fact that goal affects both processing measures and accuracy raises the issue of whether the processing changes mediate the effect of goal on accuracy. We examined the three criteria for mediation proposed by R. Baron and Kenny (1986) and found that changes in processing partially but not completely mediated the effects of goals on accuracy.

To summarize, when the incentives were structured to emphasize the goal of accuracy more than effort, we found a shift in strategies in the direction predicted by the effort–accuracy framework. These results provide the clearest evidence available to date for the effects of differences in goals on detailed process-tracing measures of decision strategies – for example, Billings and Scherer (1988) find relatively weak evidence for effects of decision importance on processing; see also J. Ford et al. (1989, pp. 101–102), for a similar appraisal.

In a second study involving risky choice problems we carried out in conjunction with Mary Frances Luce, we also found evidence of the impact of goals on processing. In particular, an accuracy goal, in comparison to a goal emphasizing effort savings, led to significantly greater time spent in making the decision, less selectivity in acquisitions across both attributes and alternatives, and more alternative-based processing. Interestingly, in this risky choice context, the impact of goals on accuracy was only marginal. Specifically, the gain scores for both the accuracy goal decision problems and the effort goal problems were essentially the same, although the probability of selecting the gamble in a choice set with the highest EV was marginally greater for the accuracy goal problems.

In these examples, we were able to make some precise predictions (e.g., about accuracy and amount of processing); others (e.g., about selectivity and pattern of processing) were ambiguous unless an individual's specific effort–accuracy tradeoffs were known. In many cases, however, fairly clear predictions can be made without knowing such tradeoffs. We now turn to such a case.

Effects of time pressure and dispersion in weights on decision processes

These experiments asked the following two questions: To what extent do people vary their information-processing behavior as a function of context effects such as the dispersion of probabilities and task effects such as time pressure? Are these changes in processing in the directions suggested by the simulation? As outlined earlier, the simulation results (see Figure 4.1) provide a fairly clear picture of what a decision maker might do to adapt to various decision environments. Specifically, the simulation results suggest that an adaptive decision maker should exhibit more attribute-based processing, greater selectivity in processing across attributes and alternatives, and a greater proportion of processing devoted to probabilities and the most important attribute in a high-dispersion environment. Such shifts in processing as a function of context would indicate that people are sensitive to changes in choice environments that affect the accuracy of strategies and not just to changes that affect processing demands – for example, the effects of number of alternatives.

Note also that simulation suggests that a decision maker who changes decision strategies in the directions mentioned previously – that is more selective with high dispersion – can maintain a high level of accuracy *and* minimize effort. Thus, the predictions for processing changes as a function of changes in dispersion *do not* require detailed knowledge of a decision maker's effort–accuracy tradeoff function.

The simulation results also indicate changes in aspects of processing that should be expected as a function of increased time pressure. In particular, the simulations suggest more attribute-based processing, greater selectivity in processing, and a greater proportion of processing focused on probabilities and the most important attribute under higher levels of time pressure.

Prior experimental and theoretical work on time pressure reinforces these predictions on time constraints derived from the simulation. For example, Ben Zur and Breznitz (1981) identified at least three ways in which people may respond to time constraints. One way to cope with time pressure is to "accelerate" processing (Ben Zur & Breznitz, 1981; Miller, 1960) by trying to process the same information at a faster rate. Another way to cope with time pressure is to process only a subset of the most important information, an idea referred to as *filtration* (Miller, 1960). Finally, one could shift processing strategies. At the extreme, this could involve random choice, or *avoidance* (Ben Zur & Breznitz, 1981; Miller, 1960). A less extreme form of contingent processing would involve a shift from a more effortful rule, such as WADD, to a less effortful rule, like EBA. The simulation results indicate that such a strategy shift could maintain relatively high levels of accuracy, even under severe time pressure.

In sum, the simulation and prior decision research lead to several hypotheses. Both higher dispersion in probabilities and higher time pressure are expected to lead to greater use of attribute-based processing, greater selectivity across attributes and alternatives, and greater focus of processing on probabilities and the most important attribute. In addition, there should be no difference in accuracy for different levels of dispersion, but there should be less effort under high dispersion (see the earlier discussion of the simulation results). Under high time pressure, accuracy should be lower and information should be processed more rapidly

Method. Two experiments were conducted in which subjects were asked to make a series of choices from sets of risky options. Each choice set contained four risky options, with each option offering four possible outcomes (attributes). For any given outcome, the probability was the same for all four options. Thus, there was only one set of probabilities for each set of four alternatives. The payoffs ranged from $.01 to $9.99. Dominated options were possible. At the end of an experiment, subjects actually played one gamble and received the amount of money that they won.

The sets varied in terms of two factors: presence or absence of time pressure, and high or low dispersion in probabilities. In terms of the simulation, the no time pressure conditions correspond to the dominance-possible, low- and high- dispersion conditions shown in Figure 4.1. The high time pressure sets correspond to conditions presented in Table 4.3. In the first experiment, the time pressure condition involved a 15-second time constraint. In the second experiment, half the subjects had a 15-second constraint. The other half had a more moderate 25-second time constraint. For comparison, the average response time for the no time pressure conditions was 44 seconds.

The design was a complete within-subjects procedure, with a total of 40 randomly ordered decision problems in an experimental session, 10 in each of the 4 dispersion-by-time-pressure conditions. This design was motivated by the desire to provide the strongest possible test of adaptivity in decision making (i.e., the same subject would be expected to switch strategies from one trial to the next). The subjects were *not* provided any accuracy feedback in these experiments, for two reasons: (1) It is the exception, rather than the rule, for probabilistic decision problems to provide immediate and

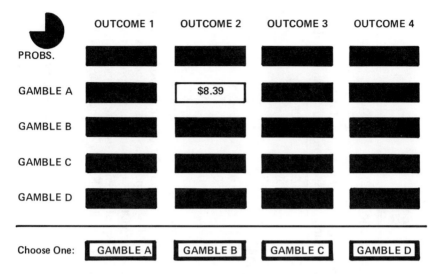

	OUTCOME 1	OUTCOME 2	OUTCOME 3	OUTCOME 4
PROBS.	■	■	■	■
GAMBLE A	■	$8.39	■	■
GAMBLE B	■	■	■	■
GAMBLE C	■	■	■	■
GAMBLE D	■	■	■	■

Choose One: GAMBLE A   GAMBLE B   GAMBLE C   GAMBLE D

Figure 4.6. Example of a stimulus display using the Mouselab system with time pressure clock. *Source*: Reprinted by permission of the publisher from "Adaptive strategy selection in decision making," John W. Payne, James R. Bettman, and Eric J. Johnson, *Journal of Experimental Psychology: Learning, Memory, and Cognition, 14* (1988), p. 543. Copyright © 1988 by the American Psychological Association.

clear outcome feedback (Einhorn, 1980); and (2) to the extent that adaptivity is exhibited in such situations, it suggests that adaptivity is crucial enough to decision makers that they will guide themselves to it without the need for explicit feedback.

Information acquisitions, response times, and choices were monitored using Mouselab. For the time-constrained trials, Mouselab ensured that subjects could not collect any additional information once the available time had expired. A clock on the display screen was used to indicate the time left as it counted down. Figure 4.6 is an example of a stimulus display with one box opened, and with the time pressure clock part way through the countdown.

Results. Four main types of dependent measures were again examined: amount of processing, selectivity in processing, pattern of processing, and relative accuracy.

The measures can be related directly to the hypotheses outlined previously. Higher dispersion in probabilities and higher time pressure should lead to lower values of PATTERN (more attribute-

Table 4.9. *Summary of process and accuracy results: Experiment 2, Day 1 results*

Dependent Measure	Group 1 (N = 16)				Group 2 (N = 12)			
	NTP, low dispersion	NTP, high dispersion	TP, low dispersion	TP, high dispersion	NTP, low dispersion	NTP, high dispersion	TP, low dispersion	TP, high dispersion
ACQ	50.8	42.1	19.5	17.2	52.8	45.2	28.8	27.7
TPERACQ	.64	.62	.48	.48	.64	.62	.52	.52
PTMI	.29	.37	.32	.43	.30	.39	.32	.41
PTPROB	.24	.27	.27	.29	.19	.20	.20	.22
VAR-ALTER	.010	.013	.009	.013	.008	.010	.008	.010
VAR-ATTRIB	.007	.018	.013	.027	.005	.017	.007	.021
PATTERN	.00	−.22	−.03	−.31	.30	.00	.33	.03
GAIN	.56	.59	.43	.42	.75	.81	.67	.64

Note: NTP = no time pressure. TP = time pressure. TPERACQ = time per information acquisition. PTMI = proportion of time on the most important attribute. PTPROB = proportion of time on the probability information. VAR-ALTER = variance in the proportion of time spent on each alternative. VAR-ATTRIB = variance in the proportion of time spent on each attribute (including both payoff and probability information). PATTERN = index reflecting relative amount of attribute-based (−) and alternative-based (+) processing. GAIN = relative accuracy of choices.

Source: Adapted by permission of the publisher from "Adaptive strategy selection in decision making," John W. Payne, James R. Bettman, and Eric J. Johnson, *Journal of Experimental Psychology: Learning, Memory, and Cognition, 14* (1988), p. 547. Copyright © 1988 by the American Psychological Association.

based processing); higher values of VAR-ALTER and VAR-ATTRIB (greater selectivity); and higher values of PTPROB and PTMI (greater focus on probabilities and the most important attribute). In addition, there should be fewer acquisitions (ACQ) and lower TPERACQ under high dispersion (less processing effort), and TPERACQ should be lower under time pressure. Finally, GAIN should be similar across levels of dispersion, but lower under high time pressure.

Overall, the results for subjects' actual decision behaviors validated the patterns predicted by the simulation. Subjects showed a substantial degree of adaptivity in decision making, although this adaptivity was not perfect. Table 4.9 provides a summary of the process and accuracy results from the second experiment. The results from the first experiment were similar.

As can been seen in Table 4.9, subjects processed less information, were more selective in processing, and tended to process more by attribute when dispersion in probabilities was high rather than low. Moreover, accuracy was equivalent in the two dispersion conditions. Thus, subjects showed ability to take advantage of changes in the structure of the available alternatives so as to reduce processing load while maintaining accuracy. Recall that this prediction was drawn from the simulation results.

At the level of individual subjects' behaviors, subjects who were more adaptive in their patterns of processing (i.e., relatively more selective and attribute-based processors in high-dispersion environments) also performed better in terms of relative accuracy scores. Importantly, this increase in performance was not accompanied by a significant increase in effort. *Hence, more adaptive subjects also appeared to be more efficient decision makers.*

Several effects of time pressure were also demonstrated. First, under severe time pressure, people accelerated their processing (i.e., less time was spent per item of information acquired), selectively focused on a subset of the more important information, and changed their pattern of processing in the direction of relatively more attribute-based processing. This general pattern of results is consistent with the simulation, which suggested that an efficient strategy under severe time pressure was one that involved selective and attribute-based processing.

The effects of time pressure were substantially less for those subjects with a 25- as opposed to a 15-second constraint. In the more moderate condition, subjects showed evidence of acceleration in processing and some selectivity in processing, but no evidence of a shift in the pattern of processing. These results suggested a possible hierarchy of responses to time pressure. First, people may try to respond to time pressure simply by working faster. If this is insufficient, people may then focus on a subset of the available information. Finally, if that is still insufficient, people may change processing strategies, for example, from alternative-based processing to attribute-based processing.

Although these results suggest high adaptivity, there was evidence to suggest that the adaptivity to time pressure was not perfect on a trial-by-trial basis. When the responses to the no time pressure condition were compared for the two groups of subjects in the second experiment, some carryover from behavior generated in response to the time pressure trials to performance on the no time pressure trials was detected. Specifically, subjects who had the severer 15-second time constraint showed comparatively more attribute-based processing, even in the no time pressure trials.

To summarize, the results of the two experiments outlined here provide strong evidence of adaptivity in decision making. Although not perfectly adaptive, our subjects were able to change processing strategies in ways that the simulation indicated were appropriate given changes in context and task features of the decision problems.

Back to the world of simulation

Empirical work can serve not only to verify implications of the simulation but also to suggest new simulation work. In the work reported here, we observed that many subjects under moderate time pressure used a strategy we had not anticipated. Subjects appeared to scan the probabilities and select the two outcomes with the highest probabilities for further processing. Then the subjects processed the alternatives one at a time, using just these two outcomes. Although many heuristics could be consistent with this observed processing pattern, we simulated the performance of one particular case, which we called the selective weighted adding heuristic. This heuristic chooses the two outcomes with the highest probabilities and then calculates a weighted sum for each alternative (as time allows), using just these two outcomes.

The relative accuracy scores for the selective weighted adding rule for various combinations of time pressure and problem size were .87 (moderate pressure, moderate size [five alternatives and five outcomes]); .42 (moderate pressure, large size [eight alternatives and eight outcomes]); .06 (severe pressure, moderate size); and .02 (severe pressure, large size). Note that the selective weighted adding heuristic performs extremely well under moderate pressure for moderate-sized problems. In fact, if we compare the performance of the selective rule with that of the other heuristics shown in Table 4.4, the selective rule is superior for this one condition. This is an intriguing result, as the empirical studies reviewed earlier used moderate-sized problems (4×4) and found processing patterns consistent with the selective rule. The relative performance of the selective heuristic does fall off dramatically, however, under severe time pressure or for large problems. An obvious prediction of the simulation, therefore, is that usage of the selective heuristic should decrease, even under moderate time pressure, for large choice problems.

These conclusions continue to hold even if the simulation is run with time weights on the EIPs. The performance of the selective heuristic is .94 (moderate pressure, moderate size), .56 (moderate pressure, large size), .51 (severe pressure, moderate size), and $-.09$ (severe pressure, large size). Interestingly, the selective weighted adding rule is the best performer in six of the eight environments characterized by crossing low or moderate time pressure with the four dispersion-dominance conditions.

The results for the selective weighted adding heuristic also demonstrate the power of selectivity. Under moderate time pressure and moderate problem size, selectivity alone, without strategy change, can lead to very good performance. The selective weighted adding rule achieves 87% of the attainable accuracy, despite examining no more than 40% of the available information for a 5×5 decision problem, and on average using only 70% as many operations as the weighted adding rule would use to run to completion for a problem of that size.

There is also evidence of a hierarchy of responses to time pressure in the empirical work we have described. People apparently first tried to respond to time constraints by accelerating processing and being more selective. Only for the severest time constraint studied was there evidence of a shift in strategies. Such a pattern is consistent with the efficient performance of the selective weighted adding technique in the moderate time pressure, moderate size problems.

These results show that the progression from simulation to empirical work to further simulation can yield fascinating results and suggest even further empirical work. The combination of simulation and process-oriented experimentation has proved quite complementary, with the richness of the simulation predictions guiding the analysis of complex process data. In sum, the two together do much more than either could alone.

Summary

This chapter has shown how computer simulation and the techniques of information acquisition monitoring and verbal protocol collection can be combined in the exploration of contingent decision behavior at a process level of analysis. The modeling of decision strategies as production systems and the use of Monte Carlo simulation techniques to explore the impacts of task and context variables on the accuracy and effort levels of strategies provide insights into how an idealized decision maker might adapt his or her behavior to task environments. More specifically, the computer simulation approach can be used to generate hypotheses about how aspects of decision processing (e.g., amount, selectivity, and pattern) will vary as a function of task variables like time pressure. Methods like the monitoring of information acquisitions provide a method for then testing the process level predictions derived from the simulation against actual decision behavior. This combination of simulation and process tracing is a distinctive feature of our approach.

In this chapter, we reviewed a program of research that provides tests of how closely the efficient processing patterns for a given decision identified by the simulation correspond to the actual processing behavior exhibited by decision makers. The results of those studies are clearly consistent with the results that would be expected given our accuracy–effort framework for understanding the contingent use of decision strategies. Reviewing work done a number of years ago, we show how sensitive decision processes are to variations in the number of alternatives available. This task complexity variable was shown in the simulation to influence greatly the relative effort levels of various decision strategies. Much more

Table 4.10. *Summary of major points from chapter 4*

The modeling of decision strategies as production systems and the use of Monte Carlo simulation techniques provide insights into how an idealized decision maker might adapt his or her behavior to changes in task environments.

A computer simulation of the problem of strategy selection in decision making indicates that:

(1) Heuristic strategies can significantly reduce the effort needed to reach a decision while providing a level of relative accuracy comparable with that obtained by more normative procedures like the weighted additive rule.
(2) Heuristic strategies vary greatly in performance as a function of task and context factors; thus, a decision maker wanting to achieve both a reasonably high level of accuracy and low effort would have to use a repertoire of strategies and change strategies across different decision tasks.
(3) Task variables such as the number of alternatives available have greater influence on the relative effort of strategies, whereas context variables such as the presence or absence of dominated alternatives tend to have greater influence on accuracy.
(4) The weighted additive rule rapidly degrades in accuracy under time constraints, whereas attribute-based heuristics like elimination-by-aspects and the lexicographic choice rule show much smaller accuracy decrements and can be the most accurate procedures in some situations.

A series of experiments using a variety of process-tracing methods, such as verbal protocols and the monitoring of information acquisition behavior, indicates that:

(1) People shift decision strategies as a function of task complexity in ways consistent with a concern for conserving cognitive effort.
(2) Decision makers explicitly consider task demands and plan processing strategies, at least some of the time.
(3) Processing becomes more extensive, less selective, and more alternative-based when greater emphasis is placed on the goal of maximizing accuracy relative to the goal of minimizing effort.
(4) Processing becomes less extensive, more selective, and more attribute-based under time pressure. People appear to use a hierarchy of responses to time pressure: acceleration of processing, then increased selectivity, and finally, changes in strategies.
(5) Although not perfectly adaptive, people generally changed strategies in ways that the simulation results indicated were appropriate given changes in features of the decision problem; furthermore, the more adaptive decision makers also appeared to be more efficient in terms of relative accuracy and effort.

recent and direct tests of specific simulation predictions were also shown to validate the patterns of processing one would expect an adaptive decision maker to exhibit when faced with tasks varying in terms of incentive schemes, time pressure (a task variable), and the dispersion of weights or probabilities (a context variable). Table 4.10 provides a summary of the main points presented in this chapter.

Taken together, we believe that the results of the simulation, the results of the experiments in adaptive decision behavior, and the studies of cognitive effort (chapter 3) provide strong and consistent support for our approach to strategy selection. We also believe that this approach provides a more systematic way to characterize the effort and accuracy considerations that often underlay strategy selection than any other currently available. Later in the book (see chapter 6), we report further applications of this conceptualization to problems of contingent strategy selection. However, in the next chapter we suggest how our top-down view of strategy selection might be expanded to allow for contingent decision behavior that is much more "opportunistic." That is, we discuss how the learning of the structure of a decision problem during the course of making the decision can lead people to change their processing to exploit this structure.

5

Constructive processes in decision making

Introduction

Over the past several chapters, we have developed our accuracy–effort framework based upon a top-down view of strategy selection. That is, we have assumed that a decision maker has a repertoire of strategies, evaluates the costs and benefits of those strategies given his or her a priori perceptions of the decision task, and then selects the particular strategy that represents the best accuracy–effort trade-off for the task at hand. As we have seen in the previous chapter, there are data supporting such a goal-directed process of strategy selection. However, assuming both the use of single prototypical strategies and the notion of a top-down process of strategy selection is certainly too restrictive. Problem solvers not only use information extracted from the original problem definition in deciding what strategy to use but also use information they have already explored to identify promising paths for further search (Langley et al., 1987). That is, as people learn more about the problem structure during the course of making a decision, they can change their processing to exploit that structure. Such a view implies that individuals *construct* choice strategies on the spot during the course of making a decision (Bettman, 1979), which is a more bottom-up or data-driven view of strategy usage. Processing, in other words, can be *opportunistic* (Hayes-Roth & Hayes-Roth 1979).

Several examples may clarify this concept. For instance, an individual may intend to evaluate a set of gambles using a weighted adding (expected value) strategy. However, if the individual noted that the probability of one outcome was extremely high (e.g., .8), then that individual might drop plans to carry out an expected value calculation and simply look for the alternative with the best payoff for the highly probable outcome. In other words, this represents a data-driven shift from a compensatory process to a noncompensatory, lexicographic strategy. We have observed such strategies in our data (Payne et al. 1988). As another example, taken from a consumer choice context, a consumer may start to compare alternatives on what is a priori the most important attribute and discover that the values on that attribute are very similar across alternatives. He or she might then edit or cancel out that attribute (Kahneman & Tversky, 1979b). Then he or she may decide to look at another attribute but find that the information available on that attribute is too hard to understand. In both these cases, individuals make spur-of-the-moment shifts in processing direction rather than merely executing some strategy determined beforehand.

In the next several sections we develop this notion of constructive processing and consider how such a view fits with our conception of contingent processing based upon accuracy–effort tradeoffs. Then we consider what is perhaps the heart of constructive processing, noticing and exploiting regularities in the decision task, in more detail. Finally, we suggest some opportunistic processing extensions to the simple production system models presented in the preceding chapter.

The nature of constructive processes

Elements of decision heuristics

The basic notion behind a constructive choice process is that the heuristic used is developed at the actual time of choice. The individual essentially makes up the strategy as he or she goes along. The individual may begin a particular choice process without any complete rule or heuristic stored in memory that is deemed applicable for that choice. Rather, a heuristic is constructed using fragments or elements of heuristics stored in memory; the overall strategy is built dynamically at the time of choice from elements or subparts. These elements or fragments may be beliefs about alternatives; evaluations; simple rules of thumb involving subsets of beliefs (e.g., "compare these alternatives on attribute A to see if they differ very much"); rules for integrating information (e.g.,"count how may attributes alternative X is best on" or "average these ratings"); rules for assigning weights (e.g., "if the values of the alternatives on attribute B are very similar, then assign a low weight to attribute B"); and so on.

Bettman and Park (1980) and Biehal and Chakravarti (1986) have argued that simple processing operations such as those already described may represent the level at which consumers store much of their information-processing repertoire in memory. Rules such as "If the values of the alternatives are similar, then assign a low weight to that attribute" are also easily representable as productions or procedural knowledge (J. Anderson, 1983).

Effects of the decision task on the construction of a heuristic

An individual may enter many decision situations with only a general plan to guide the construction of a heuristic. Thus, choice heuristics will in general vary from one situation to the next if a constructive method is used, depending upon how the elements available are put together. The elements used for a particular choice and the sequence in which they are used will be a function of such factors as what information is available (e.g., whether the same data are available for all alternatives); the format in which the information is presented (e.g., in a consumer choice, prices may not be compared if unit prices are not provided and different brands have different-sized packages); the salience of various pieces of information; intermediate processing results; and other task-specific factors.

The constructive view reinforces the argument of Yates et al. (1978) that events affecting order of attention in the real world are likely to be numerous and powerful; such events should not be dismissed as just experimental nuisance factors.[1] An example of the effect of physical proximity of items in an information display on processing is provided by Russo and Rosen (1975). Based on an analysis of eye movements, they found that 63% of all paired comparisons were between alternatives that were spatially adjacent, even though only 47% of the possible pairs were adjacent. More active ways to influence the sequence of processing include the setting of choice agendas (see chapter 2).

---

[1] Therefore, a key question is the extent to which attention drives preferences rather than preferences (values) driving attention (Jay Russo, personal communication, 1991).

If individuals build up heuristics as they go along, and the elements used are sensitive to many task-specific factors (salience, format, and so on), the resulting choice "heuristic" may consist of a sequence of elements with a less than coherent overall structure. The following sequence illustrates such a structure: (1) An individual uses the element "compare several attribute levels of standards" for each of several alternatives (a component of a satisficing rule). (2) While doing so, the individual notes an outstanding value for a particular alternative on some attribute and eliminates all alternatives still being considered that are not "close" to that value (like an element of an elimination by aspect heuristics). (3) Next, the individual compares two remaining alternatives to see which is better on more attributes (a procedure that is part of a majority of confirming dimensions rule [Russo & Dosher, 1983]), and so on. Thus, each element or short sequence of elements may be used to process only a few alternatives. Different sequences of elements may be used for different alternatives. Examples of such fragmented heuristics have been found in several studies (e.g., Payne, 1976; Bettman & Park, 1980). For a specific example of a choice among apartments from Payne (1976), see Figure 5.1. This protocol shows several features similar to those already alluded to. For example, the individual eliminates several options based upon landlord attitude in lines B119–B132 and then shifts to something like a majority of confirming dimensions strategy in statements B172–B197. For another example of a constructive decision process involving a choice among micro-wave ovens (Bettman & Park, 1980), see Figure 5.2. Lines 19–24, for example, illustrate noticing operations and an adjustment in an elimination rule cutoff. Thus, constructive processes imply that the resulting heuristics are very sensitive to specific features of the situation.

Constructive processes and labile preferences

Another implication of the opportunistic use of heuristics and the task sensitivity of constructive processes is the labile nature of preferences mentioned in chapter 1 (see also Fischhoff, Slovic, & Lichtenstein, 1980). That is, the preferences that we observe often may reflect a constructive process in which attention to information and the methods used to combine information vary across tasks.

The compatibility hypothesis of Slovic et al. (1990), discussed in

B119: I'm going to look at landlord attitude.
B120: In H it's fair.
B121: In D it's poor.
B122: B it's fair, and
B123: A it's good.
B124: In L the attitude is poor.
B125: In K it's poor.
B126: In J it's good, and
B127: in I it's poor.
B128: So, one of them ... is poor.
B129: So, that's important to me.
B130: So ... that I'm living there.
B131: Which is the landlord also.
B132: So, I'm not going to live any place where it's poor.

.

.

B172: So, eliminate those two (A & B).
B173: And decide between these two (J & H).
B174: O.K., the kitchen facilities in H are good.
B175: In J they're fair.
B176: And that's about the same to me.

.

.

B186: Landlord attribute in J is better than in H.
B187: And, that's important.

.

.

B190: Quietness of the rooms.
B191: in H it's good.
B192: In J it's fair.
B193: And that's about the same.
B194: The rents are just about the same.
B195: In both of them the cleanliness is poor.
B196: In J the rooms are larger.
B197: So, I guess, J will be better.

Figure 5.1. Verbal protocol of a constructive choice process for apartments. *Source*: Reprinted by permission from "Task complexity and contingent processing in decision making: An information search and protocol analysis," John W. Payne, *Organizational Behavior and Human Performance*, *16* (1976), pp. 379–380. Copyright © 1976 by Academic Press, Inc.

chapter 2, provides an example of such variability in preferences. According to that hypothesis, the weight given to a stimulus attribute is enhanced by its compatibility with the response mode. A study of the prediction of academic performance reported in Slovic et al. (1990) is a nice illustration of a compatibility effect in choice. In that study, subjects were presented with pairs of students and asked to choose the student in each pair who would achieve either a higher grade in history (half the subjects) or achieve a higher class rank in history (the other half of the subjects). The information to

1   Montgomery Wards.
2   Hum, a lot of information here.
3   That's not so hot. I don't like that.
4   That makes Amana a plus.
5   Is Amana the only one that comes out like that?
6   No, everything that stays below 1 would probably be acceptable.
7   I don't know, after that I would begin to become a little
        bit leery, maybe even 1.2. I'm not sure.
8   This one, Sharp.
9   And maybe this 1.2.
10 I don't know, after that, I begin to get leery about it.
11 Okay, after that, it has to have a browner.
12 So now we're in trouble.
13 I'm getting particular.
14 Probably to the cooking levels or timers.
15 But the Montgomery Wards has 7 and the Sharp number was 4.
16 I might sacrifice this, but this is so important, at least to me,
        that I might even sacrifice the other three cooking levels.
17 Then that would leave me with so much less that I would
        probably, looking at this, would go with this one.
18 But, by dollars, that is such a determining factor, I don't
        think I would go for that over this, but it would
        probably be between these two.
19 I was not aware that so many models didn't have [a browner].
20 I thought that this was something that was fairly common.
21 But I was not aware that browners were not that widespread.
22 I might eliminate the browner which goes on the oven itself.
23 And then things such as the cooking levels and the timer
        would become more important factors.
24 So, in looking them over again, this would be acceptable now.
25 No, only two cooking levels doesn't do it.
26 This one would probably be acceptable now.
27 And, I don't know, probably not this one.
28 All three of them have expanded timers so where would we go from there?
29 Probably to the amount of space I could use in cooking.
30 So this one, this one, so probably between these three at this point.
31 I still have the same two with the browner except one.
32 And now I'd go back to using the browner to eliminate.
33 Which still leaves me with the large Sharp or the large Montgomery Ward.
34 I'm going to pick the biggest model as my first choice.

Figure 5.2. Verbal protocol of a constructive choice process for micro-wave ovens.

be used to predict relative achievement was the students' prior performance levels in two other courses, English literature and philosophy. The performance in one course was given by a grade (from A+ to D), and the performance in the other course was given in terms of a class rank (from 1 to 100). As expected from the compatibility hypothesis, subjects who had to choose which student would receive a better history grade chose the student in a pair with the higher prior grade in a course significantly more often than subjects who had to decide which student would achieve a higher class rank.

The notion of compatibility also may be the basis for the effect of dimensional commensurability on the use of attribute information (Slovic & MacPhillamy, 1974), that is, that the weight of an attribute will be enhanced to the extent that values on the attribute can be more easily compared across alternatives. Once again, therefore, how individuals process information is to some extent ad hoc. In this case it is not the compatibility of an attribute with a response mode that is important, but the compatibility of attribute information across alternatives. Stone and Schkade (1991a) provide some evidence in support of this idea in a study of the effects of attribute scaling on multiattribute choice. Using the Mouselab program, they found that unique scaling of each attribute led to more attribute-oriented processing and faster decisions, whereas common scaling across attributes (e.g., 1–10) led to more alternative-based processing and more accurate decisions.

It is important to note that both the compatibility of an attribute with a response mode and the compatibility of attribute information across alternatives can be interpreted in terms of a more general cognitive effort effect. For instance, Slovic et al. (1990, p. 5) suggest that "noncompatibility between the input and the output requires additional mental operations." Thus, a decision maker may adjust his or her processing to take advantage of special features of a problem that will reduce cognitive effort. Our hypothesis is that individuals respond to such special features as they are noticed during the course of solving a problem, not just at the beginning of the decision episode.

When will constructive processes be used?

Constructive processes are not always used, of course. In cases where there is a good deal of prior experience with a particular decision, we hypothesize that the top-down use of complete heuristics is much more likely. It would be too inefficient for individuals to construct heuristics in such situations where the structure of the decision task was well known. However, when choices are made where there is little prior knowledge, constructive processes seem more likely.

Constructive processes may also be more likely as decision problems become more complex or stressful. In such situations, it may be too difficult to attempt to determine an overall strategy a priori (see also Wood & Locke, 1990; Klein & Yadav, 1989). Of course, more difficult and stressful decisions will also tend to be less familiar, so the arguments above about prior experience would also apply. Janis and his colleagues have argued that under severe stress, people evaluate information in a hasty, disorganized, and incomplete fashion (Janis, 1982, 1989; Janis, Defares, & Grossman, 1983; Janis & Mann, 1977). Keinan (1987) provides experimental evidence that people do scan alternatives in a more nonsystematic fashion under stress. If so, this suggests that we would see more data-driven processing patterns under situations of stress.

Bettman and Zins (1977) have done one of the few studies attempting to examine the frequency of constructive choice processes. They used verbal protocol data gathered from two consumers while they shopped over several shopping trips. Judges were given transcripts of the protocols and definitions of constructive choice and were asked to categorize each choice episode. In roughly 25% of the choices, the consumers appeared to be constructing a choice heuristic on the spot. This amount of constructive processing seems reasonable; in most cases, individuals will try to develop simplified rules they can merely apply for repetitive decisions, and most everyday decisions are somewhat repetitive. However, in many experimental settings, individuals will be faced with unfamiliar tasks and may exhibit constructive processes.

Accuracy–effort tradeoffs and constructive processes

Local accuracy–effort assessments

What does the notion of constructive processing imply about our accuracy–effort view of contingent decision making? In our view, the two are perfectly consistent. When individuals construct heuristics on the spot, these constructions are based upon more local, momentary accuracy–effort assessments. When an individual notes that all values on an attribute appear to be similar and shifts to another attribute, that shift in effect reflects a tradeoff of the low benefits from continued processing of that attribute versus the costs. The earlier example of a shift in processing by a consumer due to the noticing of common attribute values illustrates this point. Tversky (1972; Kahneman & Tversky, 1979b) has argued that people often disregard components that alternatives share as one method for simplifying the choice among alternatives. Such spur-of-the-moment shifts in processing direction are still based upon accuracy–effort considerations, even though the individual is building or realizing a heuristic on the spot rather than using one selected a priori (see Simon, 1956, for a related view).

A dynamic view of properties of the choice task and contingency

These arguments lead to an extension of our notions about contingent choice processes. We have mainly used examples where contingent processing is based upon relatively stable task properties of the decision (e.g., number of alternatives, time pressure) or context factors that were relatively easy to perceive quickly (e.g., dispersion in probabilities). However, the constructive view implies a more complex notion of contingency, where many properties of the "choice task" itself change as the individual progresses. Thus the elements of choice heuristics used may not even be the same for all alternatives during a given choice. The task is *not* the same for all alternatives. The elements used to process a given alternative may depend upon which alternatives have already been processed (e.g., whether a "good" alternative has appeared yet or not); upon the particular sequence of elements already used (e.g., if certain alternatives have been eliminated because of their values on a given attribute, that attribute may have a relatively restricted range when further operations involving that attribute are considered); upon which other alternatives happen to be near a given alternative in the information display (e.g., because this will affect the magnitude of the differences on various attributes); and so on.

The level of intercorrelation among the attribute values defining the choice alternatives provides another example of how the properties of the "choice task" itself may change as an individual progresses. Decision problems often may include dominated alternatives or be characterized more generally by moderately high positive correlations between attribute values (see Einhorn et al., 1979 for a discussion of the related concept of redundancy in cue values). It has often been suggested that people first eliminate dominated alternatives from consideration when making a choice (e.g., Coombs & Avrunin, 1977), making the intercorrelation structure more negative. This change in intercorrelation may then trigger the application of new decision procedures (see chapter 6). Thus, the constructive view implies a more detailed contingency notion: The *elements* of choice heuristics used at any given time are contingent upon the properties of the choice task at that particular time. Finally, a constructive viewpoint also suggests that context variables, which reflect specific values of the alternatives rather than more general structural properties of the choice task, may play an even more important role in determining decision processes.

Noticing and exploiting regularities

Throughout this discussion, one of the most important underlying concepts has been the idea that individuals can notice and exploit regularities in the decision task. That is, individuals learn about the structure of the task as they gather information, and they may then change their processing to take advantage of what they have learned. People may, in fact, often begin working on a task using some approach that generally has proved successful for them in the past, knowing that they can adjust their processing as they learn.

Interruption of current processing

These notions of noticing and exploiting regularities are very similar to the idea of interrupts and reactions to interrupts (Simon, 1967; Bettman, 1979). Once they have begun to work on a particular goal or to implement some element of a strategy, individuals do not necessarily blindly follow their original direction to completion. Rather, if conditions warrant, they can interrupt current processing, assess the situation, and switch direction if necessary. Interrupts are generally brought about by departures from expectations; unexpected events are noticed, assessed, and reacted to if necessary. This structure of interrupts and reactions is of course very parallel to that of noticing and exploiting structure in a decision task.

However, there is a cost associated with opportunistic decision processes. As J. Anderson (1983) has noted with regard to the Hayes-Roth and Hayes-Roth (1979) model, there is a problem with distractibility. Specifically, if a decision maker's attention can always be captured by a currently interesting piece of information, overload of working memory may lead to a failure to maintain a coherent decision process. This possibility of overload necessitates a theory for when information will be considered or ignored and a theory for resolving conflicts about which pieces of available information are relevant to the overall goal. Anderson offers production system models as one way to incorporate noticing and conflict resolution mechanisms into theories of human problem solving.

We conjecture that distractibility is a fairly common problem for decisions of any complexity. Important attributes may get ignored, and much too much time may be spent on relatively unimportant attributes. In fact, we would argue that one of the primary benefits of decision analysis techniques for improving decisions (see chapter 7) is that they mitigate the problem of distractibility by forcing the decision maker to consider information in a more systematic and explicit fashion.[2]

What is noticed in a decision task

Two aspects of noticing (or interrupts) are particularly relevant: *what* gets noticed, and *when* things are noticed. As we just discussed, departures from expectations are often noticed. In the context of choice situations, this could include extreme values or negative information (Fiske, 1980); missing information (e.g., if one is trying to implement a LEX rule but finds information is missing for some alternatives [Burke, 1990]); or information in a different format from other alternatives. There may also be differences in the ease of noticing different types of information. Some task factors, such as time pressure or problem size, may be relatively easy to ascertain. However, many context factors are more difficult to perceive (e.g., interattribute correlation [Crocker, 1981; Klein & Yadav, 1989]).

The ease of noticing task properties is generally related to the concept of problem "transparency" that is receiving increased attention in the decision-making literature (Hammond, 1990; Tversky & Kahneman, 1983, 1988). The idea is that a particular procedure, such as eliminating dominated options, will be used in situations when its application is transparent and will not be used in nontransparent situations. Tversky and Kahneman (1988) nicely illustrate this point with an example of dominance violations when the display makes such a relationship nontransparent (see the discussion in chapter 3). In that case, the source of the nontransparency

---

[2] Shanteau (1988) has suggested that one of the major attributes of an "expert" decision maker is the ability to ignore irrelevant information in a problem.

is the prior use of an editing operation to simplify the information display.

Hammond (1990) relates the concept of transparency to the difference between surface (immediately apparent in the display of information) and depth (not displayed or not immediately apparent) properties of a task. Nontransparency can be thought of as a situation where the surface properties of a task are inconsistent with and mask the depth properties of the task. Why would this happen? One explanation offered by Tversky and Kahneman (1990) is that rules of mental economy often result in the acceptance of a problem as presented (i.e., based upon surface properties), without the spontaneous generation of more depth-related problem representations (see also Slovic, 1972). As we discuss further in chapter 6, the issue of nontransparency of problem structure is related to failures in adaptivity.

When properties are noticed in a decision task

The distinction between task and context factors already mentioned also affects when things are noticed. Obviously task factors are much more likely to be noticed a priori or very early in the decision. Context effects, on the other hand, are often noticeable only after some information has already been examined. In general, given the importance of noticing factors to a constructive view of choice, research examining individuals' focus of attention during information gathering would be very important.

To summarize, we have argued that individuals often construct choice processes on the spot during the course of solving a decision problem. This constructive view is offered as a supplement to the top-down process of strategy selection emphasized in chapters 3 and 4. Many decisions are likely to require a mixture of both top-down and opportunistic processing. Whatever the mixture of processes, we believe that the idea of constructive processes is not a conceptual problem for our framework. Our hypothesis is that our conceptual framework still applies, but at a more detailed level of analysis. Recent work by Klein and Yadav (1989) on context effects in decision making, for example, seems consistent with a more local, bottom-up approach to accuracy–effort tradeoffs.

To implement our effort–accuracy framework at this more detailed level would require modifications to the simulation models presented in the preceding chapter. For instance, we would need to extend the set of EIPs we use to include new operators (e.g., "bookkeeping" operators to keep track of possible regularities in the decision environment). We would also need to implement more detailed elements of heuristics for our simulations. For example, the first attribute that is selected for processing might reflect more than just the relative importance or values of the attribute; the order of processing is also likely to reflect attentional factors. As suggested earlier, important "attentional" factors in decision making may include the compatibility of an attribute with a response mode, the compatibility of attribute information across alternatives, the format in which attribute information is presented, departures from expectations, and whether the information is perceived as negative or positive. Thus, one major type of extension to our simulation would be to include explicitly a set of noticing operators that would interact with information on the relative values of the attributes in determining how and when particular processing elements such as elimination procedures get applied to a specific decision problem.

In addition to better modeling of attentional factors, the notion of constructive processes may also require that we extend our models to include the notion of a decision criterion, as suggested by the work of Bockenholt et al. (1991) and other researchers. A top-down application of a particular decision strategy generally has a natural stopping point in terms of processing. A more bottom-up form of processing, on the other hand, raises the issue of when enough processing has taken place in order to generate a response. One solution to that problem is the utilization of a criterion-dependent process based on decision confidence.

These ideas for extensions to our models of adaptive decision processing are far more speculative than the ideas presented in the preceding chapter. We want to emphasize, however, that we believe that opportunistic decision processing can be modeled using similar approaches to those we outlined earlier for top-down contingent strategy selection in adaptive decision making.

In the next section, we relate the notion of constructive processing to the idea of editing as advanced by Kahneman and Tversky (1979b) and Goldstein and Einhorn (1987). We then examine the notion of problem restructuring and the possible effort–accuracy tradeoff between decision processing and problem restructuring.

Editing processes in decision making

Editing processes have been proposed as an important component of choice (Kahneman & Tversky, 1979b; Goldstein & Einhorn, 1987), with individuals supposedly editing choice problems into simpler form before choosing. Editing could involve dropping outcomes that are identical across alternatives, eliminating some alternatives, or eliminating redundant attributes, for example. To the extent that editing can simplify choice, it is potentially a major component of adaptivity to different choice environments.

Whereas Kahneman and Tversky (1979b) and Goldstein and Einhorn (1987) argue that editing processes come first, with alternatives edited and then simplified options evaluated, we argue instead that editing is opportunistic. Editing may occur throughout a choice whenever individuals notice some structure in the choice environment that can be exploited. Hence, editing can be a bottom-up process, driven by the data, as well as a priori or top-down. Editing processes may be involved earlier in the decision process the more experience one has in a given choice environment (E. Johnson & Russo, 1984).

Editing is probably also adaptive, in that the particular editing operation used may be a function of the immediately preceding processing. That is, different types of processing will leave different traces in short-term memory, and these traces will be more or less compatible with different editing operations. For example, processing a pair of alternatives one attribute at a time and noticing how one compared with the other on each attribute would enable the detection of dominance, whereas processing each alternative in its entirety without direct comparison to the other would discourage such detection. Hence, different choice strategies enable different editing operations. Therefore, different choice environment properties will affect editing because they affect processing. This is likely to be particularly true for the effects of information display. Of particular importance is Slovic's (1972) principle of *concreteness*, mentioned earlier; he argues that individuals tend to use information in the form in which it is displayed (see also Tversky & Kahneman, 1990, and the earlier discussion of problem transparency). To the extent this is true, display should exert a strong influence on editing processes by encouraging or discouraging various types of processing.

A similar argument has been offered by Kahneman and Tversky (1979b) regarding the order in which particular editing operations are carried out. They illustrate the importance of order with the following example: The gamble ($500, .20; $101, .49; $0, .31) will appear to dominate another gamble ($500, .15; $99, .51; $0, .34) if the second components of both gambles are first simplified by rounding to ($100, .50). Thus, "the final edited prospects could, therefore, depend on the sequence of editing operations, which is likely to vary with the structure of the offered set and with the format of the display" (p. 275). Further, the preference order between gambles need not be invariant across contexts due to differences in the order in which problems are edited.

This view of editing is of course very consistent with the idea of constructive processes. Note that it also implies that individuals can devote effort not only to applying a heuristic to make a choice but also to setting up the problem in such a way that further processing is made easier. In the next section, we discuss work by Coupey (1990) that considers this tradeoff between decision processing and problem restructuring in more detail.

Restructuring decision tasks

Coupey (1990) defines problem restructuring as the application of operations to a set of information to yield a new problem representation. Restructuring operations might include transformations of information (e.g., rounding off, standardizing, or performing calculations), rearranging information (e.g., the order of brands or attributes), or simplifying by eliminating information. Figure 5.3 provides a protocol that illustrates restructuring. Whereas editing and restructuring are clearly related, Coupey's definition of restructuring appears to be somewhat more general than that of editing; hence, editing could be thought of as a subset of restructuring.

The purpose of restructuring is to help make difficult decision problems more manageable. That is, by transforming, rearranging, or eliminating information, the decision maker may be able to use a processing strategy that will result in a fairly accurate choice with reasonable levels of effort. In general, decision makers can decide to put effort into restructuring in hopes that the restructuring will make later choice processing more efficient. Individuals may trade

Okay, let's see. The information isn't in the same order for
each brand. What I'm going to do is to make a table to
reorganize the information. It'll be easier to decide if I can see
everything at a glance, too. (Subject sets up a brand/attribute
matrix.) Okay, what I did was to put down all the brands and
the categories in order for each brand. Now, let's see. Hmm,
number of needles – A is best with 80, then B. That's the most
important category. Warranty, A is 56 months, B, 70 months,
C – oh, gee, that's right – they're not all in the same units. C
is weeks, so is D. E is years. Okay, what I'm going to do now
is to do some math to convert them so I can compare them
better. (Subject does calculations in notes.) Okay, that's better.
Look at the others and see if I can standardize them. Quality
rating, 2.2 out of 5, 8.8 out of 10, so A is 4.4 out of 10, 3.3
out of 5 is 7 out of 10, and E is oh, out of 100, so 7.2 out of
10. (Subject converts quality ratings mentally, noting
transformations in matrix.) Price, well, this is hard. Price per
needle or price overall? 3.39 per needle, how many needles?
Eighty, so do the math. There. 5.88 times 68. Okay, now I'm
all set. (Subject begins comparing brands.)

Figure 5.3. An example of restructuring. The task was to recommend a
knitting machine to purchase. Restructuring is used to standardize
information in order to increase processability. *Source*: Reprinted by
permission from *Decision restructuring in consumer choice*, Eloise Coupey,
Doctoral Dissertation, Fuqua School of Business, Duke University
(1990), pp. 4–5.

off restructuring effort and effort devoted to choosing among the
alternatives in the restructured problem.

Coupey examined restructuring by providing individuals with
five decision problems, each with five alternatives and from four
to six attributes. These decision problems were presented on a
computer monitor via the Mouselab system described in earlier
chapters. Two aspects of the problems were manipulated between
subjects: (1) problems were either well structured or poorly structured, and (2) information was presented either simultaneously
or sequentially. In well-structured problems, all information for a
given attribute was expressed in the same units, and information
on any given attribute was expressed in the same order within each
alternative. For poorly structured problems, the information was
presented in different units within the same attribute, and information on any given attribute could appear in a different order
within each alternative. Samples of well-structured and poorly
structured problems are given in Figure 5.4. For simultaneous
presentations, information on all alternatives and attributes was
presented on one screen in matrix form; in the sequential conditions,

WELL-STRUCTURED PRESENTATION

Brand	Price	Size (in square feet)	Durability (in months)	Difficulty to build (0 = easy, 5 = very hard)
Brand A	$1500	150	72	3
Brand B	$2352	168	50	2
Brand C	$1700	100	54	2
Brand D	$769.50	81	72	4
Brand E	$3388	121	120	1.5
Brand F	$1568	128	64	4

POORLY STRUCTURED PRESENTATION

Brand A	Total price: $1500	Size 151 x 10w	Difficulty to build: avg. (5 pt scale)	Durability 6 years
Brand B	Price per square foot $14	Durability 50 months	Size 121 x 14w	Difficulty to build: 4 out of 10 (0 = easy)
Brand C	Total price: $1700	Size 101 x 10w	Difficulty to build: easy (5 pt scale)	Durability 4.5 years
Brand D	Total price: $769.50	Durability 72 months	Difficulty to build: 8 out of 10 (0 = easy)	Size 91 x 9w
Brand E	Price per square foot $28	Difficulty to build: 29 (100 pt scale, 0 = easy)	Size 121 sq ft	Durability 10 years
Brand F	Total price: $1568	Size 161 x 8w	Durability 64 months	Difficulty to build: somewhat difficult (5 pt scale)

Figure 5.4. A sample decision: storage buildings. *Source*: Reprinted by permission from *Decision restructuring in consumer choice*, Eloise Coupey, Doctoral Dissertation, Fuqua School of Business, Duke University (1990), p. 58.

information was presented one alternative at a time. By crossing the structure and presentation conditions, four types of problems were created (well structured, simultaneous; well structured, sequential; poorly structured, simultaneous; and poorly structured, sequential). Each individual received five instances of one of the four problem types.

Choice among five storage buildings: attributes are ease to build, % preassembled, quality of materials, price, size, and length of warranty.

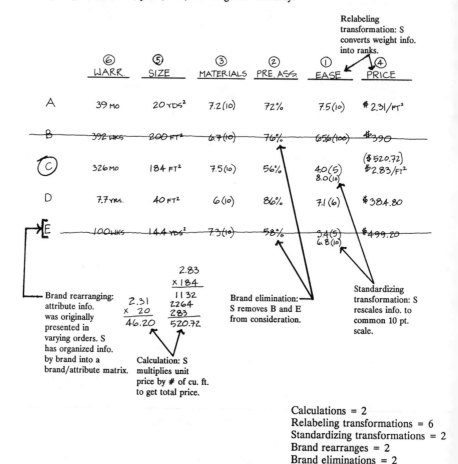

Relabeling transformation: S converts weight info. into ranks.

	⑥ WARR.	⑤ SIZE	③ MATERIALS	② PRE. ASS.	① EASE	④ PRICE
A	39 MO	20 YDS²	7.2 (10)	72%	7.5 (10)	$2.31/FT²
~~B~~	~~392 WKS~~	~~200 FT²~~	~~6.7 (10)~~	~~76%~~	~~6.56 (100)~~	~~$390~~
Ⓒ	326 MO	184 FT²	7.5 (10)	56%	4.0 (5) 8.0 (10)	($520.72) $2.83/FT²
D	7.7 YRS.	40 FT²	6 (10)	86%	7.1 (6)	$384.80
~~E~~	~~100 WKS~~	~~14.4 YDS²~~	~~7.3 (10)~~	~~58%~~	~~3.4 (5) 6.8 (10)~~	~~$499.20~~

2.83
×184
1132
2264
283
520.72

2.31
× 20
46.20

Brand rearranging: attribute info. was originally presented in varying orders. S has organized info. by brand into a brand/attribute matrix.

Calculation: S multiplies unit price by # of cu. ft. to get total price.

Brand elimination: S removes B and E from consideration.

Standardizing transformation: S rescales info. to common 10 pt. scale.

Calculations = 2
Relabeling transformations = 6
Standardizing transformations = 2
Brand rearranges = 2
Brand eliminations = 2

Figure 5.5. An example of notes coding. *Source*: Reprinted by permission from *Decision restructuring in consumer choice*, Eloise Coupey, Doctoral Dissertation, Fuqua School of Business, Duke University (1990), p. 90.

Coupey gathered information about restructuring by allowing half of the subjects to take notes and then coding the restructuring operations evident in those notes. All individuals given the opportunity to take notes did so, and 94% of those taking notes used them to restructure the information. Individuals in the poorly structured and sequential conditions used notes to create alternative by attribute matrices. For individuals receiving poorly structured input, transformations, calculations, and rearranging were used to arrive at such matrix representations. An example of notes with a coding of restructuring operations is provided in Figure 5.5. Coupey characterizes this almost universal tendency to develop matrix representations as a top-down type of restructuring, because individuals appear to carry out such restructuring almost without regard for the particular values of the information. After such a matrix is developed, individuals carry out eliminations and additional transformations in a more bottom-up fashion, depending upon the particular values of the information. In cases where the initial presentation was already in alternative-by-attribute form (the well-structured, simultaneous condition), individuals often developed rankings of the alternatives within each attribute. These transformations were not as evident in the other conditions, perhaps because individuals had already had to exert some restructuring effort simply to develop an alternative-by-attribute representation.

Individuals who restructured (i.e., almost all those who made notes) were more likely to ultimately utilize alternative-based strategies when processing the restructured information than those individuals who did not have the opportunity to make notes. Hence, one interpretation of these data is that individuals put effort into restructuring so that later they could carry out a more accurate heuristic with a reasonable amount of effort.

These descriptions of restructuring imply that restructuring occurs at early stages in the decision process. Although this may in fact be true, we should observe that the methodology of using notes to study restructuring could bias the results in this direction. That is, individuals would be likely to take notes and then do further processing based upon those notes. Therefore, although restructuring certainly often occurs in early stages of a choice process, we still believe that restructuring can occur at any time that some aspect of the choice that can be exploited is noticed.

Summary

In this chapter, we have argued that individuals will often process opportunistically, changing their processing on the spur of the moment depending upon the information they encounter. Whether or not this is constructive processing to make a choice, editing, or problem restructuring, such opportunistic processes still involve

Table 5.1. *Summary of major points from chapter 5*

Decision makers not only use information extracted from the original problem definition in deciding what strategy to use, but also use information they have already explored to identify promising paths for future processing; people construct strategies on the fly as well as select among decision strategies a priori in a top-down fashion.

A bottom-up or data-driven view of strategy usage implies that events affecting the order of attention will be powerful influences on the preferences that are observed.

The more constructive is strategy usage, the more important are context factors in determining decisions.

Constructive processes will be most likely in decision problems that involve little prior knowledge and that are stressful.

The idea of accuracy–effort tradeoffs applies to bottom-up constructive processing as well as top-down strategy selection, using more local accuracy–effort assessments.

Extensions to our production system models of decision making represent one way to incorporate opportunistic processing ideas into theories of adaptive decision behavior.

The view that individuals construct decision strategies on the spot is a potential point of contact between an accuracy–effort framework and the notion of editing processes in decision making.

People sometimes put effort into restructuring a decision problem so that later a more accurate decision strategy can be utilized with a reasonable amount of effort.

accuracy–effort tradeoffs. We simply need to bear in the mind the level of detail at which the tradeoffs are being made. Hence, our conceptual framework still applies, although new EIPs and heuristics will need to be developed for the simulations (e.g., various noticing rules could be programmed and simulated).

The processes of noticing and exploiting regularities in problem structure are crucial to all opportunistic processing. In the course of such opportunistic processing, decision makers may cycle between noticing aspects or characteristics of the choice set (e.g., extreme values across alternatives) and deciding how to exploit those aspects. As discussed in chapter 3, this depiction may represent a major opportunity for integrating accuracy–effort notions and perceptual frameworks. Perceptual frameworks may be most relevant for the noticing process, whereas cost–benefit notions may be more relevant for determining what to do to take advantage of what has been noticed. That is, some task and context effects may operate perceptually, by influencing the likelihood with which various cognitions come to mind. As noted earlier, this distinction is similar to that between interrupts and reactions or responses to those interrupts proposed by Bettman (1979). Interrupts may be more perceptually based, whereas reactions to the interrupts may be determined to a greater extent by accuracy–effort concerns.

A summary of the major points presented in this chapter is presented in Table 5.1.

Our focus throughout the first five chapters has been on the degree to which decision makers are well adapted. However, various aspects of the decision task can make adaptivity more difficult. In chapter 6, we consider some factors that can cause problems with adaptivity: difficulties in noticing choice task properties, lack of knowledge of appropriate strategies or of one's desired accuracy–effort tradeoffs, not knowing how well one is doing, and inability to execute strategies.

6

When may adaptivity fail?

Introduction

Throughout this book, we have emphasized how adaptive individuals are in their decision making. Whether by means of top-down usage of existing strategies or by constructing strategies on the fly, we have characterized decision makers as making tradeoffs of accuracy and effort that generally are reasonable and appropriate for the task at hand. However, individuals may not always exhibit such adaptivity. Even if individuals are trying to adapt, they may not be able to under some circumstances.

There are two major classes of factors associated with potential failures in adaptivity. Being adaptive requires both various types of knowledge and the ability to execute strategies. Deficits in either of these two categories can lead to the failure of adaptivity. Deficits in types of knowledge can include difficulties in assessing the task and context factors characterizing the decision environment, lack of knowledge of appropriate strategies, not being able to assess the effort and/or accuracy of a strategy in a particular situation, and not knowing one's desired accuracy–effort tradeoffs.

Even if these aspects of knowledge are present, an individual may still fail to adapt because he or she cannot execute the appropriate strategy. Such inability to execute a strategy may often be due to various environmental stressors or memory and computational difficulties.

In the following sections we consider both deficits in knowledge and inability to execute strategies as reasons for failing to adapt. Within each of these two major categories, we consider various subcategories of reasons for when adaptivity may fail.

Deficits in knowledge

Difficulties in assessing the environment

In earlier chapters, we have stressed that individuals notice properties of the decision task and then adapt by exploiting such properties. We have assumed, however, that noticing properties of the decision environment, such as task and context factors, proceeds with very little or no effort. Unfortunately, such may not always be the case. Individuals may sometimes have great difficulty assessing properties of the decision.

Such difficulties in assessment can be true for both task and context factors. In the case of task factors, for example, individuals may not know at the time they are processing exactly how much time is available or what the required response mode will be. Even the total number of available alternatives and/or attributes may not be apparent until processing has progressed substantially. An information display that appears complete provides another instance of a potential problem in assessing task factors. As noted in chapter 2, for example, the apparent completeness of a display can blind a decision maker to the possibility that some information is lacking. More generally, the assessment of task factors may be biased by a variety of information display variables that cause people to pay more attention to less important factors simply because they are more salient in the display (see MacGregor & Slovic, 1986, for an example of this problem).

Although these sorts of problems may arise in assessing task factors, in general more difficulties will arise in noticing context factors. Assessing context factors potentially requires remembering and interrelating different pieces of information to a greater extent than does assessing task factors. To assess interattribute correlation or dominated alternatives, for example, requires that one compare values for several alternatives on several attributes. There is evidence that such processes are difficult. For example, Crocker (1981) and Alloy and Tabachnik (1984) document the difficulties individuals have in assessing the degree of covariation or correlation in many settings. Furthermore, difficulties in assessing a context factor like correlation can be heightened by task factors such as information display format. For example, consider how difficult it would be to assess interattribute correlation based upon the kind of poorly structured information presentation used by Coupey (1990) and discussed in chapter 5. As shown in Figure 5.4, such information is not expressed in common units within each attribute, and information on each attribute is generally found in a different place in the display for each alternative. Attempting to assess correlation would be exceptionally hard given such a display.

In the following subsections, we consider how responses to the context factors of interattribute correlation and the range of attribute values can lead to failures in adaptivity. In addition, we discuss how the interaction of information presentation mode with context factors can result in such failures. Finally, we examine whether individuals may implicitly learn properties of the task environment.

Effects of interattribute correlation structure on processing strategies. The intercorrelational structure of a choice problem is an interesting context variable for a variety of reasons. One reason is that several authors have suggested that people should use heuristic strategies less often in negatively correlated environments and instead use strategies such as weighted adding; this suggestion follows from the argument that heuristic strategies may be relatively less accurate when attributes are negatively correlated (Newman, 1977; Einhorn et al., 1979). Because of this loss in accuracy, an effort–accuracy framework such as ours predicts that there will be less use of heuristic strategies in negatively correlated environments if the effort costs associated with various strategies are unaffected by correlation.

Another reason that correlation among attributes is of interest was mentioned earlier. There is evidence that people can be poor judges of the degree of correlation between variables. Hence, people may fail to adapt to correlation because they do not assess that correlation accurately.

We have undertaken several studies that have directly examined the relationship between the interattribute correlation structure of a set of alternatives and changes in processing strategies. In the first study (E. Johnson et al., 1989), the subjects, using the Mouselab system, were presented with choice problems involving hypothetical apartments that varied in number of alternatives (2 vs. 8) and in the level of correlation between attributes (0, maximum average negative correlation [−.33] between all pairs of attributes, and −1 correlation between the two most important attributes). While Johnson et al. found strong evidence of contingent processing due to choice set size, they found that "changes in the pattern of correlation between attributes in choice sets did not produce marked shifts in decision making strategies or evidence for a shift to compensatory rules with negative interattribute correlations" (p. 266).

The second study (Bettman et al., 1992) used a combination of Monte Carlo simulation and process tracing to study (1) the effects of variations in the interattribute correlation structure of choice sets on the performance of heuristic decision strategies, and (2) the degree to which decision makers adapt to changes in the levels of interattribute correlation.

The results from the simulation study showed that heuristics are generally less accurate for a given effort level in decision environments with negative interattribute correlation. This effect of negative correlation on performance is particularly acute when the dispersion in weights (probabilities) is low rather than high. For example, for a four-alternative, four-attribute choice problem, the equal weight strategy falls from an accuracy level of .94 for the positive-correlation, low-dispersion task environment to an accuracy level of only .30 for the negative-correlation, low-dispersion task environment. More generally, our simulation results support the conjecture of Einhorn et al. (1979, p. 480): Given positively correlated attributes, "the benefits of using one strategy or another may be so small as to make the simpler noncompensatory strategies preferable." In contrast, to obtain high levels of accuracy under negative correlation and low dispersion, one would need to devote the additional effort needed for a weighted additive strategy.

The experimental part of the Bettman et al. study again used Mouselab. The stimuli were sets of four gambles with four outcomes of the type discussed in chapter 4. Because subjects actually played some of the gambles for cash, we were able to relate choices to real consequences for the subjects. The study involved crossing two levels of correlation (positive and maximum average negative correlation [−.33] between all pairs of attributes) and two levels of dispersion in probabilities (high and low) in a complete within-subject design. Figure 6.1 illustrates a low-dispersion, negative-correlation choice problem and a low-dispersion, positive-correlation choice problem. In the experiment the boxes of the displays were closed, and the subjects had to acquire the information using the mouse.

The results of the Bettman et al. study showed significant effects

Negative Correlation

	Outcome 1	Outcome 2	Outcome 3	Outcome 4
Prob.	.18	.25	.28	.29
Gamble A	$3.97	$5.36	$6.75	$3.54
Gamble B	$2.49	$3.24	$6.99	$7.11
Gamble C	$8.84	$2.37	$4.38	$4.61
Gamble D	$6.62	$1.88	$8.66	$3.45

Choose One: Gamble A | Gamble B | Gamble C | Gamble D

Gamble D was chosen. Enter this box and click once to continue

EVs

$4.97

$5.28

$4.75

$5.09

Positive Correlation

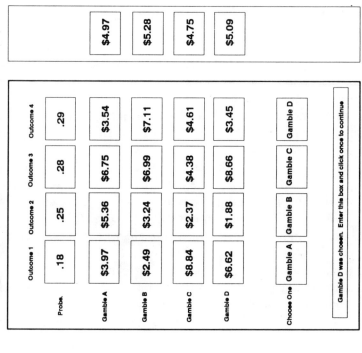

	Outcome 1	Outcome 2	Outcome 3	Outcome 4
Prob.	.18	.25	.28	.29
Gamble A	$4.83	$5.12	$6.53	$2.47
Gamble B	$3.98	$1.74	$3.72	$2.81
Gamble C	$4.34	$7.68	$3.91	$8.83
Gamble D	$9.47	$6.23	$9.58	$9.92

Choose One: Gamble A | Gamble B | Gamble C | Gamble D

Gamble D was chosen. Enter this box and click once to continue

EVs

$4.69

$3.01

$6.36

$8.82

Note: Subjects saw gamble sets only, not expected values.
Boxes were closed during the experiment.

Table 6.1. *Effects of attribute intercorrelation and dispersion in probabilities on processing and accuracy*

Dependent measure	Negative correlation		Positive correlation	
	Low dispersion	High dispersion	Low dispersion	High disperion
ACQ	46.8	32.2	32.2	28.7
TIME	48.2	33.5	33.3	30.1
VAR-ALTER	.014	.024	.022	.028
VAR-ATTRIB	.015	.044	.017	.040
PATTERN	.29	-.08	.22	-.10
GAIN	.33	.81	.88	.90

Note: ACQ = number of acquisitions. TIME = time taken. VAR-ALTER = variance in the proportion of time spent on each alternative. VAR-ATTRIB = variance in the proportion of time spent on each attribute. PATTERN = index reflecting amount of attribute-based (−) and alternative-based (+) processing. GAIN = relative accuracy of choices.

of correlational structure on decision processing. Table 6.1 shows the results for the negative- and positive-correlation problems. First, note that our standard effects of dispersion on processing were replicated: High dispersion led to less processing, more selectivity in processing, and more attribute-based processing. Second, and more important, there were effects of correlation structure. For negative-correlation problems, there was significantly more processing, less selectivity in processing across alternatives, and more alternative-based processing. Third, the effect of correlation was generally stronger for the low-dispersion problems. One interpretation of the results is that individuals attempted to process more normatively for the negative-correlation, low-dispersion problems. Effort was certainly greater in those problems, and the type of processing observed was consistent with the usage of compensatory rules. However, note that the gain score for those problems was low. The increased effort was not associated with high levels of accuracy, and hence subjects were incompletely adaptive to the differences in correlational structure.

This study shows changes in processing due to changes in the interattribute correlation structure of the choice sets. We did not attempt to measure whether the subjects were aware of the correlation levels for the different types of problems in this experiment. In a second experiment, however, half of the subjects were given a positive-correlation choice problem and half a negative-correlation problem at the end of the experiment. They then were asked to indicate their degree of agreement with the following statement (1 = disagree completely, 7 = agree completely): "Gambles in the preceding set that had a large payoff for one or two outcomes usually had small payoffs for the other outcomes." Subjects seeing a positive-correlation problem indicated marginally less agreement than subjects seeing the negative-correlation problem ($M = 3.65$ vs. $M = 4.14$, $p < .07$). Thus, there is some evidence that subjects were aware of differences among the stimuli that are indicative of the differences in interattribute correlation levels.

Our results in this study differ from those reported by E. Johnson et al. (1989), in that subjects did respond to correlation in the Bettman et al. study. However, Johnson et al. manipulated number of alternatives as well as correlation, and adaptation to the obvious task variable of problem size may have interfered with adaptation to correlation. In addition, subjects made only a limited number of decisions in each condition of their study. Adaptation to subtle context factors like correlation may require experience over many trials.

Although subjects were still somewhat adaptive in the Bettman et al. studies, it seems obvious from an examination of the stimuli given in Figure 6.1 that the detection of correlation is likely to be a more effortful process than the detection of the other context variable, dispersion in probabilities. A substantial amount of processing seems to be necessary to determine if one is facing a negative correlation problem or a positive correlation problem. Although some of our subjects may have engaged in such processing, their failure to adapt fully to correlational structure is not too surprising, given the difficulty in assessing that context factor. In addition, even if individuals assess correlation and intend to adapt to it, the weighted adding strategy may be difficult to implement in an error-free fashion, potentially leading to less accurate choices in the negative-correlation conditions where use of that strategy is more likely.

Effects of range of attribute values. The range of values on an attribute is another context variable to which individuals may not be fully adaptive. It is generally argued that the weight given an attribute should reflect the range of attribute values across the alternatives in a choice set: the greater the range, the greater the importance of the attribute. The empirical evidence on this point is equivocal, however. Although weights sometimes reflect the range of values (e.g., Goldstein, 1990), there is also evidence that weights do not reflect much consideration of the ranges of values under some conditions (Beattie & Baron, 1991).

Einhorn et al. (1979) argue that in adapting to a local decision environment, one will initially pay attention to an attribute one believes to be important based on experience in dealing with related decision problems. However, if the decision maker notices that all the alternatives are similar on the attribute, Einhorn et al. argue that he or she learns to pay less attention and may not use that attribute to make a choice. Alternatively, a decision maker may ignore an attribute initially if he or she thinks values on that attribute are likely to be similar. If there were indeed differences in values, then the individual might eventually adapt, pay more attention to the attribute, and use it to help make the decision. As noted by Einhorn et al., the implication is "that when people are in unfamiliar local environments that differ significantly from their global environments, discrepancies between attention and cue usage are likely to be large" (p. 482). That is, there may be a delay in adaptivity in moving from a familiar to an unfamiliar decision problem characterized by different levels of a particular context factor such as the range of attribute values.

Effects of information presentation mode on assessing the environment. As already suggested, some agendas or formats can exacerbate the difficulties individuals have in assessing task or context effects such as correlation, dominance, or ranges in values. For example, if alternatives are arranged so that a dominating and dominated alternative are far apart, dominance may be more difficult to detect than if these two alternatives were arranged next to one another. As another example, difficulties in assessment would be compounded if information were only available sequentially over time (i.e., some pieces of information become available, then those pieces are removed and other information appears) rather than being available simultaneously. Such sequential presentation would make such properties as the number of alternatives, dominance, range of attribute values, and correlation much harder to assess and would place greater demands on remembering earlier information. Ward and Jenkins (1965) found that sequential presentation increased the difficulty in assessing covariation relationships, for instance. Coupey (1990), as noted in the previous chapter, found that individuals made notes to attempt to cope with these problems of sequential information.

More generally, difficulties in assessing the environment are related to the concept of the transparency (or nontransparency) of the decision problem structure, as discussed in chapter 5. As noted there and in chapter 3, one might even violate the principal of dominance in situations in which dominance relationships are masked.

Implicit learning. The preceding discussion argues that individuals may have difficulty assessing task and context factors under some circumstances. There is also evidence, however, that at times individuals may act as if they had noticed features of the task environment, even if they are unable to articulate that knowledge. Reber (1989) argues that individuals may exhibit *implicit learning*, which produces insights into the structure of the environment that are acquired nonconsciously and can be used to adapt appropriately. Individuals may not be able to state explicitly such insights, however. Reber (1989, p. 233) claims that it is possible for individuals "to have an intuitive sense of what is right and proper, to have a vague feeling of the goal of an extended process of thought, to 'get the point' without really being able to verbalize what it is that one has gotten."[1] For example, Lewicki (1986) argues that subjects can respond appropriately to covariation information, even though they cannot express the degrees of covariation present. Klein and Yadav (1989) report similar results. Hence, individuals may be able to adapt even if they are unable to report specifically noticing some task or context factor. Such implicit learning is a fascinating area for further research in decision-making contexts. In particular, differentiating between situations where individuals fail to assess *and* fail to adapt and situations where individuals appear to fail to assess but still adapt will be critical.

Lack of knowledge of appropriate strategies

Individuals may fail to adapt because they do not know the appropriate strategy for a particular situation or are unable to construct such a strategy. Next we discuss how such factors as variations in the availability of strategies, problems requiring insight and difficulties of encoding or attentional focus, not knowing when and/or how to use strategies, and overgeneralization can lead to adaptivity failures.

Variations in the availability of strategies. One factor that is associated with variations in knowledge of appropriate strategies is simply stage of cognitive development. There is a good deal of evidence that young children lack knowledge of various strategies. For example, Roedder (1981) and John and Cole (1986) summarize research showing that young children do not possess several common memory strategies for encoding and retrieval. Capon and Kuhn (1980) document that younger children appear to use

---

[1] A related, but somewhat different, notion is that experts in a problem domain may also adapt appropriately without being conscious of features of the environment. However, in this case, such adaptation may stem from use of overlearned strategies whose basis is no longer easily accessible in memory.

strategies based upon one attribute rather than strategies taking more than one attribute into account. Although these data are suggestive, the authors did not attempt to determine whether this was due to lack of knowledge of multiattribute strategies. Klayman (1985) found that by 12 years of age children appeared to be knowledgeable about various strategies and task contingencies, although the children did not seem to use strategies with as much consistency or regularity as had been reported for studies involving adults (e.g., Payne, 1976). Siegler and Crowley (1991) also provide evidence that children discover new strategies over time.

Adult decision makers may also lack knowledge of appropriate strategies, although it is clear that adults generally have several strategies in their repertoires (see chapters 2 and 4). The strategies people have available for judgment and choice may derive from various sources, including natural acquisition through experience or more formal training and education. Recent work by Nisbett and Fong and their colleagues (Fong, Krantz, & Nisbett, 1986; Larrick et al., 1990; Nisbett, Krantz, Jepson, & Kunda, 1983) has shown how the teaching of statistical rules and cost–benefit principles increases the likelihood of statistical and decision theoretic reasoning processes. Nonetheless, a person may appear not to exhibit adaptivity simply due to the lack of knowledge of the more appropriate strategies for a particular decision environment.

A nice example of how variability in the knowledge of specific strategies can impact thinking is provided by Simon (1981b). Imagine that you have been asked to solve the equation $3X - 21 = 0$. How would you proceed? Most of us would start by adding 21 to both sides of the equation. Both sides would then be divided by 3, obtaining the answer: $X = 7$. In contrast, consider the following strategy used during the seventeenth century for solving similar algebra problems: First, "guess at an answer, say $X1 = 5$, and substitute it in the left side of the equation, obtaining $15-21 = -6$. We call the remainder $Y1 = -6$. Now make another guess, say $X2 = 10$. From this we obtain $30 - 21 = 9 = Y2$. Finally, compute the quantity $(X1Y2 - X2Y1)/(Y2 - Y1)$. We have $(5 \times 9 + 10 \times 6)/(9 + 6) = 105/15 = 7$" (Simon, 1981b, p. 301).

According to Simon this legitimate, but more difficult, method was used for centuries. The point is that two strategies for solving an intellectual task can differ dramatically in difficulty. Awareness of one strategy for tackling a problem can make it possible to solve

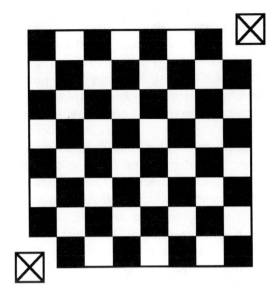

Task:

Cover the 62 remaining squares using 31 dominos. Each domino covers 2 adjacent squares.
Or: Prove logically why such a covering is impossible.

Figure 6.2. The classic mutilated checkerboard problem. *Source*: Reprinted by permission from "In search of insight," Craig A. Kaplan and Herbert A. Simon, *Cognitive Psychology*, *22* (1990), p. 378. Copyright © 1990 by Academic Press, Inc.

that problem with little effort; lack of awareness of that strategy and knowledge of another more difficult strategy may make solving the problem less likely. Simon has suggested that some cognitive strategies can be viewed as thought-saving devices in the same way shovels are labor-saving devices. As will be discussed in chapter 7, training people in strategies for decision making that save cognitive effort is of growing concern.

Problems requiring insight and difficulties with encoding/attention. Demonstrations of deficits in strategy knowledge may be particularly prevalent for problems requiring insight in their solution. For example, Kaplan and Simon (1990) discuss how individuals attempt to solve the mutilated chessboard problem (see Figure 6.2). In this problem, a standard 8 × 8 chessboard has two diagonally opposite corner squares removed. The individual's task is to determine how to cover the board by placing dominos vertically or horizontally over adjacent squares so as to cover the board completely (each domino covers exactly two squares) or to provide a proof that this is impossible. Kaplan and Simon show that without hints this is a very difficult problem; no subjects solved the problem in less than an hour without hints. However, by providing hints (e.g., that the color on the squares might help solve the problem), solution times were greatly decreased.[2] The hints enabled individuals to *construct* an appropriate strategy. Note how the difficulties with insight tasks differ from the task assessment difficulties noted previously; in insight problems, the difficulty stems from not knowing which property of the task to consider, not from any inability to assess that property. Kaplan and Simon (1990, p. 396) hypothesize that "one of the distinguishing characteristics of insightful problem solvers is that they are good noticers."

Holland et al. (1986) make a related argument about failures to adapt caused by encoding problems – that is, situations in which a person does not code elements of the environment in ways that make contact with the appropriate strategies for a situation, even if those strategies are known. They argue that erroneous rules may persist, even in the presence of feedback, simply because of a failure to attend to the factor in the environment that could lead to a better rule.

Siegler (1983) provides one example of such an encoding and attention problem and resultant failure to adapt. Siegler found that 5-year-old children were generally not able to solve balance beam problems, even when given feedback concerning the accuracy of their guesses about the movement of the balance beam under various weight and distance conditions. The difficulty seemed to be that the children were not even attending to the distance of the weight from the fulcrum. Their focus was solely on the weights on each side of the fulcrum. However, if the 5-year-olds were given practice in attending to the distance of the weights from the fulcrum (by asking them to count *both* the weights on each side of the fulcrum *and* the distance of each weight from the center in number of pegs), then they were able to learn from the accuracy feedback.

---

[2] Because a domino covers one square of each color when placed on the board, the board can only be completely covered if there are equal numbers of squares of each color. However, the two corners removed are of the same color, leaving 32 of one color and 30 of the other. Hence, the task is impossible.

We speculate that some failures to adapt in decision situations may similarly occur simply because the context factor that should guide decisions is not being attended to or encoded by the decision maker. An example is the focus on sample proportion rather than sample difference in Bayesian revision problems such as the classic bookbag and poker chip task. In a bookbag and poker chip task, an individual is given a sample containing a specified number of poker chips of two colors (e.g., seven red and three green). He or she then is asked to judge the probability that the sample was drawn from a bookbag that contained two-thirds red chips and one-third green chips versus a bookbag that contained one-third red chips and two-thirds green chips. Typically, a sample of 4 red chips and 1 green chip is judged to be more diagnostic of the mostly red bag than a sample of 8 red and 4 green chips, even though the evidence for the red bag is much stronger (16 to 1 vs. 8 to 1 odds) for the 8 red, 4 green sample than for the 4 red, 1 green sample (Kahneman & Tversky, 1972). That is, people judge the sample with the larger proportion of red chips as being more diagnostic than the sample with the larger difference between the number of red and green chips. It would be interesting to see if some errors in probabilistic reasoning (see Kahneman, Slovic & Tversky, 1982, for many examples) could be eliminated by adopting a combination of accuracy feedback *and* attention manipulations of the type used by Siegler (1983) to improve performance on balance beam problems. Note that such a combination combines elements of both cost–benefit and perceptual approaches (see chapter 3).

Finally, another way of looking at these problems requiring insight and/or attention to the appropriate factor in the situation is that picking the "right" representation for a problem can sometimes make the solution obvious. Research on variation in difficulty across problem isomorphs has also made this point (e.g., Simon & Hayes, 1976; Kotovsky, Hayes, & Simon, 1985).

Not knowing when and how to use strategies. Decision strategies like EBA and SAT can be thought of as procedural knowledge (J. Anderson, 1983), that is, as knowledge about how to solve a problem. Procedural knowledge is distinguished from declarative knowledge about facts. Gagne (1984), however, has argued that good problem solving requires a third type of knowledge, which can be called "strategic" knowledge (Greeno, 1978). The idea is that people bring to tasks "not only previously learned declarative knowledge and procedural knowledge but also some skills of *when and how to use this knowledge*" (Gagne, 1984, p. 381, emphasis added). Another source of failure to adapt due to lack of knowledge, therefore, is limits on such strategic knowledge. Some people may not have good "executive control processes" (Atkinson & Shiffrin, 1968) or metacognitive knowledge that allows them to adapt procedures to a task easily and properly. Interestingly, there is evidence to suggest that a crucial difference among students is the ability to adjust different processes (e.g., reading approaches) to different education tasks (Garner, 1987).

Overgeneralization. A related source of potential failure to adapt is not necessarily lack of knowledge of an appropriate strategy but overreliance on an inappropriate strategy. For example, the recency and frequency of activation of a decision strategy will increase its likelihood of being applied to a new decision task, even though the nature of the new task may be such that an alternative rule would be more appropriate. Ginossar and Trope (1987) demonstrate how the prior activation of different inferential strategies could impact the use or misuse of base rate information in a prediction task, for example. This idea is a variation of the idea of functional fixity (Duncker, 1945) applied to decision strategy selection.

More generally, researchers have argued that overgeneralizing the applicability of normally reasonable judgment heuristics is a typical cause of failure of adaptivity in decision making (e.g., J. Baron, 1988; Klayman & Ha, 1987). That is, individuals often apply rules or heuristics that are generally useful across a wide variety of situations to new situations where those rules are not appropriate. Klayman and Ha, for instance, argue that in hypothesis testing, people overrely on a "positive test strategy" that often works very well but can lead to systematic errors in some situations. They suggest that the use of more optimal strategies may require that the relationship between task variables and strategy performance be highly transparent.

Experts in a domain often develop specific rules for recurring, highly familiar tasks. As a result, experts do not always display overgeneralization biases to the same extent as novices (e.g., see J. Smith & Kida, 1991, for evidence on auditors' judgments). Holland et al. (1986), however, point out that such specific rules still compete with more general heuristics for application rather than substituting for them. Therefore, the same experts who avoid some biases by using a specific rule to deal with a highly familiar task may fall prey to overgeneralizing a more generic heuristic when dealing with a task containing unfamiliar elements (J. Smith & Kida, 1991).

Difficulties in assessing effort and accuracy

Our model of strategy selection assumes that the decision maker assesses the benefits and costs of various processing strategies and then chooses (or constructs) the strategy that is best for the task at hand. Thus, for an individual to adapt strategies to a particular decision task, he or she must have at least vague ideas about the degree of accuracy and effort characterizing his or her decision process. This notion suggests several questions. For example, what cues are used to assess likely accuracy and effort and how are those cues combined? What biases might occur in such assessments? Although we are far from having answers to all of these questions, we can make hypotheses about the accuracy of assessments of expected effort and accuracy in decision making. Following discussions of factors influencing the goodness of individuals' assessments of effort and accuracy, we consider empirical findings on the effects of effort and accuracy feedback on processing and performance. We try to show that adaptivity depends upon both the type of feedback and decision difficulty.

Assessments of effort. We anticipate that judgments of effort may be reasonably accurate, particularly for decisions in which the individual has some experience. *Process feedback* (Anzai & Simon, 1979) could easily provide information on the effort involved in using a strategy. Process feedback is information about the course of one's own decision processes. In the course of solving a decision problem, an individual has a fairly rich database available about how effortful and/or difficult he or she is finding the problem. Thus, information on how hard one is working at a task is usually available and salient. The kinds of task factors that affect effort (e.g., number of alternatives) are also usually salient. In many situations, therefore, likely effort can be assessed based upon prior experience or obvious task factors (note that such an assessment does place an additional processing demand on the decision maker).

However, effort may be difficult to assess in some cases (e.g., a new decision task, or sequential information presentation). The following example from Payne (1982) illustrates the potential uncertainty associated with estimating effort in dynamic decision situations. Assume you have to select one of a large set of alternatives. Because the task is complex, you decide to use a cognitively less costly elimination-by-aspects (EBA) strategy. Unfortunately, just as you have reached a decision, you are told that your chosen alternative is no longer available. What do you do next? Do you start an EBA process over again? It would probably be preferable just to select the next best alternative. The idea of a next best alternative, however, implies a ranking of alternatives, which an elimination process does not necessarily provide. It may be that if a possibility exists that a preferred alternative may become unavailable, a decision maker's *expected* effort would be less using a more compensatory strategy from the beginning. Such a strategy would allow the identification of a next best alternative. However, such a strategy selection decision requires an accurate a priori judgment of anticipated effort, which is unlikely given the dynamic aspects of the task.

Assessments of accuracy. Although effort may be somewhat easy to judge, gaining information on likely accuracy from process feedback would seem more problematic. One often does not know exactly whether the final decision is a good one or not. A self-generated notion of accuracy is possible to some degree if we assume that individuals have general knowledge about the properties of a reasonable strategy, at least for some decision tasks (see also the ideas of Siegler & Jenkins, 1989, about goal sketches, which specify the objectives a satisfactory strategy must meet). For example, decision makers might believe that a "good" strategy involves first looking at the most important information for all alternatives, and then looking at other information as desired or as time allows (Payne et al., 1988 report data supporting this notion). An individual could then observe how well his or her choice process as executed matched this general notion of a "good" strategy. For example, if time ran out before some important information could be considered, then the individual might decide that the process should be changed. Such use of process feedback to assess accuracy is similar to ideas of Reder (1987), who suggests that people generate "feelings of knowing" about the quality of their performance during the course of problem solving.

However, such feelings of knowing may not always be easy to access. Brehmer (1990), for example, has argued that knowing one is being suboptimal in solving a complex and dynamic decision problem is not a primary perceptual datum. Instead, "it is an inference based on a normative model of the task, and, if the decision maker does not have a well-developed model of the task, the possibility of doing better will not be detected" (Brehmer, 1990, p. 267).

Even if one assumes that assessments of accuracy are made, there is no guarantee that they will be accurate. Indeed, one of the most well-established errors in judgment is the overconfidence bias. That bias is said to exist when individuals are inappropriately confident in their ability to estimate an uncertain quantity (Bazerman, 1990). Typically, we think we know more than our answers really indicate. Although the typical overconfidence study has involved the estimation of the uncertainty associated with the answers to factual knowledge questions (e.g., the length of the Nile), the results of such studies suggest that people may be overconfident in their ability to generate a good decision when using a particular decision strategy.

One factor that may contribute to an overconfident assessment of decision accuracy is the hindsight bias (Fischhoff, 1975) or the "I knew it all along" phenomenon (see Hawkins & Hastie, 1990, for an excellent review). Such a belief that they knew it all along may cause individuals not to appreciate fully the limits of their decision making and judgmental processes. In the words of François, Duc de La Rochefoucauld (1678), "Everyone complains of his memory, and no one complains of his judgments" (Maxim 89).

Therefore, we hypothesize that individuals may overestimate the accuracy they will achieve with particular decision heuristics. If true, this suggests that people may select heuristics that will save effort but not produce the expected level of accuracy.

This discussion suggests that people may be biased in their assessments of accuracy; another possibility is that accuracy is given less than appropriate weight in selecting strategies simply due to the difficulty in knowing how well one is doing. Einhorn (1980), among others, has pointed out how difficult it can be to get relevant information on the quality of one's judgment. Often the decision environment provides outcome information that is incomplete, ambiguous, and delayed.[3] In the extreme, it has been argued that learning seldom occurs even under optimal presentation of outcome feedback (Brehmer, 1980).

Although accuracy may be difficult to assess, we have argued that cues to effort are more available and salient. Because assessments of effort may be easier than assessments of accuracy, effort may be overweighted relative to accuracy in strategy selection.

Effects of accuracy and effort feedback on processing and performance. Because of these questions concerning assessment of accuracy and effort, we examined how decision makers may learn to adapt when presented with explicit accuracy feedback and/or effort feedback (Creyer et al., 1990). Recall that some results of this study were presented earlier in chapter 4. Briefly, subjects made choices for 32 sets of four-alternative, six-attribute decision problems. The sets varied on four factors: (1) the dispersion of the weights provided for the attributes (high or low); (2) the explicit goal of the decision maker for the set (minimize effort or maximize accuracy); (3) effort feedback (present or absent); and (4) accuracy feedback (present or absent). The first two factors (dispersion and goal) were within-subject factors; the two feedback factors were between-subject.

Before discussing the hypotheses and results, we must first consider the feedback manipulations. One between-subject factor was the presence or absence of explicit accuracy feedback. Before defining the form of such feedback, we must first consider how to define subjects' accuracy levels. As in earlier chapters, we measure the accuracy of a decision by comparing the weighted additive value for the alternative selected from a set to the best and worst possible values for that set:

Relative Accuracy

$$= \frac{\text{Weighted Additive Value}_{\text{Choice}} - \text{Weighted Additive Value}_{\text{Worst}}}{\text{Weighted Additive Value}_{\text{Best}} - \text{Weighted Additive Value}_{\text{Worst}}}.$$

This measure was used to provide accuracy feedback to subjects via Mouselab. For each choice set, the relative accuracy score corresponding to each option was computed. After the subject had

---

[3] It is in environments that provide complete, unambiguous, and rapid feedback that individuals can learn to be well calibrated about accuracy (e.g., weather forecasters) (Murphy & Winkler, 1977).

made a choice for a problem set, a scale ranging from 0 to 1 appeared on the screen. The letters A through D, corresponding to the four alternatives in the set, were positioned on the scale to correspond to their relative accuracy scores. For example, if the weighted additive values for alternatives A to D were 125, 200, 150, and 100, then the relative accuracy scores would be 0.25, 1, 0.5, and 0 respectively. Alternative D would be placed above the left end of the scale, alternative A would be one-quarter of the way toward the right end of the scale, alternative C would be above the midpoint of the scale, and alternative B would be above the right end of the scale.

Subjects could see the relative positioning of the alternatives and thus receive visual feedback. In addition, subjects could move the mouse along the scale to correspond to the letter for any alternative. The exact relative accuracy score for that alternative would then be displayed.

The second between-subject factor was the presence or absence of explicit effort feedback. For the subjects in the effort feedback condition, a clock was displayed in the top left corner of the screen for each set of alternatives presented. The clock, initially a completely shaded circle, began to disappear when the subject started to gather information about the alternatives and stopped when the subject selected an alternative. The extent to which the circle was no longer shaded was an indication of the amount of time used by the subject to decide among the alternatives.

The notions about process feedback we have outlined suggest some interesting hypotheses in this experimental situation. For example, the presence of explicit accuracy feedback should only improve the quality of decisions for problems where individuals do not have strong notions of a "good" strategy. Thus, the effects of accuracy feedback should vary across decision tasks. For instance, the general notion of a "good" strategy outlined previously (i.e., look at the most important information first) is less easy to execute when faced with problems involving low dispersion, because one cannot easily be selective. Payne et al. (1988) also found that low-dispersion problems took longer to solve. In addition, subjects report when asked that decisions with low dispersion are more difficult and that they have less confidence in their decisions when dispersion is low.[4]

---

[4] In a study with 32 subjects exposed to decision problems varying on dispersion, presence or absence of dominated alternatives, and incentives, subjects rated

Given these perceptions, process feedback seems less likely to suffice. Hence, we predict that explicit accuracy feedback will have greater effects on low-dispersion decision problems. The impact of accuracy feedback will be to increase the use of more normative decision strategies like the weighted additive rule. Such strategies are characterized by a substantial amount of processing; an amount of processing that is not selective but rather is consistent across alternatives and attributes, indicating more compensatory processes (Payne, 1976); and processing that is alternative-based rather than attribute-based.

Because individuals are able to generate fairly accurate notions about their own effort levels, the addition of explicit effort feedback should have little effect. Although the study also considered additional complex interaction effects of feedback and goals, the hypotheses already noted are the focus here (see Creyer et al., 1990, for more details).

The results generally confirm the hypotheses. Accuracy feedback increases the number of acquisitions and marginally increases the time spent on information in the boxes. Hence, more processing is done with accuracy feedback. There is also limited evidence for low selectivity with accuracy feedback, as feedback leads to decreased variance in processing across attributes. However, there was no effect of accuracy feedback on the proportion of time spent on the most important attribute or the variance in processing across alternatives. Finally, accuracy feedback leads, as hypothesized, to relatively more alternative-based processing. However, there was no main effect of accuracy feedback on relative accuracy.

Although these main effects are roughly in the expected directions, our hypothesis was that the main effects would be qualified by an accuracy feedback by dispersion interaction, with accuracy feedback exhibiting stronger effects for the more difficult low-dispersion problems. This hypothesis received support, as there were accuracy feedback by dispersion interactions for number of acquisitions, time spent acquiring information from the boxes, variance in processing

low-dispersion problems more difficult than high-dispersion choices (means of 4.93 vs. 3.91 on a scale where $0 =$ not at all difficult and $10 =$ extremely difficult, $p < .0001$). In addition, the subjects stated that they were more confident about their choices for high-dispersion problems than for low-dispersion problems (means of 7.36 vs. 6.54 on a scale where $0 =$ not at all confident and $10 =$ extremely confident, $p < .0001$).

across attributes, and relative accuracy. Three of these interactions have the predicted form: Accuracy feedback has greater impact for low-dispersion problems than for high-dispersion problems for acquisitions, time spent on information in the boxes, and relative accuracy. For variance in processing across attributes, the low-dispersion condition shows the lowest selectivity, as predicted, but there is a greater effect of accuracy feedback under high dispersion. Only one variable, the degree of alternative-based versus attribute-based processing, displays a main effect for accuracy feedback without the qualifying interaction with dispersion.

The effects of effort feedback can be described simply. There were no significant main effects of effort feedback on any process measure or on relative accuracy. There were also no significant accuracy by effort feedback interactions and no significant effort feedback by dispersion interactions.

In summary, accuracy feedback can lead to more normative types of processing, particularly in cases where decisions are more difficult. For such problems, process feedback and general knowledge of what makes for a "good" strategy are less applicable, and feedback becomes more necessary. Explicit effort feedback, on the other hand, had no impact. Individuals appear to be able to generate adequate assessments of their own effort levels for the repetitive type of task used in the study. Further research examining how individuals assess accuracy and effort across a broad range of decision tasks would be most enlightening.

Although this study by Creyer et al. shows that accuracy feedback improves performance for more difficult low-dispersion problems, it has also been shown that outcome feedback can sometimes lead to poorer performance in probabilistic judgment tasks (Arkes et al., 1986). In the Arkes et al. study, a simple rule provided the best expected performance, although the rule did not select the best option for each trial. Their study found that incentives led to poorer performance when feedback was provided. The reason offered by Arkes et al. was that the presence of incentives increased the frequency with which subjects shifted strategies after a bad outcome was experienced. That is, subjects given incentives and feedback were less consistent in their use of the rule that gave the best performance on average but was not perfectly accurate. Hence, feedback can lead to failures to adapt if that feedback makes poor strategies more salient.

Lack of knowledge of one's desired
accuracy–effort tradeoffs

Individuals may also fail to adapt because they do not know their desired tradeoff between accuracy and effort. This may not be an uncommon situation. Hogarth (1987), for example, has argued that individuals find conflict and making explicit tradeoffs emotionally uncomfortable and difficult. If individuals are not able to decide upon such tradeoffs, then the accuracy–effort tradeoff they achieve will only be determined after the strategy they use has been implemented. This realized accuracy–effort tradeoff may not prove to be satisfactory after the fact.

Inability to execute strategies

Individuals may fail to adapt even when they know an appropriate strategy if they are unable to execute that strategy. One set of factors that can make strategies too difficult to execute is environmental stressors. Such factors as severe time pressure, heavy levels of distraction, noise, and heat may interfere with an individual's ability to implement a strategy, even if that strategy is known.

A second factor that may affect the ability to execute a strategy is the difficulty of the required computations. A weighted adding strategy may simply be too difficult if the numbers to be combined are complex.

Simon (1981b) illustrates this source of problem difficulty with the following example. Think of two numbers such as 1776 and 1492. Keeping those two numbers in working memory is probably not too hard for those knowledgeable about American history. Now, without using paper and pencil, multiply 1776 by 1492. For most of us, this will be difficult due to the constraints that limited working memory places on our ability to keep track of the interim products of the calculations. Now we obviously could solve this problem with paper and pencil. The problem would be even easier with a calculator. However, the point is that as a problem becomes more complex, the need to deal with many interim inputs and outputs of processes may exceed working memory capacity fairly quickly, even though each individual operation is within our capacity.

In our study of cognitive effort in decision making, discussed in chapter 3 (Bettman et al., 1990), we found that people had increasing difficulty in executing a strategy like weighted adding as the problem became more complex. Also, as discussed in chapter 2, there is research showing that changing the format of numbers to make them more complex, such as decimals to hard fractions (E. Johnson et al., 1988), causes people to shift away from more calculation-based strategies. Finally, as suggested by the work of Kotovsky et al., (1985) on the sources of problem difficulty, alternative (but isomorphic) representations of a problem can impose different levels of working memory demands on a problem-solving strategy. Thus, people may fail to solve different representation of the same problem simply because one representation makes certain operations more difficult.

A related point is that individuals may actually be *less* accurate when using a supposedly normative strategy than when using a heuristic if their computations for the normative strategy are more prone to error. An individual may desire a certain level of accuracy and choose a strategy to attain it but fail because of computational errors. A less error-prone heuristic might actually result in higher accuracy levels for less effort. A similar notion is the Hammond et al. (1987) hypothesis that analytical forms of cognition lead to fewer, but larger, errors due to the failure to execute an analysis properly (see chapter 3).

In the case of complex decisions problems, adaptivity also may fail due to an inability to keep one's various goals and subgoals straight. J. Anderson (1983) makes the point that a goal structure is a data structure in working memory and is no different from other memory structures. Given limits on working memory, there will be limits on the number of goals that can be kept in working memory at any one time; others would have to be retrieved from long-term memory. Assuming that memory retrieval is fallible, one may well come to points in solving a complex decision problem where one simply is unable to remember what one planned to do next.

Anderson also argues that the effect of losing track of a hierarchical goal structure can be to make behavior seem more opportunistic (see chapter 5). That is, a subject who forgets his or her current goal, analyzes the current state, and constructs some partial solution to it in response to its special properties will be seen by an observer as being much more data-driven than he or she intended to be. We would argue that in addition to appearing more opportunistic, the failure to keep track of a goal structure can lead to failures in adaptivity.

Table 6.2. *Summary of major points from chapter 6*

Failures in adaptivity can occur due to deficits in knowledge resulting from:
(1) difficulties in assessing task and context factors;
(2) lack of knowledge of appropriate strategies;
(3) difficulties in assessing the effort and/or accuracy of a strategy in a particular situation;
(4) not knowing one's desired accuracy–effort tradeoffs.

Information display factors may bias the assessment of important task and context factors and cause important factors to be ignored simply because they are less salient in a display.

In general, there will be greater difficulty in properly assessing and adapting to context factors than task factors.

Factors that affect the availability of appropriate decision strategies include:
(1) stage of cognitive development;
(2) training;
(3) prior experiences with particular strategies;
(4) whether elements of the environment are coded in ways that make contact with the appropriate strategies for a situation.

A major source of failure to adapt is overreliance on (overgeneralization of) an inappropriate strategy.

Assessment of strategy effort is easier than assessment of strategy accuracy; this may make effort considerations more salient in the selection of a decision strategy.

In addition to deficits in knowledge, a second major source of failures in adaptivity is factors that make strategies difficult to execute, such as:
(1) environmental stressors;
(2) difficulty of required computations;
(3) some forms of problem representations;
(4) more generally, any aspects of a decision task that increase working memory demands.

Summary

As the sections above document, there are many ways in which decision makers may fail to be adaptive. Table 6.2 presents a summary of the major points regarding failures in adaptivity identified in this chapter.

Our proposed framework for contingent strategy selection, therefore, does not imply that an individual always will be perfectly adaptive. There are limits to adaptivity that can make the strategy selected for solving any given decision problem an inappropriate choice. In chapter 7 we discuss how the ideas presented in the previous chapters can be used to help decision makers make better decisions. In effect these techniques try to help minimize those factors that can cause adaptivity to fail.

7

Improving decisions and other practical matters

Introduction

We have provided a view of adaptive decision making over the previous several chapters that focuses on considerations of accuracy and cognitive effort. This perspective has helped us to understand when decision makers are adaptive and when they may go astray (see chapter 6) and provides us with a framework for considering how to aid decision makers. For example, we have argued that some exact operators for integrating information, such as addition or multiplication, are often quite difficult, whereas other operations, such as comparisons, are relatively easy. In addition, implementation of some strategies may be more error prone than others, given the difficulty of the task. Our perspective, therefore, suggests that we can improve decisions by creating a better match between task demands and the information-processing capabilities and preferences of the decision maker. We can improve that match by helping to reduce the effort required and/or by helping the decision maker increase the accuracy of the choice.

One way we can encourage decision makers to be more normative (more precisely reflect their values and beliefs) is by reducing the cognitive effort demands of the task. That is, complex decision problems can be restructured to make them easier for the decision maker. For example, the basic divide-and-conquer approach of decision analysis is an attempt to reduce cognitive effort in complex multivariate decision problems by asking for simpler judgments (Slovic, Fischhoff, & Lichtenstein, 1977).

Another approach to improving decisions is to help the decision maker make a more accurate choice. As we note in chapter 6, even though individuals are often adaptive, there are times when they cannot make accurate choices on their own. Replacement of at least some part of the decision process by an external aid (e.g., a model or formula) is one path to decision improvement in such cases. Another potential approach to better decisions in these instances is training the individual to use new strategies.

The adaptive decision-making approach raises some significant issues not just for decision aiding, but also for modeling decision makers' preferences. Many applications of decision research attempt to measure and predict the preferences of individuals for both business and public policy purposes. For example, market researchers have long been interested in understanding consumer preferences for product features. In addition, public policy decision makers are increasingly interested in the systematic study of people's preferences and beliefs as inputs to societal decisions. For instance, environmental management decisions may be guided by responses to questions such as how much to spend to improve air quality (see Lichtenstein, Gregory, Slovic & Wagenaar, 1990, for a discussion of some of the dilemmas facing a societal decision maker). The problem that an adaptive perspective poses for such applications is potentially serious: If decision makers often change decision rules in response to changes in the decision environment, how can a single model predict the outcomes of these choice processes? More generally, as noted in chapter 1, the extent to which people have values for all (most) objects is a critical issue. Perhaps in many cases preferences for objects of any complexity are often constructed, not merely revealed, in the generation of a judgment or choice (Fischhoff, 1991). Given the importance of such applications, we will want to consider how they might be affected by accuracy and effort considerations.

Accordingly, the purpose of this chapter is to suggest implications of our adaptive decision-making perspective for decision aiding, the measurement of preferences, and other practical matters. The chapter is organized into two major sections. The first section explores the implications of contingent and constructive decision making and our accuracy–effort framework for decision aiding. We discuss, for example, the concern that the highly adaptive nature of human decision behavior has generated among decision analysts, whose techniques require coherent judgments of preference and belief as inputs. The second section considers implications of adaptive decision behavior for problem areas such as the measurement of consumer preferences and assessing the value of public goods. We examine, for instance, what the contingent usage of multiple decision strategies might imply about the ability of simple tradeoff models to represent consumer values.

Approaches to decision aiding

Several approaches to decision improvement are identifiable in the literature. Fischhoff (1982) offers a taxonomy of these approaches that is based on whether the responsibility for errors in judgment and choice is laid at the doorstep of the task, the judge, or some mismatch between the two.

As we have emphasized throughout the book, the nature of the decision task is of critical importance in determining decision behavior, and decision makers can have problems if the task is too difficult. Many approaches to decision support, therefore, emphasize changes in the information environment facing the decision maker as a way to improve judgments and choices. In particular, the environment can be changed to make processing easier. For example, given that decision behavior varies as a function of the way in which information is presented, decisions can often be improved through rather straightforward, inexpensive changes in information presentation.

Other approaches to aiding decision making stress changes in the capacity of the decision maker for dealing with decision tasks. For instance, the processing capacity of a decision maker can be increased by the provision of external aids such as decision analysis or computer-based decision support systems. Such aids are often used to replace the decision maker in carrying out those components of the decision task that are most prone to error or are the most difficult for the decision maker.

Another approach to improving the capacity of a decision maker to cope with difficult problems is through training the decision maker. In some cases, a decision may be difficult because the individual lacks knowledge of appropriate strategies or operations. In these situations, decision adaptivity might be improved by increasing the individual's repertoire of judgment and choice strategies. Training can also impact the relative effort that might be associated with more normative types of strategies. Training is an example of an approach to decision improvement based on the belief that judges can be perfected (Fischhoff, 1982).

Table 7.1. *Approaches to decision aiding*

Approach	Difficulty addressed
Changing information environments	Task is too difficult, but changing information presentation can make more accurate operations or strategies feasible.
Increasing processing capacity with external aids	Decision makers can only perform some components of the task accurately and with reasonable effort.
Training	Decision makers may lack knowledge of appropriate strategies or operations.
Replacing the decision maker	The task is too difficult, and the decision maker cannot be helped to perform the task with reasonable accuracy and/or effort.

Finally, one could take the view that some problems are so difficult and the variability in human decision behavior is so great that we would be better off replacing the human judge with a formula or model. Fischhoff (1982) sees this approach as being based on the belief that individuals are "incorrigible" as decision makers. We will discuss the merits of the idea of replacing man with a model; however, we will mainly focus our attention on using both man and model as parts of a decision-making system.

To summarize, we have outlined four basic approaches to decision aiding: changing information environments, increasing processing capacity with external aids, training, and replacing the decision maker. As noted, each of these approaches attempts to deal with a particular source of difficulty: Changes in information environments deal with difficult tasks whose processing can be made easier; increasing processing capacity using external aids assists with a task where the decision maker can perform some but not all components of the task accurately and with reasonable effort; training is most useful when problems in performance are due to lack of appropriate knowledge or strategies; and replacing the decision maker is resorted to when the task is too difficult and cannot be made easier. Each of these approaches, summarized in Table 7.1, will be considered in more detail.

Finally, note that decision analysis, decision support systems, training, and replacement of the decision maker by a model are very active forms of decision support. Changes in the nature of the decision environment (e.g., how product information is presented to consumers) represent a more passive form of decision aiding.

Changing information environments to aid decisions

The processability of information. Adaptivity in decision making opens up many possibilities for improving decisions by changing the information environments in which decisions are made. One simple idea is to enhance decisions by focusing on cognitive effort and making the processing of information easier. That is, the focus is on improvements in the processability of currently available information, not through making more information available. By making existing information easier to process, we lower cognitive effort costs and possibly increase that information's impact.

A now classic study emphasizing the distinction between the processability and availability of information was conducted by Russo (1977). He showed that the use of unit price information by consumers increased when the information was presented to shoppers in the form of a sorted list where the available brands were ranked by increasing unit price (see Figure 7.1). This list, when it appeared on the supermarket shelf, resulted in consumers saving about 2%, on average, compared with a normal unit price display with separate tags for each item.

Russo argued that the information display he designed worked because it made price comparisons easier for the shoppers. To illustrate, Russo and Leclerc (1991) recently estimated that the time required to make a comparison among roughly 20 different brands/sizes in a product category using an ordered list was approximately 30 seconds. In contrast, the estimated time required to achieve the same result with unit prices displayed on separate shelf tags beneath the stock of each brand/size was about 3 minutes. Thus, Russo and Leclerc argue that the ordered list intervention saved a substantial amount of cognitive effort. By reducing the cognitive effort required, the consumer can then use a potentially more accurate strategy.

Additional evidence showing format effects on how people respond to information in real world settings has been provided by a number of researchers since Russo. For example, the importance of improved formats has been borne out in studies of hazard

LIST OF UNIT PRICES
Listed in Order of Increasing Price Per Quart

PAR 48 oz.	54¢	36.0¢ PER QUART
PAR 32 oz.	38¢	38.0¢ PER QUART
SWEETHEART 32 oz.	55¢	55.0¢ PER QUART
BROCADE 48 oz.	85¢	56.7¢ PER QUART
SWEETHEART 22 oz.	39¢	56.7¢ PER QUART
SUPURB 32 oz.	59¢	59.0¢ PER QUART
WHITE MAGIC 32 oz.	59¢	59.0¢ PER QUART
BROCADE 32 oz.	63¢	63.0¢ PER QUART
BROCADE 22 oz.	45¢	65.5¢ PER QUART
SUPURB 22 oz.	45¢	65.5¢ PER QUART
WHITE MAGIC 22 oz.	45¢	65.5¢ PER QUART
BROCADE 12 oz.	27¢	72.0¢ PER QUART
SUPURB 12 oz.	29¢	73.3¢ PER QUART
IVORY 32 oz.	80¢	80.0¢ PER QUART
DOVE 22 oz.	56¢	81.5¢ PER QUART
IVORY 22 oz.	56¢	81.5¢ PER QUART
LUX 22 oz.	56¢	81.5¢ PER QUART
PALMOLIVE 32 oz.	85¢	85.0¢ PER QUART
IVORY 12 oz.	32¢	85.3¢ PER QUART
PALMOLIVE 22 oz.	60¢	87.3¢ PER QUART
PALMOLIVE 12 oz.	34¢	90.7¢ PER QUART

Figure 7.1. A sample list of unit prices. *Source*: Reprinted by permission from "The value of unit price information," J. Edward Russo, *Journal of Marketing Research*, 14 (1977), p. 194. Copyright © 1977 American Marketing Association.

warning labels on household products (Viscusi et al., 1986), in the provision of the results of home energy audits (Magat, Payne, & Brucato, 1986), and the provision of information on radon levels in homes (Smith, Desvousges, Fisher, & Johnson, 1988). It is now clear that the processability of presented information matters greatly in determining the decisions people make.

Changes in the information environment can improve decisions; however, it is worth noting that such changes do not always have the desired effect. For example, Russo et al. (1986) found that using an organized display to provide nutritional information on proteins, minerals, and vitamins had little impact on consumer behavior. On the other hand, when the nutritional information concerned negative attributes, such as sodium, sugar, and calories, the organized information display had an impact. Russo et al. offer a cost–benefit explanation for this difference in results: Most consumers were not worried about having deficiencies in vitamins, but they were concerned about getting too much sodium, sugar, and calories.

Format and processing congruence. The processability of information depends on the congruence between the format and organization of the information and the type of processing to be done. There are two basic approaches to congruence. The first, a reactive approach, is to attempt to determine how decision makers are currently processing information and to make that processing easier. Typical displays of information in *Consumer Reports* illustrate this approach. Consumers would generally like to compare information on several attributes across several alternatives – Coupey (1990), for example, shows that individuals actively try to put information into matrix form (see chapter 5). By providing matrix displays of such information and by using rating scales that are comparative, *Consumer Reports* makes any comparison process easier. As another example, Norman (1988) presents many illustrations of the design of everyday things that demonstrate the importance of how design and normal processing patterns interrelate. For example, he argues that multiple controls, such as the controls for burners on a stove, should be arranged to correspond physically to the layout of the burners. He calls this principle of effective design the use of natural mappings, which is very similar to the notion of congruence already discussed.

A second approach to the design of decision information environments, particularly relevant for policy issues, is more proactive. The policy maker determines how he or she feels that people *should* process information (e.g., making more price comparisons across brands) and designs formats that facilitate such processing. For example, the form in which car mileage information is presented on window stickers and in advertisements facilitates the comparison of a particular model's expected mileage against that of other cars within the same class of vehicle. In particular, such a label provides the range of values for available options, indicates where the particular model falls within that range, and provides a standardized format across brands. Energy usage labels for appliances facilitate processing in a similar fashion.

As another example, Bettman, Payne, and Staelin (1986) formulated general principles relevant for designing labels that would encourage the use and comparison of information about product hazards: Make important information more salient via color and/or type size; use a common organization for information on all labels; design this common organization hierarchically and in a manner compatible with the scheme used by most consumers to store information about the product; use symbols that quickly convey the concept, when possible; collect information on benefits in one place on the label; collect information risks in one place on the label; organize the label so that the information on benefits and risks is in close proximity; provide information in a relative or comparative format; and consider in-store comparative lists in addition to labels. An example of a label for household drain opener designed in accordance with these principles is provided in Figure 7.2. Evidence of the effectiveness of such a label in comparison with more traditional label designs is provided in Viscusi et al. (1986).

Displays for decision aids. Issues of information display are also a major factor in the design of active decision support systems such as computer-based decision aids. Although we will have more to say about such computer-based systems later, it is appropriate at this point to discuss how the effort–accuracy framework for strategy selection might be useful in the design of computer-based information display systems.

D. Kleinmuntz and Schkade (1990) have been among the leaders in relating the concept of strategy selection to research on information displays in computer-supported decision making. As noted by Kleinmuntz and Schkade, there has been a substantial amount of research concerned with the impact of different display options (e.g., alphanumeric vs. graphical) on the effectiveness of computer-based decision systems.

MacGregor and Slovic (1986) provide a nice example of such work relating graphical representations to the use of judgmental information. In that study, they show the importance of a match between the relative importance of an item of information for judgment and the psychological salience of the display's graphic features. For example, judgmental accuracy was greater when the

UNSTOP LIQUID DRAIN OPENER
READ ENTIRE LABEL BEFORE OPENING OR USE

PRODUCT USES	POTENTIAL HAZARDS

UNSTOP Liquid Drain Opener Opens clogged drains Keeps drains open Will not harm pipes   or septic tanks

Swallowing	🐢🐢
Contact	🐢🐢🐢🐢
Breathing	🐢🐢🐢
Flammability	NONE

DANGERS	HOW TO AVOID DANGERS

HARMFUL OR FATAL IF SWALLOWED	⟹	KEEP OUT OF REACH OF CHILDREN Store on high shelf Store in locked cabinet Always keep safety cap on bottle
CAUSES SEVERE EYE DAMAGE ON CONTACT	⟹	Keep away from eyes and face
CAUSES BURNS ON SKIN CONTACT	⟹	Protect hands by wearing rubber gloves Keep away from skin and clothing Do not get Unstop on your hands

CAN SPLATTER
IF MISUSED
	⟹	Keep hands and face away from drain
		Do not mix with other chemicals or
		  drain openers
		NEVER use with a plunger or
		  pressurized drain opener
		NEVER cover a drain while using
		NEVER use a garbage disposer

WILL HARM SOME MATERIALS	⟹	Keep away from aluminum, wood, and painted surfaces

DIRECTIONS FOR USE

TO OPEN: Place bottle on flat, steady surface. Press down on cap while turning in a counter-clockwise direction. Do not squeeze bottle.
TO LOCK: Turn cap onto threads in a clockwise direction until it no longer turns. Then press down cap and turn to seal.

KEEP DRAINS OPEN: Every week remove drain sieve. Keep bottle away from face at all times. Use 1/4 bottle. Let stand 10 minutes. Flush with hot water from faucet.

OPENING CLOGGED DRAINS: Remove sieve and any standing water from sink, wash-bowl, or tub. Keep bottle away from face at all times. Use 1/2 bottle. Allow to work 30 minutes. Flush with hot water when drain clears. Repeat if necessary. For tough jobs, let stand overnight before flushing with hot water. Keep face away from drain.

44600 00102

EMERGENCY TREATMENT: IF SWALLOWED: Do NOT induce vomiting. Give large quantities of water or milk. Seek medical care immediately. IN EYES: Immediately flush with water for at least 15 minutes. Seek medical care immediately. ON SKIN: Flood area with water for at least 15 minutes. If irritation persists, seek medical care.

Figure 7.2. Test label for Unstop Drain Opener. *Source*: Reprinted by permission from "Cognitive considerations in presenting risk information," James R. Bettman, John W. Payne, and Richard Staelin, chap. 2 in *Learning about risk*, W. Kip Viscusi and Wesley A. Magat, Harvard University Press (1987), p. 37. Copyright © 1987 by the President and Fellows of Harvard College.

more important item of information (cue) was represented by the more salient display feature. This finding regarding the matching of display salience and cue importance reflects the concreteness principle of Slovic (1972) discussed previously. That is, for reasons of cognitive effort minimization, people will use cues that are more salient. Hence, an individual might use a less important cue simply because it is more salient in the display (see the discussion in chapter 6 on such failures of adaptivity due to information display). In a related series of experiments dealing with cognitive effort considerations and the design of computer displays for decisions, Jarvenpaa (1989, 1990) found that the sequence of information processing tended to be consistent with how graphic displays were organized (e.g., by alternative or by attribute).

More generally, MacGregor and Slovic (1986) suggest that matching of information displays with decision processes would be enhanced through the development of two taxonomies, one that would describe the essential dimensions along which graphic displays vary and a second that would characterize decision-making responses in terms of their basic cognitive and behavioral properties. For instance, a useful distinction in regard to displays is between those elements of the display that involve individual information items (e.g., the numeric, verbal, or graphic display of an attribute value) and those elements of a display that reflect relationships among information items (e.g., a matrix or hierarchical display) (D. Kleinmuntz & Schkade, 1990). A basis for the response taxonomy might be the elementary information processes that are involved in many judgment and choice strategies (e.g., reads, comparisons, and eliminations). As noted by Kleinmuntz and Schkade, different display changes will differentially impact different decision subprocesses such as the extraction of attribute values versus the comparison of values.

Although some useful research exists, Kleinmuntz and Schkade argue that progress on the design of decision displays has been limited due to a relative lack of theory and a focus simply on decision outcomes, not both processes and outcomes. They suggest the adoption of an effort–accuracy framework in the design and implementation of display research. Specifically, they propose that differences in displays change the anticipated effort and accuracy of available strategies ("cognitive incentives"). Consistent with the theory presented in this book, they then argue that decision makers will adapt their processing to do the cognitive operations the display makes easier and avoid those operations that the display makes more difficult. As an example, they suggest that people will avoid multiplying operations when information is displayed in verbal form (e.g., the visibility is fair) rather than in numeric form (e.g., the visibility is 10 miles). Schkade and Kleinmuntz (in press) find that the organization of information (i.e., the use of matrices or lists) strongly influenced information acquisition, whereas the form of information (i.e., the use of numbers or words) strongly influenced information combination and evaluation. Thus, display changes may impact not only what information is used (MacGregor & Slovic, 1986) but also how that information is used. The evidence provided by E. Johnson et al. (1988) on strategy shifts as a function of information format is consistent with this hypothesis.

Much of what Kleinmuntz and Schkade discuss fits within the effort–accuracy view of adaptive decision making; however, it is important to acknowledge that their ideas on displays for computer-based decision systems are based more on speculation than on data. What Kleinmuntz and Schkade have done is to propose an agenda for research that might serve as a bridge between the more passive approach to decision aiding typified by Russo's work and the more active approaches of decision analysis and decision support systems. The latter two related approaches both attempt to improve processing capacity by providing external aids.

Increasing processing capacity with external aids

Decision analysis. Decision analysis is a set of models and methods for helping people to deal with complex, confusing, and stressful decisions. The operating assumption of decision analysts is that a decision maker wishes to select the action that has the highest expected utility. The methods include tools for structuring decisions (e.g., decision trees) and tools for eliciting beliefs (probabilities) and values (utilities) (Watson & Buede, 1987). As noted earlier, the divide-and-conquer approach, in which complex decision tasks are decomposed, is also an important feature of decision analysis (Henrion, Fischer, & Mullin, in press; MacGregor & Lichtenstein, 1991; Ravinder & Kleinmuntz, 1991). Some evidence for the general value of decision analysis is provided by Politser (1991).

Decision analysis replaces unaided expression of preferences with the systematic use of assessment techniques and replaces intuitive combination with a systematic combination rule. Thus decision analysis is really a bet that the inputs derived using value assessment are more accurate than those generated without an aid, and that the systematic combination rule will be more accurate than intuitive aggregation of values.

Because decision analysis still depends heavily on human judgments of beliefs and/or preferences as inputs, decision analysts are sensitive to the evidence for the constructive and contingent (adaptive) nature of decision behavior. However, as noted in chapter 1, Amos Tversky (1988b, p. 612) has argued that "we should not overreact to the lability of preferences and conclude that decision analysis cannot be used to help. In fact, it could be argued that the psychological research shows that people need a great deal of help, and formal training. Rather than abandoning decision analysis, we should try to make it responsive to the complexities and limitations of the human mind."

A key way in which decision analysts are trying to be responsive to the adaptive nature of judgment and choice is in terms of the methods used to elicit the beliefs and values necessary to operationalize decision models. New methods are being proposed that will, hopefully, avoid some of the context factors influencing probability and preference assessments. For instance, the most common procedure for assessing utility functions involves the matching of a sure thing option with a gamble. For example, a respondent might be presented with the sure thing of receiving $500 and a gamble offering a p chance of winning $1,000 and a $1 - p$ chance of winning $0. The respondent's task is to specify a value of p – for example, 0.7 – that makes the two options equal in value to the respondent. If we let the $U(\$1,000) = 1.0$ and the $U(\$0) = 0$, then this implies that $U(\$500) = .7$, if one assumes the expected utility model holds. Unfortunately, this procedure is subject to the so-called certainty effect (Tversky & Kahneman, 1986), in which outcomes that occur with certainty are given more weight. Thus the utility elicited for $500 might be too large. As an alternative method, McCord and De Neufville (1986) have suggested a utility assessment method that involves the comparison of one gamble against a second gamble. In their procedure, one would be presented with one gamble offering a .5 chance of $500 and a .5 chance of $0 versus a second gamble offering a q chance of $1000 and a $1 - q$

chance of $0. The respondent's task in this case is to specify the value of q (q will be less than .5) that would make the two gambles equal in value for that individual, e.g., .3. Again assuming the expected utility model holds and assigning the values of $U(\$1,000) = 1.0$ and $U(\$0) = 0.0$, one can easily show that the $U(\$500) = q/.5$ or .6, a lesser utility than that found with the standard procedure.[1]

There is merit to the development of assessment tools that may avoid biases such as the certainty effect. However, one might ask whether we are just exchanging a simple biased response for a possibly more complex biased response. Therefore, another common approach suggested for dealing with contingent judgments is sensitivity analysis, in which utility is measured in several ways and any discrepancies are explicitly reconciled by the decision maker (von Winterfeldt & Edwards, 1986). Edwards (1990) makes a strong case for multiple elicitations of the same beliefs or values by different procedures, followed by a discussion of discrepancies, followed by revision of the elicited quantities by the respondent. The belief is that asking respondents to think harder (expend more cognitive effort) and reconcile conflicting estimates will enhance the validity (accuracy) of the assessed preferences and beliefs. That belief is in some ways consistent with an effort–accuracy framework; nonetheless, the Edwards argument has the flavor that incentives (the encouragement of the analyst) will always lead to more normative behavior. As noted earlier, it is not clear that incentives do always lead to the use of more optimal response strategies. Increased effort does not necessarily result in more adaptive responses. In addition, there also is the danger that the analyst will become too much a part of the construction of the decision maker's values (See Fischhoff et al., 1980, for a discussion of how an elicitor can affect the expression or formulation of values.) We agree with Edwards (1990) that more data on the effects of multiple elicitations would help a great deal.

A third approach to dealing with the sensitivity of assessment procedures to task and context effects is discussed by D. Kleinmuntz

---

[1] One reviewer of this book pointed out that the results of McCord and De Neufville are illustrative of the format and processing congruence approach to improving decisions. Thus, one may want to avoid introducing a certainty element in evaluation tasks that are designed to uncover risky preferences (see Barron, von Winterfeldt, & Fischer, 1984, for more on the possible relationships between risky and riskless utility assessment).

(1990). That approach involves building error theories that can help predict the cumulative effects of assessment errors given that a complex problem has been decomposed into a series of simpler judgment tasks. Each judgment is seen as having an expected value (systematic portion) and a standard deviation (random portion). Kleinmuntz proposes that the expected value not be viewed as a true internal opinion but as jointly determined by the person, task, and context. Thus, systematic error due to shifts in strategies resulting from task and context changes is explicitly included in the error theory along with the more commonly considered random error portion of judgment. Elaborating on the idea of multiple assessments of preferences and beliefs, Kleinmuntz suggests that if the direction and size of the systematic errors can be predicted, then it should be possible to select a portfolio of assessment procedures in such a way that biases cancel each other out. This idea is similar to the approach of structured intuition that Kahneman and Tversky (1979a) have suggested as one way to overcome biases in prediction. Finally, Kleinmuntz notes that decision makers' great concern with conserving cognitive effort suggests that simplified modeling techniques might be preferred in practice (see Behn & Vaupel, 1982; von Winterfeldt & Edwards, 1986, for examples), although Politser (1991) has argued that simple problem analysis may not always provide the greatest gains.

Decision support systems. A decision support system is a computer-based, interactive system that provides the decision maker with models and data to support semistructured or unstructured decision making tasks. The core of decision support systems is option evaluation and selection, although decision support can also include problem definition and structuring, forecasting, and option generation, among other activities (Andriole, 1989). In the past 10 years, the revolution in microcomputer technology has made at least simple decision support systems widely available. For example, @RISK (Palisade Corporation) aids in the modeling of effects of uncertainties, DECISION PAD (Apian Software) and HIVIEW (London School of Economics) help with the evaluation of multiattribute alternatives, and ARBORIST (Texas Instruments) aids in the construction and analysis of decision trees and risky choice problems. Thus, like the intuitive decision maker, the computer-supported decision maker now has available a repertoire of alternative programs ("strategies") that can be adaptively used to solve different types of decision problems.

One of the major advantages of the new computer-based packages for decision support is the ease with which sensitivity analysis can be performed on judgmental inputs (see the previous discussion on the use of multiple elicitation procedures for dealing with contingencies in judgment). Our personal experience in both the teaching of decision analysis and decision support systems and their applications suggests that the ability to do, and easily display, the results of sensitivity analysis is a crucial feature of computer decision-aiding packages and helps to increase the use of decision analysis. People appreciate that there are contingencies in judgments and feel more confident about an analysis if the impact of those contingencies can be examined directly.

In the discussion of information environment design already presented, a distinction was made between a reactive and a proactive approach. A similar distinction exists in the design of computer-based decision support systems. Consider, for example, the following statement by Rasmussen (1988, p. 227): "In intelligent decision support systems it should be possible to let a computer analyze the user queries in order to identify the strategy a user is trying to apply and then to supply the required support in displays and messages of the proper from." That is, the computer system could react to the preferred decision strategy of the individual. For instance, if there are individual differences in preferences for quantitative versus qualitative decision reasoning, as suggested in chapter 3, then the computer system might detect those preferences and change how information is presented. An example of a decision support system with some elementary adaptive features is provided by Cohen, Laskey, and Tolcott (1987). The Cohen et al. system, for instance, allows preferences to be incorporated in one of three ways: direct tradeoffs, cutoff levels, and derived weights from a policy capturing routine. Further, the Cohen et al. decision support system allows the decision maker to use several different decision strategies, including EBA.

A key issue in the reactive approach to decision support systems is the identification of the strategy being employed by the individual. We have not explored this issue in any depth; nonetheless, some of our ideas on the measurement of adaptive decision behavior might be useful for the purpose of identifying decision strategies. For example, the analysis of "user queries" suggested by Rasmussen (1988) might be aided by adopting the concept of strategies as a collection of EIPs and using the process-tracing measures illustrated in chapters 3, 4, and 5. One could imagine the development of an expert system that would infer the strategy being used on the basis of data like those generated by the Mouselab system. The decision support system would then supply the required support for that strategy.

As illustrated in the verbal protocol data of Payne (1976) (see chapter 4), there is evidence that a decision-making episode often involves the use of more than just one decision strategy. For example, decision processing frequently involves both noncompensatory strategies like EBA and compensatory methods like AU, with EBA used to screen options and therefore reduce task complexity. Further, as indicated in the simulation results presented in chapter 4, the use of such combined strategies can be efficient in terms of decision accuracy. Beach (1990) argues that decision support systems (aids) "ought to provide for two steps, using the first step to screen candidates and the second to choose the best candidate when there are multiple survivors of the first step" (Beach, 1990, p. 172). Some commercially available computer-based decision support systems provide the capability to mark options that fail a screening test (e.g., DECISION PAD). More generally, our perspective suggests that allowing for the use of multiple and combination strategies as part of a decision aid is valuable.

Intelligent, adaptive, decision support systems appear to be a promising idea. We should acknowledge, however, that prior efforts to tailor the design of a decision aid to fit particular users have not been that successful (D. Kleinmuntz, 1987). In particular, prior efforts to match systems with individuals using very broad personal characteristics such as "cognitive style" have proved disappointing (G. Huber, 1983). The importance of task factors as well as individual difference factors in determining strategy selection suggests that any intelligent, adaptive decision support system will have to reflect how people adapt to the demands of the specific decision task being faced.

In addition, as noted throughout this book, a number of decision strategies used by people have the potential for substantial decision error – for example, the status quo bias and intransitivities in preference. Thus, it would seem prudent to design more proactive intelligent decision support systems with the capability to warn the decision maker if his or her preferred strategy may not be an efficient one for the particular decision environment. Cohen et al. (1987), for example, discuss advisory prompts that would alert the decision maker to potential errors such as only searching for confirmatory information and the consideration of dominated options. A related idea would be to use knowledge derived from the use of a heuristic strategy like EBA (e.g., attribute importance) to alert the decision maker to other possible "good" options. More specifically, one could use the information on the relative importance of attributes gathered to implement an EBA strategy to construct a linear model that could then be used to evaluate options in a database, with those options that score highly brought to the attention of the decision maker.

Of course, the effort and accuracy framework may also have an even more direct role to play in the design of computer-based decision aids. Todd and Benbasat (1991), for example, provide evidence that decision aids can be used to induce more compensatory processing by reducing the relative effort needed to execute certain operations (e.g., calculations of differences between options on various attributes). This proactive approach to decision aiding emphasizes directing decision makers toward the use of more normative strategies, with effort reduction being the lever used to encourage strategy change.

Finally, the contingent nature of decision behavior is causing decision analysts to do more than just develop new methods for assessing beliefs and values or designing new computer-based decision support systems. Bell (1985), for example, suggests that the models used in most decision-aiding exercises (i.e., expected utility) may need to be modified to allow the incorporation of psychological concerns such as regret or disappointment. That is, a context-related concept like regret could be explicitly built into prescriptive models of how people should make decisions as opposed to treating it as an "error" to be overcome.

At another level, Keeney (1988, 1992) suggests that instead of the alternative-focused thinking that is used in most decision problems, people would be better served by a more value-focused approach. In such an approach, one considers whether one could do better in achieving one's values than is suggested by the most readily apparent alternatives. Building on the ideas of Keeney and others, L. Keller and Ho (1988) offer suggestions for how new alternatives might be constructed. Interestingly, Keller and Ho note that even at the stage of alternative generation there may be examples of contingent processing, such as agenda effects due to the order in which values are considered in the construction of new options.

Training for decision making

Throughout this book, we have stressed that a decision maker has available a repertoire of strategies (methods) for solving decision problems. However, some more approximately normative decision procedures and principles may not be known by all (most) people. Thus one approach to decision improvement is simply to train people in better (more normative) strategies for reasoning about uncertainties and preferences and for making choices. An adaptive decision maker potentially can be more effective if his or her repertoire of strategies is larger. Obviously, there is much interest in this approach to decision improvement. Both private firms and public agencies have long paid to send people through courses on decision making. Increasingly, there is interest in teaching such reasoning and judgment skills at the primary and secondary levels of education.

What evidence, however, is there that knowledge of normative principles of decision making leads to better decision outcomes? Also, what evidence is there that such knowledge can be conveyed in simple training programs? A recent program of research by Richard Nisbett and his colleagues has sought to answer those questions (Fong et al., 1986; Fong & Nisbett, 1991; Larrick et al., 1990). In Larrick et al. (1990), for example, people trained in the principle of ignoring sunk costs seemed to reason more normatively about novel decision problems even a month after the time of the training. Further, there was some weak evidence suggesting that the training had an impact on actual decisions.

As we have emphasized, the use of heuristics often involves ignoring potentially relevant problem information. Another difficulty in decision making, however, is that sometimes one uses irrelevant information to make a judgment. E. Johnson and Schkade (1989), for example, showed that the subjects using an anchoring and adjustment heuristic not only underweighted relevant information but also were subject to an irrelevant manipulation of the anchor. Numerous other studies have shown how irrelevant information can adversely influence judgments, even those of experts (e.g., Gaeth &

Shanteau, 1984; Alba & Marmorstein, 1987). However, as Gaeth and Shanteau have also shown, relatively simple training procedures can help experts learn to ignore irrelevant information and improve accuracy. Gaeth and Shanteau found that interactive training was particularly effective. The training consists of the expert's making judgments where irrelevant information is present and then showing the expert that such information had an impact on his or her judgment. Based on the Gaeth and Shanteau result, we hypothesize that a similar interactive training program might be effective in helping a decision maker understand the biases associated with the use of different decision strategies.

Much more research on the effects on actual decision behavior of training individuals in various decision strategies is clearly needed. From the perspective of this book, however, two issues are worth mentioning. First, training programs should be sensitive to the major role that considerations of cognitive effort seem to play in how people decide how to decide. Arkes (1991) makes a related point when he argues that efforts to improve intuitive predictive judgments can be facilitated by considering the costs and benefits of various cognitive strategies underlying those judgments. Also, as suggested by Behn and Vaupel (1982), the emphasis should be on the teaching of decision procedures that may not only be approximately correct but that are also simple to use.[2] Second, as noted in chapter 6, there is evidence from the domain of reading skills that good readers have better metaknowledge about how to read differently in different situations (Garner, 1987). Wade and Reynolds (1988) make the related argument that reading skills be developed, in part, through instruction in the utilities of various reading strategies and when and where the strategies should be used. More generally, Gagne (1984) argues that good problem solving requires strategic knowledge of when and how to use procedural and declarative task knowledge. Coupled with the evidence for adaptive decision processing presented in this book, this argument suggests that training programs might emphasize an understanding of the

---

[2] It has also been suggested that decision aids or procedures will be more acceptable to people to the extent they reduce perceived decisional conflict (Kottemann & Davis, 1991). This suggestion points out once again that multiple goals may underlie strategy selection and decision aid selection (see the discussions in chapters 1 and 2).

relationships between task structure and decision strategy effectiveness and efficiency. For example, the training might emphasize how task knowledge that the environment has positively correlated attribute values can allow a person to identify when simple procedures like equal weighting will be very efficient.

Replacing the decision maker: Models or/and heads

The focus of this book has been on understanding the strategies a decision maker uses to process information in his or her head. Alternatively, a decision maker could use a mathematical or mechanical procedure to combine the information when asked to make a judgment or choice. One argument for the use of models to combine information is that the variability of cognitive combination processes due to subtle – and sometimes nonrelevant – task, context, and individual difference factors is so great that the consistency needed for good decision making is unlikely if information is combined in the head.

Combining information in the head is often referred to as clinical judgment. Combination of information using a formula or model can involve simply the automation of the judge's decision rules, or reflect empirically established relations between data and the outcomes of interest, an actuarial approach (Dawes, Faust, & Meehl, 1989). Numerous studies have shown that judgments are generally better if made using a formula instead of combining information in the head (Dawes et al., 1989; B. Kleinmuntz, 1990), and organizations do use formulas instead of clinical judgment for some decision problems. The use of model-based judgment in place of clinical judgment is more the exception than the rule, however. Consequently, recent decision research has emphasized two questions. First, what are the factors influencing the use of an automated decision procedure? Second, how can models and man be utilized as complements to one another rather than as competing decision systems?

Dawes et al. (1989) suggest several reasons why we still use our heads instead of formulas: lack of familiarity with the evidence showing the benefits of formulas, a belief that the evidence does not apply to case-by-case decisions, and an inflated belief in the accuracy of clinical judgment. Note the connection between an "inflated belief in the accuracy of clinical judgment" and the discussion in chapter 6 on why adaptivity might fail due to an overconfidence in the accuracy of decisions.

B. Kleinmuntz (1990) offers several other reasons why formulas are not often used, including the error possibilities in the execution of a formula (Hammond et al., 1987; Ashton, Ashton, & Davis, 1990). In addition, Arkes et al. (1986) show empirically that a simple decision formula was used *less* in solving a probabilistic judgment task when incentives for performance existed, when outcome feedback was available, and when people felt they had more domain expertise. Apparently, under the conditions of incentives, feedback, and felt expertise, people frequently shift strategies in the hope that they will be able to beat the odds inherent in the probabilistic nature of the judgment task.[3]

Einhorn (1986) suggests that people generally find it difficult to accept some level of explicit error associated with the use of a decision rule, even though the use of the statistical rule would lead to fewer overall errors in prediction. Einhorn argues that the fact that the use of a formula will lead to better performance on average should be a compelling argument for its use. He acknowledges, however, that one might view the clinical approach as a high-risk strategy that potentially could allow predicting every outcome perfectly.

Einhorn (1986) also suggests that the degree to which one decides to use a statistical formula depends on whether one believes the phenomenon being predicted is inherently random or systematic in nature. As Einhorn notes, people have a tendency to believe even random events are systematic. Similarly, Kahneman and Tversky (1982) hypothesize that the laws of probability are more likely to be accepted (and used) when uncertainty is attributed to the external world and a distributional mode of reasoning is adopted. Given the contingent nature of probabilistic reasoning reviewed earlier in chapter 2, one might be able to frame problems as being more external and distributional and thus increase the acceptability of formal statistical and decision models. Kahneman and Lovallo (1992) have made the related suggestion that framing an apparently unique risky decision as part of a much larger set of risky choices

---

[3] As noted in chapter 3, the Arkes et al. study nicely illustrates that increased incentives do not necessarily lead to increased effort *and* increased accuracy. Sometimes increased effort (e.g., the search for alternative strategies in their study) can result in poorer performance.

may lead to behavior more in line with a considered tradeoff of beliefs and values.

In sum, the debate about models versus heads can be seen as a debate concerning what part of the decision process is most errorful and should be replaced. Even the strongest advocates of using models to replace heads acknowledge the role of experts in encoding cues; recently, there is growing agreement that expert human decision makers can provide some inputs that are both accurate and are not provided by models (E. Johnson, 1988). Therefore, attention has turned to approaches that use models as a partial (but not complete) replacement for the judge, reviving an old idea (B. Kleinmuntz, 1990).

One combination approach is to use experts to measure the inputs to a model but to combine the subjective inputs mechanically (e.g., Libby & Libby, 1989). Of course, this is just a variant of the method used in decision analysis, in which people provide values and beliefs that are then combined using a logical rule. At a more aggregate level, a judgment from an actuarial or statistical model and intuitive judgment might be integrated in several other ways. The model might be used as one input to be combined with other information in the head of the decision maker (Peterson & Pitz, 1986). The model also could be used as a baseline judgment, which should only be modified by the decision maker in special cases. For example, in the 1980s, the U.S. Parole System adopted a procedure for deciding when someone should be released on parole that required that any deviation from the decision suggested by the guidelines (model) be documented in writing. The idea was that the parole decision should reflect the guidelines for the vast majority of decisions, while still allowing for "special" cases. Finally, the judgment by formula and the judgment in the head might be aggregated using another formula, for example, 50% head and 50% model (Blattberg & Hoch, 1990).

The measurement and prediction of preferences

Measuring the values (preferences) of people is important in a number of different domains. Marketing, for example, has long been concerned with understanding and predicting the preferences of consumers in the hope that such understanding will lead to better managerial decisions. Sophisticated methods for measuring preferences are also being used to guide decisions in a variety of other areas, such as medicine, law, and public policy (Keeney, von Winterfeldt, & Eppel, 1990). In the following sections, we examine the implications of contingent strategy use for current approaches to measuring a person's preferences in marketing research and to assessing the value of public goods.

Marketing research applications

The idea that consumers make tradeoffs between all the relevant attributes of a product and form overall evaluations of each alternative brand or product considered plays a central role in marketing research. Models or techniques for representing consumer preferences that are based on such a compensatory process enjoy wide popularity and have spawned many applications. These include pretest marketing systems (e.g., Silk & Urban, 1978), sales–response analysis of mature products (e.g., Guadagni & Little, 1983), and new product design and brand management (e.g., Green & Srinivasan, 1990).

Of course, as described in this book, it is clear that people often use noncompensatory strategies in making choices and judgments. Do those results suggest that the most common technologies for representing consumer preferences are in error? Many marketing researchers believe that there is no cause for alarm. Compensatory multiattribute preference models are widely believed to be capable of mimicking a wide range of consumer decision processes, provided two conditions are met: attributes are related monotonically to consumers' preferences, and there is error or uncertainty about these preferences (Dawes & Corrigan, 1974). Because these conditions are thought likely to be satisfied in most applied contexts, compensatory models are widely used even when presumed not to reflect the actual process by which decisions are made (e.g., Cattin & Wittink, 1982). Confidence in such an approximation is widespread, as illustrated in Green and Srinivasan's (1978, p. 107) conclusion about the potential dangers of misspecifying consumers' decision rules: "The compensatory model of conjoint analysis can approximate the outcome of other kinds of decision rules quite well ... even if the respondent's information processing strategy and decision model are complex, the compensatory models can usually produce good predictions."

In the spirit of this book, E. Johnson and Meyer (1984; E. Johnson et al., 1989) have explored how well simple linear models represent preferences when the nature of the decision environment is varied and where one has reason to believe such changes in task and context will lead to the use of noncompensatory decision processes.

Variation in task. As noted earlier in this book, perhaps the clearest example of contingent processing in decision making is the shift to noncompensatory elimination strategies that is observed when the number of alternatives is increased. One therefore might hypothesize that the linear compensatory model would be less able to represent preferences in the case of more complex decision situations involving multiple alternatives. E. Johnson and Meyer (1984) used an apartment choice task similar to that used by Payne (1976) to test whether the predictive ability of the linear model would decrease as the number of alternatives in the choice set to be predicted increased. The somewhat counterintuitive result was that compensatory models were *more* accurate predictively in the case of the larger choice sets. This improved predictive accuracy was in clear contradiction of the process evidence for more noncompensatory processing in the larger choice sets. Johnson and Meyer suggested that the most likely explanation was that when faced with larger set sizes, subjects tended uniformly to adopt a simplified choice strategy that emphasized the most important attribute. Hence, the decrease in fit due to the increased use of a noncompensatory heuristic may have been offset by an increased homogeneity in the strategies being used to make choices.

E. Johnson and Meyer (1984) make an important distinction between errors in prediction due to misspecifying the underlying evaluation rule used by consumers and errors in prediction due to misspecifying the weights (importances) given to the attributes used in the preference decision. Interestingly, it may be that the increased prominence of the most important attribute associated with the use of heuristics like EBA and LEX may, in some situations, allow a simple linear model to predict better.

Variation in choice context. E. Johnson et al. (1989) argue that simple linear compensatory models may not be as robust to errors in specifying the correct underlying decision process as popular wisdom often maintains when changes in the context of choice are considered. In particular, they argue that the linear model may fail if the consumer is using a noncompensatory decision heuristic *and* the choice context is one characterized by a negatively correlated attribute structure.

They examine this issue by using a simulation approach like those described in chapter 4. That is, various decision rules were represented as production systems, and the choices yielded by those rules in different task environments were measured using Monte Carlo techniques. The results strongly suggest that the standard modeling approach used by market researchers could fail in the case when consumers use noncompensatory heuristics in a task environment with negatively correlated attributes. Specifically, the average predictive validity of a linear compensatory rule in modeling the choices generated by the EBA, LEX, and SAT heuristics dropped from .80 to .34 (measured by Pearson) when the choice environment changed from a 0 average correlation among attributes to a −.33 average correlation.

In interpreting these results, several other pieces of evidence must be considered. First, there is evidence that some consumer choice environments can have negative interattribute correlations (Hjorth-Anderson, 1984, 1986; Curry & Faulds, 1986). Second, Green, Helsen, & Shandler (1988) find no difference in the predictive ability of linear additive conjoint analysis models estimated in orthogonal and negatively correlated environments, which fails to replicate Johnson et al. Finally, the Bettman et al. (1992) correlation studies find that individuals adapt to negative correlation by increased use of compensatory processing rather than increased use of noncompensatory heuristics, although adaption is not perfect.

This additional information makes the interpretation of the Johnson et al. results more complex. At this point, it is difficult to make strong claims about the effect of correlation on the robustness of linear compensatory models of choice. However, we would offer the following thoughts. It is clear that people use heuristics in a contingent fashion to solve decision problems. It is also possible that there are situations in which the use of simple linear compensatory models to represent heuristic and contingent processes can lead to substantial predictive errors. What is a market modeler to do? One approach is to try to represent, as faithfully as possible, the salient characteristics of the actual decision environment in the environment used to estimate a choice model. For example, using realistic interattribute correlations, numbers of alternatives, or portraying attributes in a realistic manner may increase the predictive validity of a choice model.

Market research studies of preferences, such as those cited, typically involve brands or classes of products for which the consumers would be expected to have substantial experience or knowledge. Sometimes, however, public policy decisions require information about the preferences of people for items that are not normally traded in the market place – for example, environmental goods like air quality. We next discuss how values might be assessed in such contexts.

Contingent valuation

The method of contingent valuation (Cummings, Brookshire, & Schulze, 1986; Fischhoff & Furby, 1988; R. Mitchell & Carson, 1989) is a method for measuring preferences that is increasingly being used to assess the value of environmental goods, both for the purpose of guiding policy decisions regarding environmental protection and for establishing liability in the case of environmental damages. A contingent valuation (CV) study typically involves the assessment of tradeoffs by a large sample of respondents. Essentially, CV studies assess preferences by asking a respondent to match an option defined by an environmental good (level of air quality) at a clearly specified level (1) and a wealth level (1) against a second option defined by an environmental good at a specified second (more preferred) level (2) and an alternative (less preferred) wealth level (2). In the typical willingness-to-pay (WTP) task, the respondent is asked to specify an amount by which he or she would be willing to reduce his or her current wealth level (i.e., move from level 1 to level 2) in order to gain an improvement in the environmental good from level 1 to the better level 2. Alternatively, in a willingness-to-accept (WTA) task, the respondent is asked to specify an amount by which he or she would need to have his or her current wealth increased (i.e., move from level 2 to level 1 in wealth) in order to accept a decrement in the level of the environmental good (i.e., go from level 2 to level 1). Increasingly, contingent valuation studies also use a choice mode in which the respondent is simply asked which of two combinations of the environmental resource and wealth he or she prefers. Contingent valuation has been applied to many issues, including visibility in the Grand Canyon, wilderness areas in the western United States, and environmental damages due to oil and chemical spills.

A subject of much practical import is the extent to which the assessed value of a public good (e.g., clean air) using the CVM is contingent on a host of procedural variables, such as the order in which questions are asked, whether one matches by considering a potential gain (WTP) or a potential loss in the level of a public good (WTA), or whether an event to be assessed (e.g., environmental damage) may occur or has already occurred (Kahneman & Knetsch, 1992; Schulze & McClelland, 1990). As noted in chapter 2, often WTP does not equal WTA; the amount needed to accept a loss is usually several times more than the amount one is willing to pay to achieve an equivalent level of environmental improvement. This difference appears much larger than could be accounted for by wealth effects. One explanation for the disparity between WTP and WTA is the notion of loss aversion (Tversky & Kahneman, 1990). Other possible explanations for why WTP and WTA responses might differ are discussed in R. Mitchell and Carson (1989). In addition, given what we know about the different processing strategies used in matching and choice, it seems possible that the preferences inferred from the matching procedure used in WTP and WTA studies might differ from the preferences that would underlie actual choices among public policies (Fischer & Hawkins, 1993).

For example, Irwin, Slovic, Lichtenstein, and McClelland (1993) showed that respondents were willing to pay more for improvements in consumer goods than for improvements in air quality when responding with WTP; however, they favored improvements in air quality when making a direct choice between the two. That is, preference reversals were obtained in the domain of contingent valuation. Viscusi et al. (1986) and Desvouges et al. (1992) have found that the choice response mode produced significantly higher valuations for an environmental good than open-ended WTP responses. Thus, factors discussed earlier in this book, such as possible changes in strategies due to response modes and influences on preferences due to the prominence effect, may impact important policy decisions if the contingent valuation method is used.

In addition to being sensitive to factors that are irrelevant from the standpoint of economic theory, contingent valuation responses are insensitive to some theoretically relevant factors, such as the inclusiveness of the resource. For example, Kahneman and Knetsch (1992) have demonstrated what they call an "embedding" effect, in which the expressed value for a subset of a resource was essentially the same as the value for the entire resource (e.g., the value for cleaning up one lake in a region is similar to that for cleaning up all lakes in that region). Kahneman and Knetsch interpret their responses in terms of the feelings of "moral satisfaction" achieved through payments rather than in terms of reasoned tradeoffs. Using verbal protocols, Schkade and Payne (1992) found that responses to willingness-to-pay questions about protecting a natural resource often included explicit statements reflecting feelings of moral satisfaction and the symbolic value of the expressed response.

More generally, the constructive nature of human preferences, particularly in domains where people do not commonly make trade-off decisions, raises the question of to what extent any preference assessment technique such as CV creates values as much as it reveals them. Fischhoff and Furby (1988) emphasize a careful provision of information to the respondent as one response to the labile (constructive) nature of values. Of course, one needs to be careful to avoid information overload and the potential for a less than considered response strategy. A variation on the information provision approach is actually to bring a group of citizens together in a forum where extensive information on the policy options is provided by experts, the values held by the citizens are elicited using decision analysis, and the constructed preferences are then viewed as such and used by the policy maker (Keeney et al., 1990). Finally, Gregory and McDaniels (1987) suggest the explicit construction of values using multiattribute decision analysis.

One should also ask whether there is an alternative to the measurement of individual values, however flawed, as input to policy decisions. Ignoring the value of an environmental good because it is difficult to measure is a questionable response. Using an unstructured intuitive approach to judge the value of some environmental good may be even more biased. (See Carson & Navarro, 1988, for a discussion of some of the fundamental issues in the use of CVM and other assessment techniques.) Hopefully, increased understanding of the details of adaptive decision processes can lead to the development of better value assessment tools, at least for the purpose of guiding public policy decisions.

Modeling constructive preferences

One goal of choice modeling is the construction of representations of decision making that are predictive in spite of changes of context. Much of the work discussed in this book suggests that caution is in order in such endeavors. If choices are changed by seemingly minor changes in either the task or context, then the "portability" of models of preference across situations may be called into question.

Although linear models are often very robust and are relatively insensitive to misspecification (Dawes & Corrigan, 1974), some of the findings we have reviewed are more than cautionary. For example, the changes in revealed attribute weightings that are associated with response mode effects can change revealed preferences, and differences in preferences caused by asking about buying and selling prices seem troubling if we are to use them pragmatically to aid policy decisions.

One could identify two alternatives to coping with this problem, which we will call the context-matching and the reconciliation approaches. The first simply suggests that the analyst tries to match, as closely as possible, the relevant factors that affect preferences. For example, we have argued that factors such as the number of alternatives and the correlation among attributes could change choice processes and consequently the preferences revealed by a choice model of these preferences. The goal of the environment-matching technique is to minimize these process changes by attempting to approximate, at the time of elicitation, the decision environment in which the model will be applied. This approach is more predictive in emphasis.

In contrast, the reconciliation approach attempts to point out to the decision maker the inconsistencies that are revealed by differences in contexts or tasks. Such attempts have been an important part of the practice of decision analysis. This approach seems to be compatible with a constructive view of preferences (see Fischhoff, 1991).

Whether matching environments or reconciliation is a useful approach depends, in part, on why the choice is being modeled. If simple prediction is the goal, then matching environments seems to be reasonable. In fact, if, as in many market research examples, one is trying to generalize from a sample to a population, it is the only feasible tactic. However, if part of the goal is not just prediction, but aiding, then reconciliation seems appropriate. Reconciliation, however, should be recommended with caution. A theory of the construction of values is just emerging, and principled reconciliation of values would seem to depend crucially on both a theory of how values are constructed and the ability of individuals to predict their future happiness. As pointed out by Kahneman and Snell (1990), this is not an easy endeavor.

Summary

In this chapter we have summarized some of the applied implications of the adaptive nature of human decision behavior for the design of information environments, the practice of decision analysis, the design of man–model decision systems, and the measurement of values. More generally, we believe that the highly contingent nature of decision behavior means that an understanding of how decisions are actually made in different task environments is crucial for efforts to improve and predict decision. In the final chapter, we summarize our framework and results and provide a brief discussion of topics for future research.

8

The adaptive decision maker:
A look backward and a look forward

Introduction

This book reports on an ongoing program of research concerned with adaptive decision behavior. Although we believe that much has been learned about how decision makers adapt to task and context demands, we also believe that there is much more yet to be learned. Therefore, this concluding chapter has two purposes: First, we offer a summary of the major concepts and findings of our program of research to date; second, we sketch ideas for several major directions in which we think the effort and accuracy framework presented in this book might be extended.

What have we learned?

The framework and research presented in the previous chapters yield several generalizations about the adaptive decision maker. First, people clearly use a variety of strategies to solve decision problems, contingent upon task and context factors. Often those strategies are heuristic processes that ignore potentially relevant problem information. Thus, while people frequently make reasonable judgments and choices, the use of heuristic decision strategies sometimes can lead to decision errors.[1]

Second, given that decision makers have limited information-processing capabilities, strategy selection can be seen as the result of a compromise between the desire to make the most accurate decision and the desire to minimize cognitive effort. Further, because the

---

[1] As noted in the Preface, our program of research draws upon the work of many other decision researchers. The conclusions presented here should therefore more properly be viewed as our summary of both our own work and that of others.

accuracy and effort of different heuristics will vary across task environments, a decision maker concerned with both accuracy and effort will have to use strategies in a contingent fashion in order to be adaptive.

Third, the cognitive effort required to make a decision can be usefully measured in terms of the total number of elementary information processes needed to solve a particular problem using a specific decision strategy. In addition, individual differences in decision behavior may be related to differences in how effortful various elementary information processes are to the individuals. Production system models of strategies based upon such elementary information processes can be used in simulations that characterize the effort and accuracy levels of different strategies in different task environments and lead to predictions about adaptive strategy selection.

Fourth, there is clear evidence that people often use decision strategies adaptively: They exhibit intelligent, if not optimal, responses to changes in such task and context variables as the number of alternatives available, the degree of time pressure, the dispersion in the weights for attributes, and differing goals for accuracy and effort. Such adaptivity may reflect a hierarchy of response strategies in some cases (e.g., responses to time stress). The use of process-tracing methodologies such as Mouselab is extremely valuable in gathering detailed data documenting adaptivity.

Fifth, individuals often process opportunistically, changing their strategies on the fly as they learn about the task environment. This view, that individuals construct choice strategies during the course of decision making, represents a more bottom-up or data-driven perspective on strategy usage. Whether the focus is on making a choice, editing, or problem restructuring, however, such constructive processing still involves accuracy–effort tradeoffs. Noticing and exploiting regularities in the environment are major components of constructive processing.

Sixth, although people often select strategies adaptively, failures in adaptivity do occur. These failures can be traced to such factors as difficulties in assessing task and context factors, deficits in knowledge of appropriate strategies or the related problem of overreliance on inappropriate strategies, difficulties in assessing effort and accuracy, and lack of ability to execute appropriate strategies. These limits to adaptivity also help to explain why increased incentives, while generally leading to greater effort expenditures, do not necessarily lead to more accurate decision making.

Seventh, the design of information environments, the practice of decision analysis, the design of man–model decision systems, and the measurement of values can be enhanced through consideration of how people adapt their decision behavior due to effort and accuracy concerns.

Although we are excited by the progress made thus far, there are aspects of our framework for understanding adaptive decision behavior that are incomplete. We have tried to identify several of these important areas for further research in the previous chapters of the book. For example, the notion of opportunistic processing requires a better understanding of what aspects of the environment are noticed and of the control elements of decision making than we present in this book. In addition, the accuracy–effort and perceptual frameworks also need to be better integrated, more work is needed on how people assess effort and accuracy and respond to feedback, and research characterizing the detailed effects of training in different processing strategies would be valuable. In addition to these ideas, which represent extensions of ideas outlined in previous chapters, there are also several areas of importance for understanding decision behavior that we have not yet considered. In the next section of this chapter we examine three of these new directions for future research on adaptive decision making: problem structuring, the social context of decisions, and contingent judgment processes.

New directions for future research

Problem structuring

As discussed in chapter 2, most studies of decision behavior use relatively well structured tasks. For example, a preferential choice problem typically consists of a specified set of alternatives and attribute values to be used in solving the problem. The focus of such studies is on the strategies used to evaluate and combine the given information into a judgment or choice. Thus, it often makes sense for purposes of experimental control to use well-structured decision tasks. It is also the case that we are sometimes presented with such decision tasks – for example, the selection among a set of graduate applicants for a fellowship. In many cases, however, information is less well structured. For example, decision making can include problem-structuring activities such as the generation of alternatives and the delimitation of a consideration set of alternatives.

There is a growing interest in the problem-structuring elements of decision behavior, although the amount of such research is relatively small. As noted in chapter 5, one can think of problem structuring as an ongoing, opportunistic process that also includes the restructuring of initially presented problems. We believe that the accuracy–effort framework presented in this book can be extended to understand better the processes of problem structuring. In the rest of this section we briefly explore two streams of research on problem structuring that might serve as starting points for such an extension, alternative generation and consideration sets.

Alternative generation. How well do people generate high-utility alternatives when faced with unstructured decision problems? As noted already, the research on this question is limited. However, work by Gettys et al. (1987) suggests that people often fail to generate potential actions that might solve a decision problem. Further, such failures are not due to lack of motivation. Gettys et al. found that subjects in their experiment generated the same number of alternatives whether or not there was an explicit incentive tied to the quantity or quality of the options generated.

Many of the problems with alternative generation have been traced to how human memory is structured and the processes that are used to access that memory. L. Keller and Ho (1988), for example, have discussed how an associative network structure for memory, in combination with the use of heuristics like representativeness and availability, may account for biases in option generation. For instance, people sometimes find it difficult to generate a substantially different option once a single alternative has been made salient. This may be particularly true if the first alternative generated seems highly representative of the class of problems under consideration. More generally, Keller and Ho argue that the number and quality of options generated is often affected by the effort needed to retrieve options from memory.

How might alternative generation be improved? L. Keller and Ho (1988) suggest several strategies that are either attribute-based, state- or event-based, or option-based. Each strategy can be viewed as a different way to improve memory access, with the strategies differing in terms of the cognitive unit (attribute, state, or option) that is brought into working memory to stimulate further search. An example of an attribute-based procedure is to present, one at a time, each of the attributes that will be used to judge the value of the outcomes and to elicit options that will help attain that individual attribute. Pitz, Sachs, and Heerboth (1980) present evidence supporting the effectiveness of such a procedure. A similar state-based procedure is to present the possible states of nature one at a time, eliciting options that will be effective in each individual state. Option-based procedures include such things as the use of examples to elicit more options, although this may lead to only generating variations on the example. Finally, Keller and Ho also discuss such general creativity techniques as brainstorming.

As noted by L. Keller and the Ho (1988), there is need for research to examine how the effects of incentives for accuracy "as well as how differing levels of cognitive effort may influence memory search strategies" (p. 725). We agree and suggest that strategies for alternative generation, like strategies for alternative evaluation, may be usefully investigated from an effort–accuracy framework.

Consideration sets. In the last subsection, we talked about problem structuring in situations where the alternatives are not given but have to be generated. In many consumer decisions, the issue facing the decision maker is different: There can be an overabundance of alternatives. For example, in deciding on a new car to buy, a consumer has several hundred alternatives available in the marketplace. When faced with a purchase decision, however, consumers generally do not seriously consider all of the available brands (alternatives) in the relevant product class. Instead, a subset of the brands is considered. Further, the consideration set, as it is called by market researchers, is frequently only a small subset of the available brands. Hauser and Wernerfelt (1990) summarize a series of studies dealing with the size of consideration sets and report that the consideration set is most often between 3 and 4 brands, although the number of brands available in the product classes studied ranged from 6 to 47.

The size and the composition of the consideration set is an extremely important aspect of decision making. For example, Hauser and Wernerfelt (1990) argue that consideration sets have implications for the measurement of consumer preferences, responses to advertising, competitive pricing strategies, and the benefits from being a pioneer brand in a product class.

What factors determine the size and the content of the consideration set? Hauser and Wernerfelt (1990) offer a model of the addition (or deletion) of brands to a consideration set that is similar to the cost–benefit framework presented in this book. They propose that the size and content of a consideration set will reflect a trade-off between "decision costs" (effort) and the incremental benefits of choosing from a larger set of brands (accuracy). Hauser and Wernerfelt then suggest how changes in decision costs through such means as advertising will effect the likelihood of adding a brand to a consideration set and the separate likelihood of dropping a brand from the set. Such advertising changes are related to the general topic of changes in the information environment of decisions explored in the previous chapter.

Hauser and Wernerfelt also speculate on how decision costs will vary as a function of the number of brands in the set. Are decision costs, for instance, a linear function of the number of brands in a set? In their model, Hauser and Wernerfelt assume a linear function, but acknowledge that the function may be nonlinear. As we have shown earlier, the question of how decision costs (effort) vary with the size of the option set will be a joint function of the strategy being used, the number of alternatives, and various context factors (see chapters 4 and 6). Thus, there are possibilities for the ideas about cognitive effort and decision making presented in this book to help us better understand the nature of consideration sets.[2]

Another reason we suggest the issue of consideration sets as a future research direction is that it is a topic, like that of alternative generation, where the role of memory will be crucial. Alba et al. (1991), for instance, discuss a variety of potential effects of the structure and processes of memory on consideration sets. More generally, we see both the topics of alternative generation and the size and composition of consideration sets as areas in which the more stimulus-based choice problems of the type described in this book (i.e., all relevant information is directly present when the choice is made) can be extended to problems that are both stimulus-based and memory-based (Lynch & Srull, 1982; Lynch, Marmorstein, & Weigold, 1988).

---

[2] Note that phased strategies like EBA + WADD could be seen as developing a consideration set in the EBA phase.

The social context of decisions

In this book, we have emphasized considerations of accuracy and effort in the decision on how to decide. However, as acknowledged in chapters 1 and 3, other considerations may also be relevant in strategy selection. An important class of those additional considerations reflects the fact that decisions are generally not made in a social vacuum. Sometimes, for example, we are accountable for our decisions to someone else. At other times, our individual decision processes are invoked within the context of a group making a judgment or choice. In this section, we explore how decision strategy selection might be influenced by such social factors as (1) the need to justify a decision to someone else, (2) being part of a group decision process, and (3) being part of a competitive decision-making situation.

Accountability and decision processing. Beach and Mitchell (1978) identified accountability as one factor that might influence strategy selection. They argued that the more one is accountable to others for a decision's result, the greater the pressure to be correct. Thus, they viewed greater accountability as leading to the increased use of more accurate decision strategies (for evidence in support of this view, see McAllister et al., 1979). In that regard, accountability is just another way to manipulate the incentive structure of a decision problem.

It is not clear, however, that the need to justify a decision to another (accountability) will always lead to more normative types of decision processes. Tetlock (1991), for instance, offers a social contingency model of judgment and choice that allows for both effort-minimizing as well as accuracy-seeking responses to accountability. He argues that one strategy used by people to cope with accountability demands is to adopt decisions that they feel are likely to gain the favor of those to whom they feel accountable. That is, you might adopt the decision strategy of simply choosing that option that you think the other person would prefer. Tetlock views this strategy as the least effortful way to deal with accountability. However, when people do not know the views of the prospective audience, it is assumed that "accountability will motivate them to abandon their cognitive-miserly ways and to become relatively flexible, and self-critical thinkers" (p. 457). In general, this greater level of thought is assumed to lead to better judgments (see Tetlock & Kim, 1987 for supporting evidence). The exception to this hypothesis occurs when a person has already irrevocably committed himself to a course of action. In that case, accountability motivates cognitive effort, but in this case the thought will be rigid, defensive, and directed to explaining why one is right and one's critics are wrong.

Tetlock (1991) also notes that the increased use of information motivated by accountability can be nonadaptive if the additional information that is used is nondiagnostic or nonrelevant to the task. Tetlock and Boettger (1989), for example, found a greater dilution effect of nondiagnostic information on judgments under conditions of accountability. Also, as discussed in chapter 2, Simonson (1989) found that the asymmetric dominance effect tended to be stronger among subjects who expected to justify their decisions to others, because the asymmetric dominance structure provided an argument for choosing one alternative. To the extent that susceptibility of preferences to such a context variable is a bias, as we would argue, Simonson's results also support the argument that increased accountability does not necessarily lead to more normative (better) decision making.

Finally, it is worth remembering that one of the reasons offered by Tversky (1972) for the attractiveness of an EBA strategy was that it was easy to justify a decision made using that strategy. The point is that what makes a decision strategy more justifiable may not be the same as what makes a decision strategy more accurate. Furthermore, it may well be that the ease with which a particular decision strategy can be justified will vary across task and contexts, just as accuracy and effort vary. In any event, we agree with Tetlock (1985; 1991) that the social context of decisions has been a neglected part of decision research and that it is an area worthy of much greater study.

Social loafing. Imagine that you are an undergraduate participating in a study of college student work preferences. You are asked to evaluate a series of job descriptions representing kinds of part-time summer jobs. The jobs differ on such dimensions as flexibility of hours and the friendliness of co-workers. In one case you are told that "although many students will participate in this study, you are

the only one who will evaluate this particular set of job descriptions."
How might you go about making a judgment about the attractiveness of each job? Now, imagine that in the other case you are told
that "you are 1 of 16 students who will be evaluating this particular
set of job descriptions. As soon as you make your evaluation, it is
automatically averaged with the other students' to form one evaluation for each job description." Would your decision processes be the
same when you are making a judgment as an individual as when
you are making the judgment as one of a group of judges?

The two scenarios presented here were taken from a study
conducted by Weldon and Gargano (1985). They found that the
judgment processes seemed to differ. Under the individual condition, the judgments of the subjects were better fit by a linear compensatory model involving greater use of information. The judges in
the group condition seemed to use less information, although still
primarily in a linear compensatory fashion. Thus, there was evidence
of "social loafing" (Latané, Williams, & Harkins, 1979) for decisions
made within a group context. In a later study, Weldon and Mustari
(1988) found more evidence for the use of heuristics rather than a
linear compensatory rule under the group condition. They suggest
that feelings of dispensability may be the underlying cause of the
findings in the group condition.

At one level, the work by Weldon and her associates shows that
social context can affect the accuracy–effort tradeoffs that people
make in a judgment task. Under conditions of greater felt dispensability, people will emphasize effort minimization more than accuracy.
Obviously, it would be nice to see if a shift in strategies could also
be observed in a choice task under the conditions of individual
versus group responsibility identified by Weldon. More generally,
however, we suggest that it would be useful to examine the impact
of groups, and different types of groups and group structures, on
how the individuals that make up a group decide how to decide. In
that regard, we endorse the recent call by Schneider (1991) for
research on the effects of social variables on cognitive processes.

Competitive decision making. We have concentrated on decisions in
which the outcomes connected to the actions are either certain or
determined by random events. However, for one class for problems,
the outcomes we experience depend upon the actions selected by
others, and at times those others may be trying to maximize their

outcomes at our expense. Such competitive decisions are the domain of game theory, a subdiscipline within economics.

A natural extension of our own work would be to examine competitive decisions. Traditionally, the emphasis in game theory has been on normative description, or determining what players in competitive games *should* do. The goal of such research is that the normative prescriptions of decision makers' strategies would be descriptively accurate, at least for experienced players. However, there has been an increase in interest in how decision makers may be able to identify these strategies: "Equilibrium analysis dominates the study of games of strategy, but even many of its foremost exponents are troubled by its assumptions that players immediately and unerringly identify and play a particular vector of equilibrium strategies, that is, by the assumptions that the equilibrium is common knowledge. An alternative (and to some extent complementary) approach to analyzing behavior in games focuses on learning" (Milgrom & Roberts, 1991, p. 82).

This emphasis on learning is quite consistent with our notions of adaptivity. A major conclusion of our work is that decision makers can do almost as well as normative strategies by employing a repertoire of heuristic strategies and knowing when each is appropriate. Similarly, Milgrom and Roberts (1991, p. 84) conclude that "These results ... indicate that the 'rationality' of any particular learning algorithm is situation dependent: An algorithm that performs well in some situations may work poorly in others. Apparently, real biological players tailor rules-of-thumb to their environments and experience: They learn how to learn."

An example of the study of adaptative decisions in competitive environments is provided by E. Johnson, Camerer, Sen, and Rymon (1991). They explain the failure of players to select the equilibrium payoff in a fairly simple bargaining game by arguing that the players do not completely evaluate all possible moves, but rather concentrate on a subset of moves that are incompletely evaluated. In many ways, this is much like the description of decision makers faced with complex choice sets (see chapter 2). Using Mouselab, Johnson et al. showed that players' search was related to the quality of the decision outcomes: the more the search, the more normative the offer in the bargaining game. Much more research on the processes by which players "tailor" their heuristics to the environment seems warranted.

Contingent judgment process

Judgment ≠ choice. The focus of this book thus far has been on the adaptive use of information-processing strategies leading to a choice among alternatives. Choice is one major way in which a person's preferences may be expressed, and, as we have seen, there are different strategies that people use in making choices. Thus, understanding the factors that determine which strategy will be used in making a choice is of crucial importance. However, choice is not the only way in which preferences are expressed. Often a person's values are expressed in terms of a judgment about a single alternative. For example, a candidate for a job might be rated on a 10-point scale, where 1 = poor and 10 = excellent.

At one time, it was assumed that judgment and choice were equivalent; judgments were made for all available options, and the option with the best overall evaluation was selected, as in the weighted adding rule. However, as noted in chapter 2, many heuristics yield a choice among options without providing evaluations of each alternative (e.g., EBA, LEX, SAT). In addition, many striking examples of contingent decision behavior indicate that judgment is not the same as choice. As one example, the large body of research on preference reversals discussed in chapter 2 shows that expressed preferences can be reversed depending upon whether a choice or judgment response mode is used. In the words of Einhorn and Hogarth (1981), judgment "is neither necessary nor sufficient for choice" (p. 73).

Contingencies in judgment. There is also a good deal of evidence that judgment responses are contingent upon properties of the task. For example, Goldstein and Einhorn (1987) demonstrate that preference reversals can be obtained within judgment; they obtained different preference orders by changing from a dollar scale to a 20-point attractiveness scale. Schkade and Johnson (1989) and Mellers, Ordonez, and Birnbaum (1992) argue further that preference reversals may be caused by changes in processing strategies across different response modes. Other research demonstrates contingencies in judgment depending upon response mode compatibility (Tversky et al., 1988; Slovic et al., 1990; also see chapters 2 and 5), differences in utility assessment tasks (E. Johnson & Schkade, 1989), and differences in tasks requiring updating of information (Hogarth & Einhorn, 1992).

Based upon such evidence, several researchers have suggested that contingencies in judgment responses, like those associated with choice responses, can be understood in terms of the application of multiple judgment strategies, contingent upon task demands (Hogarth & Einhorn, 1992; E. Johnson & Schkade, 1989; Mellers et al., 1992). We agree, and we suggest further that the study of judgment could be approached using the same type of accuracy–effort framework presented in this book. In the rest of this section, we briefly sketch how that framework might be applied to judgment processes.

Strategies for judgment. In order to apply our framework to judgment, we first need to enumerate the strategies that might be used in generating a judgment response. Unfortunately, unlike choice, for which there are many well-known alternative heuristics, there have been fewer heuristics proposed for judgment. As discussed in chapter 1, one simple judgment heuristic for familiar problems is affect referral: A prior evaluation is simply retrieved from memory (P. Wright, 1975). However, we will focus on judgment tasks of some complexity and novelty.

For these more novel judgment tasks, the most frequently proposed models of judgment are weighted additive or averaging models. A particularly influential formulation of such a model is provided by N. Anderson (1981):

$$r = \sum_i w_i s_i$$

where the w_i is the weight for attribute i and s_i is the subjective scale value for attribute i. The response of the decision maker, r, represents the result on a internal scale; this internal response then can be transformed to the external response required by the situation by a response mapping process. The w_i are assumed to add to 1 in the averaging form of the model; initial impressions or additive constants can also be added to account for certain response biases.

This additive or averaging model of judgment clearly is related to the weighted additive or expectation models of choice described in chapter 2. Although these models of judgment do not claim normative status (N. Anderson, 1986), the models make very similar cognitive demands upon decision makers. That is, all information is processed, and effortful EIPs such as PRODUCT are used. Hence, the additive or averaging models of judgment demand a good deal of cognitive effort.

Because we have shown that individuals often use simplifying heuristics in choice, it seems reasonable to argue that simplifying heuristics are also employed for judgment. Indeed, several alternative models of judgment have been proposed that represent possible simplifications that people might use in making a judgment. The most-discussed simplifying heuristic for judgment is anchoring and adjustment (Slovic & Lichtenstein, 1971). As noted in chapter 2, in this heuristic one item of information about an alternative is used as an anchor or starting point for an initial judgment. That initial judgment is then adjusted to take additional information into account, but the adjustment is often insufficient.

Although the anchoring and adjustment heuristic can be represented in a mathematical form that is similar to that used for adding models (see, e.g., Hogarth & Einhorn, 1992), it is often argued that the anchoring and adjustment process is easier than that implied by the usual additive or averaging model. For example, Lopes (1982) has offered a process model of anchoring and adjustment involving an analogue process of adjustment that she argues is cognitively less demanding than a multiplication. The general insufficiency of the adjustment to the anchor may also reflect the application of less cognitively effortful (and less accurate) processes.

A key characteristic distinguishing an anchoring and adjustment model from the most straightforward adding or averaging model is the presence of order dependence. The item of information that serves as an anchor will have greater impact on judgment than the item of information used as the basis for the adjustment (see Hogarth & Einhorn, 1992, for an extensive discussion of one class of order effects in judgment). If one assumes an anchoring and adjustment process is being used by an individual, the key research question then becomes understanding the factors that affect the selection of the anchor, for example, compatibility effects (Slovic et al., 1990).

Other simplifications in judgment that have been proposed include the equal weight model (Einhorn & Hogarth, 1975) and the rule for counting the frequency of good and bad features proposed by Alba and Marmorstein (1987). Both of these heuristics can also be used for choice and were described in chapter 2.

Accuracy–effort tradeoffs in judgment. Like heuristics for choice, the simplifications used in making a judgment can be characterized in terms of accuracy and effort. Obviously, strategies like anchoring and adjustment and counting the frequency of good and bad features can lead to biases (errors) in judgment, such as preference reversals. Simpler judgment strategies also can save cognitive effort.

Several researchers have suggested that tradeoffs between accuracy and effort are made in judgment. Individuals may sometimes increase effort if they realize a simple strategy is insufficient. For instance, Mellers et al. (1992) suggest that a change in decision context caused a change in decision processes from an adding model to a more complicated multiplicative combination rule because certain stimuli highlighted "problems" with additive strategies. In other cases, people may settle for less accuracy if too much effort seems necessary. For example, Slovic (1967) argued that the loss of accuracy represented by preference reversals might be due to subjects not exerting the cognitive effort needed to use probabilities precisely. Similarly, Tversky et al. (1988) argued that compatibility effects may result because dealing with noncompatibility requires more effort than subjects sometimes provide. E. Johnson et al. (1988) specifically showed that more effortful displays led to strategy changes. Finally, N. Anderson (1981) noted that subjects make judgments of motivation by subtracting ratings of ability from those of performance, rather than dividing performance by ability, which would be expected from the classic performance = motivation × ability formula. N. Anderson (1981, p. 55) speculated that the reason is "that the dividing rule is difficult and subjects tend to slip into an easier, subtracting mode."

Measuring cognitive effort in judgment. Thus, there is some agreement that an accuracy–effort framework is relevent for judgment. However, as in the case of choice, to implement our framework we require measures of how effortful various judgment strategies are in different task environments.

Our approach to measuring cognitive effort, outlined in chapter 3, involves using a set of elementary information processes (EIPs) to model heuristics. Unfortunately, the set of EIPs proposed in chapter 3 does not appear sufficient for modeling judgment heuristics. While many of the EIPs presented in chapter 3 (e.g., READ, COMPARE, DIFFERENCE, ADD, PRODUCT, MOVE) apply directly to some judgment heuristics, additional mental operators are needed. For example, the judgment heuristics outlined previously invoke a valuation process, in which an item of information is transformed onto some internal scale of likability that is common across different types of information (e.g., developing the subjective scale values s_i). Hogarth and Einhorn (1992) also have stressed that even if identical strategies are used to combine information, different encodings of information (e.g., comparative versus absolute) will lead to different judgment outcomes. Hence we need to add a VALUATION EIP to model judgment heuristics. Such a cognitive operation is similar to extracting the utility or value of an attribute, briefly mentioned in chapter 3. One weakness of the EIP framework for choice presented in this book is that we have tended to ignore such valuation issues. Thus, extending our framework to judgment by adding a VALUATION EIP could help in understanding choice behavior as well.

Because anchoring and adjustment is a commonly invoked heuristic for judgment, EIPs for modeling that heuristic are necessary. In particular, we require EIPs for selecting an anchor and for the adjustment process. One option, of course, is simply to use ANCHOR and ADJUST EIPs; however, it might be desirable to model selecting an anchor and making an adjustment in more-detail, with component EIPs to reflect this detail. Unfortunately, the processes of selecting an anchor and making an adjustment have not been addressed in great detail to date. Hence, more detailed, process level conceptualizations of anchoring and adjustment are needed before more detailed EIPs can be suggested.

Another EIP that has been stressed in judgment research is EXPRESSION, which represents the transformation of the internal scale value of a stimulus onto the external response scale. As mentioned in chapter 2, Goldstein and Einhorn (1987) attribute preference reversals to the expression of preferences rather than to the formation of the preferences. Note that both the VALUATION and EXPRESSION EIPs are very aggregate in nature; that is, each may involve constructive and retrieval processes that we have not included in our framework to date.

We believe that applying an accuracy–effort approach to understanding contingent judgment processes is an extremely promising direction for additional research. The obstacles to progress include a lack of process level descriptions of some judgment heuristics and the aggregate nature of such EIPs as VALUATION and EXPRES-

SION. However, such obstacles provide great opportunities for significant extensions to our approach.

Summary

Throughout this book we have sought to convey the highly contingent nature of human decision behavior. Although some may view the fact that decision processes are not invariant across task environments as a difficulty for decision research, we view it as a source of excitement and opportunity. As we ask questions about the conditions under which different decision processes are more likely to be used, generalizations about decision behavior are emerging. Those generalizations hold promise for both a better understanding of how people make decisions and the development of better methods to aid decisions.

Appendix: The Mouselab system

Introduction

Throughout this book we have described studies carried out using the Mouselab system for monitoring information processing. This appendix provides additional detail about the properties of that system.[1]

The two process-tracing methods of greatest interest to decision researchers have been verbal protocol analysis and the analysis of information acquisition behavior. (See J. Ford et al., 1989, for a recent summary of process-tracing studies of judgment and choice.) The Mouselab system focuses on monitoring information acquisition behaviors, such as what information the subject seeks, the sequence of acquisition, how much information is acquired, and for what duration information is examined. Such data on information acquisitions are important for several reasons. First, the evaluation strategies that have been proposed in the decision literature imply certain patterns of search (Payne, 1976). Second, studying information acquisition can yield insight into the role of attention and memory in decision making (Einhorn & Hogarth, 1981). Finally, understanding the amount, types, and pattern of information acquisition is important in the design of decision aids.

If one wants to monitor information acquisition, what is the best technique to use? At one extreme are simple information board procedures. For example, in Payne (1976) the information board

[1] Eric J. Johnson and John W. Payne have been equally responsible for the bulk of the development of the Mouselab system. Valuable initial work was carried out by David A. Schkade, and James R. Bettman has provided inputs at later stages. The programming assistance of James Christy, Kim Collins, Stuart Shapiro, and David Rovin is gratefully acknowledged. Particular thanks are due to Mark T. Jones, now at Argonne National Laboratory, for the design and implementation of the most recent features.

consisted of a matrix of envelopes attached to a sheet of cardboard. To obtain the value on a particular dimension for a particular alternative, the subject had to pull a card out of the appropriate envelope, turn it around, read the card, and place it back into the envelope. The value was printed on the back of the card. Similar types of information boards had been used successfully in a number of studies (e.g., Jacoby et al., 1976; Thorngate & Maki, 1976; Wilkins, 1967). A major criticism of information boards, however, is the time and effort required to acquire a piece of information (Arch, Bettman, & Kakkar, 1978).

At the other extreme is the monitoring of information acquisition using sophisticated techniques for the recording of eye fixations. Russo and his associates have been the primary users of eye movement recording to study decision behavior. For example, Russo and Dosher (1983) used a photoelectric sensing device and a computer for recording and analyzing the fixations. While eye movement recording provides dense data, there are disadvantages. The equipment is complex and nontrivial to use, it is quite costly, and analyses of the data are time consuming and difficult.

In one of the few efforts to directly compare various information monitoring techniques, Russo (1978) reports that eye movements typically required a minimum of 200–300 milliseconds. On the other hand, a physical retrieval of information from an information display board could involve 3–4 seconds. One consequence of this difference in acquisition time (effort) was that subjects seldom reacquired information in information display board studies. Russo (1978) reviews several information display board studies and his own work using eye movement recording and reports that the reacquisitions rate with eye movements was as high as 56%. Although differences in stimulus materials make comparisons across studies somewhat imprecise, the reacquisition rate is likely to be much higher with eye movements. More generally, information display boards yield a much sparser pattern of observations than eye movement recording. Consequently, Russo argues that there is a danger that the less dense data set may yield misleading conclusions about a decision maker's strategies.

Mouselab, like other computer-based information acquisition procedures (e.g., Brucks, 1988; Dahlstrand & Montgomery, 1984; Jacoby et al., 1984; Payne & Braunstein, 1978), is an alternative to simple information boards and to expensive and difficult-to-use eye movement recording. By employing computer graphics to display information that is accessed using a pointing device called a mouse, Mouselab comes close to the recording of eye movements in terms of speed and ease of acquisitions, while minimizing instrumentation cost and the difficulty of use for both subject and experimenter. The rest of this appendix documents this methodology.

The mouse as pointing device

There are a number of computer-based pointing or position entry devices, such as a light pen, joystick, directional cursor keys or other keyboard keys, and mouse; several of these devices have been used in prior computer-based information acquisition systems (e.g., Jacoby et al. [1984] use a light pen, whereas Payne & Braunstein [1978] and Dahlstrand & Montgomery [1984] use the keyboard). Of these devices, the mouse has three marked advantages (Card et al., 1983). The first advantage of a mouse as a pointing device is ease of learning. Card et al. (1983) compared the mouse, joystick, and two key-operated devices for selecting text on a screen. Although each of the devices yields improved performance with practice, research indicates that the mouse and joystick provide a significantly faster rate of learning than do cursor keys. In our experience, even people unfamiliar with computers are relatively comfortable with the mouse after a brief training period of 5 to 10 minutes.

A second major advantage of a mouse is its rapid movement. Card et al. found the mouse to be significantly faster than the other devices they tested. An earlier study by English, Englebart, and Berman (1967) found the mouse to be faster than a lightpen and several other devices. An analysis of the time to move the mouse from point to point suggests that this follows Fitts' Law (Fitts, 1954; Card et al., 1983), a basic equation in the human factors literature. Fitts' law states that Time to Position $= K_o + I_m(D/S + .5)$ (in seconds), where D is the distance to the target box, S is the size of the target, $I_m = .100$ seconds/bit, and K_o is a constant. Card et al. suggest that the time to move a mouse is primarily limited by the central information-processing capacities of the eye–hand guidance system. In other words, the major limitation in speed is due to the time it takes to think where to point, not in the movement of the mouse. Further analysis of the performance of the mouse indicated that it was within 5% of this optimal pointing device described by Fitts' Law.

We have done an analysis of two of our decision tasks using Fitts' Law. The size of the target S and the distance between targets D varies across the different displays possible with the Mouselab program. Consequently, time to position will differ across the displays. However, it is useful to consider two displays that will involve large differences in the time to position the mouse cursor in a box, the gamble schema and the matrix schema (these displays will be described in more detail). The gamble schema involves the smallest number of boxes spread across the greatest width of the screen. The boxes are 1.2 cm high and 3.0 cm wide. They have a maximum distance of 7 cm. For such a display, Fitts' Law yields a value of $K_o + 245$ milliseconds. A matrix display involving just two alternatives and two attributes is one that is likely to yield the fastest times to position the cursor. The boxes are 8 cm high and 8 cm wide. They have a maximum distance of 8 cm. For such a display, Fitts' Law yields a value of $K_o + 82$ milliseconds. Of course, these values for time to position depend on a value for K_o. Card et al. (1983) present values for K_o that range from 600 to 1,100 milliseconds. However, those values are likely to be overestimates of the K_o's for our task. Unlike some of the pointing devices and tasks studied by Card et al., in our task the subject's hand is always present on the mouse.

Thus, for a simple matrix display, it is possible that subjects could move between information cells in less than 100 milliseconds, a figure we have occasionally observed with practiced subjects. Surprisingly, these times are of similar magnitude to eye movements, or about 160–200 milliseconds per bit of information (Card et al., 1983). This suggests that reactivity due to the effort of moving the mouse might be minimal.

The third advantage of the mouse is its error rate, the percentage of times that the device is used to select an incorrect item of information. Card et al. (1983) report that the mouse has a significantly lower error rate than other devices.

Despite these advantages, the use of the mouse does have limitations. In order to precisely monitor what information is acquired at a particular point in time, it is necessary to structure the decision task so that only one item of information is visible at a time. This was done by setting up the decision task so that the relevant information is hidden in boxes on the screen until the subject moves the mouse to point at a box. At that time, the box opens and the information is revealed. This procedure eliminates the possibility of the subject's acquiring information from peripheral vision, as might be the case in a more normal visual information environment. Our task is more similar to those used in research in reading, which manipulates the display to remove any peripheral information from around the current eye fixation (Rayner, 1975; McConkie & Rayner, 1976). Apparently, such manipulations have little effect upon the overall ability of an individual to understand text. The manipulations, however, do seem to increase the average time of each fixation and to diminish the length of the distance covered by each fixation. By analogy, the mouse may have the same effect on search patterns. Specifically, we might see fewer transitions between distant areas of the display. However, reacquisition of information is often seen with the mouse, suggesting that much of the reactivity discussed by Russo is not present.

Ultimately, of course, the comparison of eye movement recording to a mouse-based information acquisition system will require a series of empirical studies. Nonetheless, the existing evidence suggests that with a mouse-based system the time and effort to acquire a piece of information from a computer display are relatively small. This should reduce the reactivity of studies that examine decision behavior through the monitoring of information acquisition behavior. We can say at this time that studies of the effects of number of alternatives on processing (Johnson et al., 1989) and of preference reversals (Johnson et al., 1988) in which Mouselab was used yield results that agree with those of previous studies that did not use a mouse. The next sections of this appendix briefly describe the features of the Mouselab system. A more complete description of the Mouselab system is provided in Johnson, Payne, Schkade, and Bettman (1991).

Overview of the Mouselab system

The core of the mouse-based system for doing decision studies is a program called Mouselab. The program can be used to present the instructions for an experiment, present decision problems using one of four general types of screens or "schemas," and automatically record what information was acquired, the duration of the acquisition, search order, and the final judgment or choice. Response times are recorded to an accuracy of 1/60th of a second. In addition to

Mouselab, the decision laboratory software includes a program that can be used in the analysis and reduction of the data generated from the process-tracing studies and a set of programs that allows for the randomization and counterbalancing of Mouselab input files.

Each Mouselab screen or display has two major components. The schema type determines the manner in which information is displayed on the screen. The response mode determines the manner in which the subject is to respond to the information presented in the schema. Any schema type may be used in conjunction with any response mode. Mouselab currently supports four different schemas (text, matrix, gamble, and multiple risky choice) and three different response modes (boxes, scale, and keyboard input). Each of these is now briefly described.

Mouselab schemas

Text schema. A text schema simply presents lines of text that the researcher wishes to present to the subject (e.g., a set of instructions). Up to 24 lines of text can be presented on a screen. To present additional information on additional screens, the text schema is just evoked repeatedly. See Display Example 1 for a sample text schema.

Matrix schema. A matrix schema presents a matrix of boxes, M rows by N columns, which can be opened to display information. The information presented in a box can be of three types: numbers, letters, or graphics (this is a special feature, to be described). Labels can be specified for the rows and columns. Boxes used to choose one of the alternatives appear at the bottom of the screen. The maximum size matrix we have used corresponded to an eight-alternative by eight-attribute decision problem. This schema is useful for presenting nonrisky, multiattribute decision problems and certain types of gambles with multiple outcomes. See Display Example 2. Payne et al. (1988) used this schema to present their sets of four-outcome gambles.

Gamble schema. The gamble schema presents a two-outcome gamble and a certain outcome in a format appropriate for either a probability equivalence or a certainty equivalence judgment. See Display Example 3. A study of preference reversals using this schema is reported in E. Johnson et al. (1988).

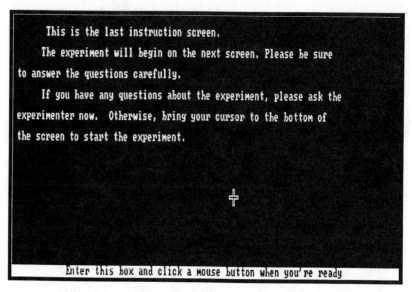

Display Example 1. Sample text schema.

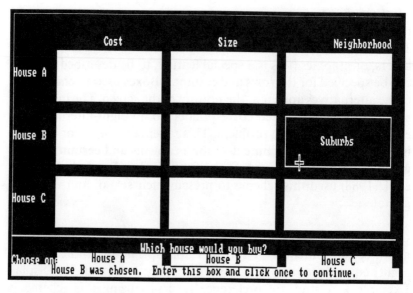

Display Example 2. Sample matrix schema.

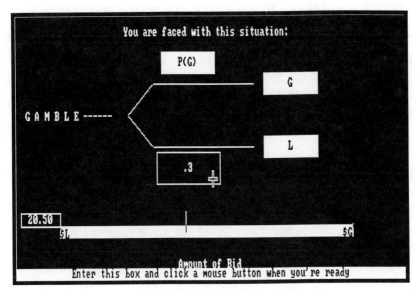

Display Example 3. Sample gamble schema.

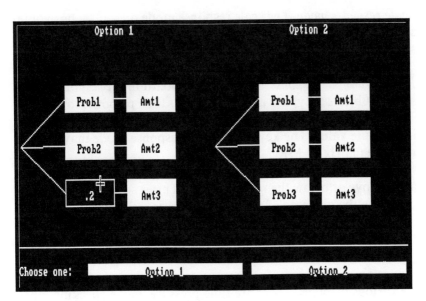

Display Example 4. Sample MRC schema.

Multiple risky choice (MRC) schema. An MRC schema can be used to present any number of different gambles in a decision tree format. The gambles in a set can have different numbers of outcomes and attributes, although each gamble in a set must have the same structure. This schema can also be used to present nonrisky, multiattribute problems by setting the number of outcomes equal to one. An example of a MRC display is shown in Display Example 4.

Mouselab response modes

In any schema, an experimenter can choose between three different response modes: response boxes, response scales, and keyboard input responses. Choices are made using the boxes response mode, whereas judgments are made using the scale response mode. The keyboard input response mode can be used for either choices or judgments.

Boxes response mode. The boxes response mode presents a variable number of labeled choice boxes at the bottom of the screen. To choose a response, the subject simply moves the cursor into the desired response box and clicks to register a response.

Scale response mode. The scale response mode presents a horizontal scale for responses. Scale labels and the numbered divisions of the scale can be specified (see Display Example 5).

Keyboard input response mode. The keyboard input response mode allows subjects to type in a real number as their response to a screen. The number must be a real number less than approximately 32,000 in absolute value. The keyboard input response mode may be used with the matrix or MRC schema types.

All response modes provide for a one-line message either immediately above or below the response area. This is sometimes useful for clarifying the meaning of possible responses.

Other Mouselab features

Mouselab also supports four general features that can be used with the various displays. These are time pressure, move checking, open boxes, and graphics.

Display Example 5. Sample response scale.

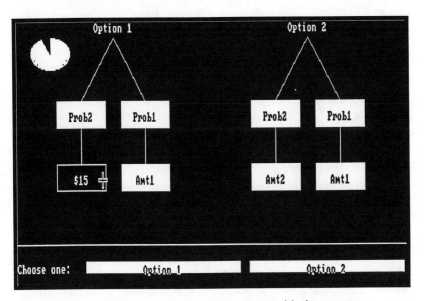

Display Example 6. Sample MRC schema with time pressure.

Time pressure. Time pressure is implemented by depicting an analog clock that counts down for a specified number of seconds. The clock is displayed on the screen along with the information contained in a schema. When the allotted time has expired, the request "Please make a choice or indicate a value" is displayed at the top of the screen. Several other things can happen to the screen, depending on the option specified. For example, after the clock has finished, the information boxes can be closed so that no additional information can be acquired, and the subject must make a decision based on only the information acquired up to that point. See Display Example 6 for a sample MRC schema with a clock. The time pressure feature was used with the matrix schema in a study of adaptive decision behavior by Payne et al. (1988).

Move checking. On occasion, an experimenter will want to make sure that subjects acquire information in a certain order, perhaps to ensure that a certain decision strategy is followed. One could, for example, use the move-monitoring feature to ensure that a subject used an elimination-by-aspects strategy (Tversky, 1972). To implement this feature, the experimenter must specify the desired sequence of boxes. If the subject enters any box out of sequence, the box will not open and the computer will emit a beep and record in the output file the time and location of the cursor. Bettman et al. (1990) provide an example of how this feature might be used to estimate the cognitive effort associated with the elementary information processes making up various decision strategies.

Open boxes. This option uncovers all boxes within a given screen, displaying their normally hidden contents. This feature is useful for instructional purposes – for example, to familiarize subjects with the experimental stimuli before introducing the task of acquiring stimuli. Display Example 7 contains a sample of a matrix with open boxes.

Graphics. In addition to typing in values for boxes in a matrix or MRC schema, the experimenter can "call in" graphics, such as figures and graphs, from external files. These files, which are stored in a PCX format, can serve as the basis for subjects' choices and judgments.

Other features in Mouselab modify the appearance of some schemas or change how data are recorded. These features include data tracing, transpose, orientation, scale tracking, and suppressed alternatives.

Data tracing. The data tracing option allows the researcher to suspend tracing and recording of subject activity within a display. This option is also useful for instructional screens, where there may be no need to monitor a subject's behavior.

Transpose. The transpose option allows a matrix schema to be rotated so that rows become columns and vice versa. For example,

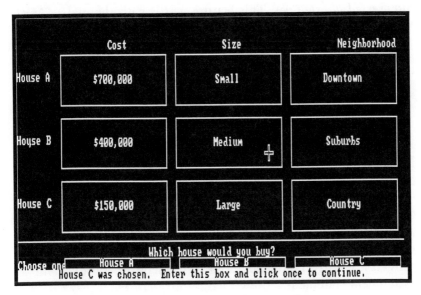

Display Example 7. Matrix schema with open boxes.

the standard form of display for the matrix schema is to consider the rows as alternatives and the matrix columns as attributes. With the transpose feature, the same input format is used, but the columns become the choice alternatives while the rows become attributes. The transposition feature can be used to make the display look better or to counterbalance the possible impact of the normal left–right reading order on search behavior.

Orientation. The orientation feature does for MRC schemas what TRANSPOSE does for matrix schemas, displaying the gambles in either horizontal or vertical orientation.

Scale tracking. Normally, when a subject is manipulating a scale, Mouselab only records the value of the scale each time the subject changes its value. Scale tracking allows the researcher to monitor the scale adjustment, recording the time and scale value each time the subject changes the direction of adjustment. This feature might be useful for studying anchoring and adjustment processes (see Schkade & Johnson, 1989, for an example of the usage of this feature).

Suppressed alternatives. This feature works with the matrix MRC schema to prevent row labels from appearing as choice selections. For instance, if the first row of a matrix was needed to reflect attribute weights, then this option would be used to make sure that "weights" was not one of the choice boxes at the bottom of the screen.

The Mouselab programming language

Mouselab now has a fairly complete programming language. This allows the experimenter to alter a succeeding display according to the previous responses of the subject. The language both provides certain predeclared variables that contain information about how the subject behaved on each trial and allows experimenters to declare their own variables as well. In addition, the Mouselab language provides a fairly complete set of arithmetic operations and an assignment statement.

Predeclared variables allow the experimenter to access data from a previous screen. For example, a variable could be used to retrieve the subject's choice from the previous screen. This information could then be used to determine which alternatives will be presented in the current decision matrix.

The experimenter may also create his or her own variables in the input file. For example, the experimenter could create non-Mouselab variables like name and age. When the subject is prompted to type in his or her name and age, the Mouselab program records the responses in the output file. These variables can also be assigned values and used to determine flow of control. An example of this use would be the creation of a variable that determines the amount of time a subject can spend in a given matrix screen as a function of time spent on earlier screens. The experimenter can "set" the clock time to any desired length of time by assigning the variable a time value based on the earlier decision.

A set of Mouselab flow-of-control commands is available to control the order in which Mouselab commands are executed. These flow-of-control commands can be used, for example, to execute the same set of Mouselab statements several times or to execute conditionally a set of Mouselab statements. Mouselab provides a fairly complete set of control constructs similar to any block-oriented programming language.

Running Mouselab

Equipment needed. The current version of Mouselab is written in Microsoft Pascal, Version 4.0. Some of the auxiliary programs for data analysis are written in Borland's Turbo Pascal.

Mouselab runs on an **IBM-PC XT, AT, PS/2** or equivalent under **IBM PS/DOS**. Because of the real-time processing load, the original IBM PC's system requires an Intel 8087 coprocessor to run Mouselab effectively. Faster processors do not need a coprocessor. A recommended system configuration would include an IBM-PC with at least 384K of free memory, a hard disk with at least two free megabytes of disk space, and a Microsoft mouse or other mouse that will emulate the Microsoft mouse. The monitor can be monochrome or color. A graphics card is required; currently Hercules, IBM CGA, EGA and VGA displays and compatibles are supported.

Designing Mouselab displays. The details of the specific commands used for designing Mouselab displays are beyond the scope of this appendix. These details can be found in E. Johnson et al. (1991).

Mouselab output. Mouselab generates an output file that can be processed further. The file contains pairs of lines that record the box a subject was in and the time of entry and exit from that box. When the subject chooses a response, that response and the time of the response are written into the file. Finally, other information is also included in the file to indicate special conditions: the end of the countdown under time pressure, reading time for a text screen, indications if the subject moved to the wrong box when move checking was in force, the output from print statements inserted in the commands for designing the displays, and indications of a change in the direction of response scale adjustment if scale tracking is used.

A utility program called Bisect is used to analyze the output file. Bisect produces a file that includes a line for each box entered by the subject. The line contains the subject's identification, the trial number, the box number, the elapsed time in the box, the time from entering that box until actually entering the next box, a sequence number indicating the order of acquisition, and any response for that box. The data in the file produced by Bisect are then analyzed using an appropriate statistical package. We have generally used SAS for our analyses.

Obtaining Mouselab. If the reader is interested in obtaining a copy of the Mouselab program and manual, we request a $25 fee, payable to the Trustees of the University of Pennsylvania. This covers only our reproduction costs and labor. In return, permission is given to use Mouselab for not-for-profit research and educational uses only. Please contact Professor Eric Johnson, Wharton School, University of Pennsylvania, Philadelphia, PA 19104 to obtain a copy of Mouselab or if you wish to use Mouselab for applications other than not-for-profit research or educational uses.

Summary

This appendix has documented a procedure for monitoring information acquisition behavior using a microcomputer-controlled pointing device called a mouse. The procedure also employs a number of flexible graphics and data-recording routines. There are several thousand different display and experimental condition combinations that can be used. Included are relatively new capabilities, such as checking the order of information acquisitions to ensure that the subject is following a specified decision strategy. Using Mouselab offers a decision researcher a viable way to obtain the high temporal density of observations regarding a subject's predecision behavior that appears necessary to develop and test process models of decision behavior.

References

Alba, J. W., & Hutchinson, J. W. (1987). Dimensions of consumer expertise. *Journal of Consumer Research, 13,* 411–445.

Alba, J. W., Hutchinson, J. W., & Lynch, J. G. (1991). Memory and decision making. In T. S. Robertson & H. H. Kassarjian (Eds.), *Handbook of consumer behavior* (pp. 1–49). Englewood Cliffs, NJ: Prentice-Hall.

Alba, J. W., & Marmorstein, H. (1987). The effects of frequency knowledge on consumer decision making. *Journal of Consumer Research, 14,* 14–26.

Alloy, L. B., & Tabachnik, N. (1984). Assessment of covariation by humans and animals: The joint influence of prior expectations and current situational information. *Psychological Review, 91,* 112–149.

Anderson, J. R. (1982). Acquisition of cognitive skill. *Psychological Review, 89,* 369–406.

Anderson, J. R. (1983). *The architecture of cognition.* Cambridge, MA: Harvard University Press.

Anderson, N. H. (1981). *Foundations of information integration theory.* New York: Academic Press.

Anderson, N. H. (1986). A cognitive theory of judgment and decision. In B. Brehmer, H. Jungermann, P. Lourens, & G. Sevón (Eds.), *New directions in research on decision making* (pp. 63–108). Amsterdam: Elsevier Science Publishers.

Andriole, S. J. (1989). *Handbook of decision support systems.* Blue Ridge, PA: Tab.

Anzai, Y., & Simon, H. A. (1979). The theory of learning by doing. *Psychological Review, 86,* 124–140.

Arch, D. C., Bettman, J. R., & Kakkar, P. (1978). Subjects' information processing in information display board studies. In H. K. Hunt (Ed.), *Advances in consumer research* (Vol. 5, pp. 555–560). Ann Arbor, MI: Association for Consumer Research.

Arkes, H. R. (1991). Costs and benefits of judgment errors: Implications for debiasing. *Psychological Bulletin, 110,* 486–498.

Arkes, H. R., Dawes, R. M., & Christensen, C. (1986). Factors influencing the use of a decision rule in a probabilistic task. *Organizational Behavior and Human Decision Processes, 37,* 93–110.

Aschenbrenner, K. M. (1978). Single-peaked risk preferences and their dependability on the gambles' presentation mode. *Journal of Experimental Psychology: Human Perception and Performance, 4,* 513–520.

Aschenbrenner, K. M., Bockenholt, U., Albert, D., & Schmalhofer, F. (1986). The selection of dimensions when choosing between multiattribute alternatives. In R. W. Scholz (Ed.), *Current issues in West German decision research* (pp. 63–78). Frankfurt: Lang.

Ashton, R. H. (1990). Pressure and performance in accounting decision settings: Paradoxical effects of incentives, feedback, and justification. *Journal of Accounting Research, 28* (Supplement), 148–180.

Ashton, R. H., Ashton, A. H., & Davis, M. N. (1990). White-collar robotics. Unpublished working paper, Fuqua School of Business, Duke University.

Atkinson, R. C., & Shiffrin, R. M. (1968). Human memory: A proposed system and its control processes. In K. W. Spence & J. T. Spence (Eds.), *The psychology of learning and motivation: Advances in research and theory* (Vol. 2, pp. 89–195). New York: Academic Press.

Baron, J. (1988). *Thinking and deciding.* Cambridge: Cambridge University Press.

Baron, R. M., & Kenny, D. A. (1986). The moderator–mediator variable distinction in social psychological research: Conceptual, strategic, and statistical considerations. *Journal of Personality and Social Psychology, 51,* 1173–1182.

Barron, F. H., von Winterfeldt, D., & Fischer, G. W. (1984). Theoretical and empirical relationships between risky and riskless utility functions. *Acta Psychologica, 56,* 233–244.

Batsell, R. R., & Polking, J. C. (1985). A new class of market share models. *Marketing Science, 4,* 177–198.

Bazerman, M. H. (1990). *Judgment in managerial decision making* (2nd ed.). New York: Wiley.

Beach, L. R. (1983). Muddling through: A response to Yates and Goldstein. *Organizational Behavior and Human Performance, 31,* 47–53.

Beach, L. R. (1990). *Image theory: Decision making in personal and organizational contexts.* Chichester: Wiley.

Beach, L. R., Barnes. V. E., & Christensen-Szalanski, J. J. J. (1986). Beyond heuristics and biases: A contingency model of judgmental forecasting. *Journal of Forecasting, 5,* 143–157.

Beach, L. R., & Mitchell, T. R. (1978). A contingency model for the selection of decision strategies. *Academy of Management Review, 3,* 439–449.

Beattie, J., & Baron, J. (1991). Investigating the effect of stimulus range on attribute weight. *Journal of Experimental Psychology: Human Perception and Performance, 17,* 571–585.

Behn, R. D., & Vaupel, J. W. (1982). *Quick analysis for busy decision makers.* New York: Basic Books.

Bell, D. E. (1982). Regret in decision making under uncertainty. *Operations Research, 30,* 961–981.

Bell, D. E. (1985). Disappointment in decision making under uncertainty. *Operations Research, 33,* 1–27.

Ben Zur, H., & Breznitz, S. J. (1981). The effects of time pressure on risky choice behavior. *Acta Psycologica, 47,* 89–104.

Berg, J. E. & Dickhaut, J. W. (1990). Preference reversals: Incentives do matter. Unpublished manuscript, University of Chicago.

Berg, J. E., Dickhaut, J. W., & O'Brien, J. R. (1985). Preference reversal and arbitrage. In V. Smith (Ed.), *Research in experimental economics* (Vol. 3, pp. 31–72). Greenwich, CT: JAI Press.

Bettman, J. R. (1979). *An information processing theory of consumer choice.* Reading, MA: Addison Wesley.

Bettman, J. R., Johnson, E. J., Luce, M. F., & Payne, J. W. (1992). Correlation, conflict, and choice. Unpublished working paper, Fuqua School of Business, Duke University.

Bettman, J. R., Johnson, E. J., & Payne, J. W. (1990). A componential analysis of cognitive effort in choice. *Organizational Behavior and Human Decision Processes, 45,* 111–139.

Bettman, J. R., & Kakkar, P. (1977). Effects of information presentation format on consumer information acquisition strategies. *Journal of Consumer Research, 3,* 233–240.

Bettman, J. R., & Park, C. W. (1980). Effects of prior knowledge and experience and phase of the choice process on consumer decision processes: A protocol analysis. *Journal of Consumer Research, 7,* 234–248.

Bettman, J. R., Payne, J. W., & Staelin, R. (1986). Cognitive considerations in designing effective labels for presenting risk information. *Journal of Marketing and Public Policy, 5,* 1–28.

Bettman, J. R., & Sujan, M. (1987). Effects of framing on evaluation of comparable and noncomparable alternatives by expert and novice consumers. *Journal of Consumer Research, 14,* 141–154.

Bettman, J. R., & Zins, M. A. (1977). Constructive processes in consumer choice. *Journal of Consumer Research, 4,* 75–85.

Biehal, G. J., & Chakravarti, D. (1986). Consumers' use of memory and external information in choice: Macro and micro processing perspectives. *Journal of Consumer Research, 12,* 382–405.

Biggs, S. F., Bedard, J. C., Gaber, B. G., & Linsmeier, T. J. (1985). The effects of task size and similarity on the decision behavior of bank loan officers. *Management Science, 31*, 970–987.

Billings, R. S., & Marcus, S. A. (1983). Measures of compensatory and noncompensatory models of decision behavior: Process tracing versus policy capturing. *Organizational Behavior and Human Performance, 31*, 331–352.

Billings, R. S., & Scherer, L. M. (1988). The effects of response mode and importance in decision making strategies: Judgment versus choice. *Organizational Behavior and Human Decision Processes, 34*, 1–19.

Blattberg, R. C., & Hoch, S. J. (1990). Database models and managerial intuition: 50% model and 50% manager. *Management Science, 36*, 887–899.

Bockenholt, U., Albert, D., Aschenbrenner, M., & Schmalhofer, F. (1991). The effects of attractiveness, dominance, and attribute differences on information acquisition in multiattribute binary choice. *Organizational Behavior and Human Decision Processes, 49*, 258–281.

Bostic, R., Herrnstein, R. J., & Luce, R. D. (1990). The effect on the preference-reversal phenomenon of using choice indifferences. *Journal of Economic Behavior and Organization, 13*, 193–212.

Brehmer, B. (1980). In a word: Not from experience. *Acta Psychologica, 45*, 223–241.

Brehmer, B. (1990). Strategies in real-time dynamic decision making. In R. M. Hogarth (Ed.), *Insights in decision making: A tribute to Hillel J. Einhorn* (pp. 262–279). Chicago: University of Chicago Press.

Brucks, M. (1988). Search monitor: An approach for computer-controlled experiments involving consumer information search. *Journal of Consumer Research, 15*, 117–121.

Burke, S. J. (1990). The effects of missing information on decision strategy selection. In M. E. Goldberg, G. Gorn, & R. W. Pollay (Eds.), *Advances in consumer research* (Vol. 17, pp. 250–256). Provo, UT: Association for Consumer Research.

Calvin, W. H. (1986). *The river that flows uphill.* New York: Macmillan.

Capon, N., & Kuhn, D. (1980). A developmental study of consumer information-processing strategies. *Journal of Consumer Research, 7*, 225–233.

Card, S. K., Moran, T. P., & Newell, A. (1983). *The psychology of human–computer interaction.* Hillsdale, NJ: Erlbaum.

Carpenter, P. A., & Just, M. A. (1975). Sentence comprehension: A psycholinguistic processing model of verification. *Psychological Review, 82*, 45–73.

Carroll, J. S., & Johnson, E. J. (1990). *Decision research: A field guide.* Newbury Park, CA: Sage.

Carson, R. T., & Navarro, P. (1988). Fundamental issues in natural resources damage assessment. *Natural Resources Journal, 28,* 815–836.

Casey, J. T. (1991). Reversal of the preference reversal phenomenon. *Organizational Behavior and Human Decision Processes, 48,* 224–251.

Cattin, P., & Wittink, D. R. (1982). Commercial use of conjoint analysis: A survey. *Journal of Marketing, 46,* 44–53.

Chase, W. G. (1978). Elementary information processes. In W. K. Estes (Ed.), *Handbook of learning and cognitive processes. Vol. 5, Human information processing* (pp. 19–90). Hillsdale, NJ: Erlbaum.

Chi, M. T. H., Glaser, R., & Farr, M. J. (Eds.). (1988). *The nature of expertise.* Hillsdale, NJ: Erlbaum.

Christensen-Szalanski, J. J. J. (1978). Problem-solving strategies: A selection mechanism, some implications, and some data. *Organizational Behavior and Human Performance, 22,* 307–323.

Christensen-Szalanksi, J. J. J. (1980). A further examination of the selection of problem-solving strategies: The effects of deadliness and analytic aptitudes. *Organizational Behavior and Human Performance, 25,* 107–122.

Christensen-Szalanski, J. J. J. (1984). Discount functions and the measurement of patient values: Women's decisions during childbirth. *Medical Decision Making, 4,* 41–48.

Cohen, M. S., Laskey, K. B., & Tolcott, M. A. (1987). A personalized and prescriptive decision aid for choice from a database of options. Unpublished report, Decision Sciences Consortium, Reston, VA.

Coombs, C. H. (1964). *A theory of data.* New York: Wiley.

Coombs, C. H., & Avrunin, G. S. (1977). Single-peaked functions and the theory of preference. *Psychological Review, 84,* 216–230.

Coombs, C. H., Donnell, M. L., & Kirk, D. B. (1978). An experimental study of risk preferences in lotteries. *Journal of Experimental Psychology: Human Perception and Performance, 4,* 497–512.

Coupey, E. (1990). *Decision restructing in consumer choice.* Unpublished doctoral dissertation, Duke University.

Crandall, C. S., & Greenfield, B. (1986). Understanding the conjunction fallacy: A conjunction of effects? *Social Cognition, 4,* 408–419.

Creyer, E. H., Bettman, J. R., & Payne, J. W. (1990). The impact of accuracy and effort feedback and goals on adaptive decision behavior. *Journal of Behavioral Decision Making, 3,* 1–16.

Crocker, J. (1981). Judgment of convariation by social perceivers. *Psychological Bulletin, 90,* 272–292.

Cummings, R. G., Brookshire, D. S., & Schulze, W. D. (1986). *Valuing environmental goods: An assessment of the contingent valuation method.* Totowa, NJ: Rowman & Allanheld.

Curry, D. J., & Faulds, D. J. (1986). Indexing product quality: Issues, theory, and results. *Journal of Consumer Research, 13,* 134–145.

Curry, D. J., & Menasco, M. B. (1983). On the separability of weights and scale values: Issues and empirical results. *Journal of Consumer Research, 10,* 83–92.

Dahlstrand, U., & Montgomery, H. (1984). Information search and evaluative processes in decision making: A computer based process tracing study. *Acta Psychologica, 56,* 113–123.

Dansereau, D. F. (1969). *An information processing model of mental multiplication.* Unpublished dissertation, Carnegie Mellon University.

Dawes, R. M. (1964). Social selection based on multidimensional criteria. *Journal of Abnormal and Social Psychology, 68,* 104–109.

Dawes, R. M. (1979). The robust beauty of improper linear models in decision making. *American Psychologist, 34,* 571–582.

Dawes, R. M., & Corrigan, B. (1974). Linear models in decision making. *Psychological Bulletin, 81,* 95–106.

Dawes, R. M., Faust, D., & Meehl, P. E. (1989). Clinical versus actuarial judgment. *Science, 243,* 1668–1674.

Debreu, G. (1960). Review of R. D. Luce, *Individual choice behavior: A theoretical analysis. American Economic Review, 50,* 186–188.

Desvousges, W. H., Johnson, F. R., Dunford, R., Boyle, K. J., Hudson, S., & Wilson, K. N. (1992). *Using contingent valuation for natural resource damage assessments: An experimental evaluation of accuracy.* Center for Economics Research Monograph, Research Triangle Institute.

Dube-Rioux, L., & Russo, J. E. (1988). An availability bias in professional judgment. *Journal of Behavioral Decision Making, 1,* 223–237.

Duncker, K. (1945). On problem solving. *Psychological Monographs, 58* (No. 270).

Edwards, W. (1990). Unfinished tasks: A research agenda for behavioral decision theory. In R. M. Hogarth (Ed.), *Insights in decision making: A tribute to Hillel J. Einhorn* (pp. 44–65). Chicago: University of Chicago Press.

Einhorn, H. J. (1970). The use of nonlinear, noncompensatory models in decision making. *Psychological Bulletin, 73,* 211–230.

Einhorn, H. J. (1980). Learning from experience and suboptimal rules in decision making. In T. S. Wallsten (Ed.), *Cognitive processes in choice and decision behavior* (pp. 1–20). Hillsdale, NJ: Erlbaum.

Einhorn, H. J. (1986). Accepting error to make less error. *Journal of Personality Assessment, 50,* 387–395.

Einhorn, H. J., & Hogarth, R. M. (1975). Unit weighting schemes for decision making. *Organizational Behavior and Human Performance, 13,* 171–192.

Einhorn, H. J., & Hogarth, R. M. (1981). Behavioral decision theory: Processes of judgment and choice. *Annual Review of Psychology, 32,* 53–88.

Einhorn, H. J., & Hogarth, R. M. (1986a). Decision making under ambiguity. *Journal of Business, 59,* S225–S250.

Einhorn, H. J., & Hogarth, R. M. (1986b) Judging probable cause. *Psychological Bulletin, 99,* 3–19.

Einhorn, H. J., Kleinmuntz, D. N., & Kleinmuntz, B. (1979). Linear regression and process-tracing models of judgment. *Psychological Review, 86,* 465–485.

Eisenhardt, K. M. (1989). Making fast strategic decisions in high velocity environments. *Academy of Management Journal, 32,* 543–575.

English, W. K., Englebart, D. C., & Berman, M. L. (1967). Display-selection techniques for text manipulation. *IEEE Transactions on Human Factors in Electronics, 8,* 5–15.

Ericsson, K. A., & Simon, H. A. (1984). *Protocol analysis: Verbal reports as data.* Cambridge, MA: MIT Press.

Feldman, J., & Lindell, M. K. (1990). On rationality. In I. Horowitz (Ed.), *Organization and decision theory* (pp. 83–164). Boston: Kluwer.

Fischer, G. W. (1991). Range sensitivity of attribute weights in multi-attribute utility assessment. Unpublished working paper, Fuqua School of Business, Duke University.

Fischer, G. W., & Hawkins, S. A. (1993). Strategy compatibility, scale compatibility, and the prominence effect. *Journal of Experimental Psychology: Human Perception and Performance, 19.*

Fischhoff, B. (1975). Hindsight ≠ foresight: The effect of outcome knowledge on judgment under uncertainty. *Journal of Experimental Psychology: Human Perception and Performance, 1,* 288–299.

Fischhoff, B. (1982). Debiasing. In D. Kahneman, P. Slovic, & A. Tversky (Eds.), *Judgment under uncertainty: Heuristics and biases* (pp. 422–444). Cambridge: Cambridge University Press.

Fischhoff, B. (1983). Predicting frames. *Journal of Experimental Psychology: Learning, Memory, and Cognition, 9,* 103–116.

Fischhoff, B. (1991). Value elicitation: Is there anything in there? *American Psychologist, 46,* 835–847.

Fischhoff, B., & Furby, L. (1988). Measuring values: A conceptual framework for interpreting transactions with special reference to contingent valuations of visibility. *Journal of Risk and Uncertainty, 1,* 147–184.

Fischhoff, B., Slovic P., & Lichtenstein, S. (1978). Fault trees: Sensitivity of estimated failure probabilities to problem representation. *Journal of*

Experimental Psychology: Human Perception and Performance, 4, 330–344.

Fischhoff, B., Slovic, P., & Lichtenstein, S. (1980). Knowing what you want: Measuring labile values. In T. Wallsten (Ed.), *Cognitive processes in choice and decision behavior* (pp. 117–141). Hillsdale, NJ: Erlbaum.

Fishburn, P. (1991). Nontransitive preferences in decision theory. *Journal of Risk and Uncertainty, 4,* 113–124.

Fiske, S.T. (1980). Attention and weight in person perception: The impact of negative and extreme behavior. *Journal of Personality and Social Psychology, 38,* 889–906.

Fiske, S. T. (1982). Schema-triggered affect: Applications to social perception. In M. S. Clark & S. T. Fiske (Eds.), *Affect and cognition: The 17th Annual Carnegie Symposium on Cognition* (pp. 55–78). Hillsdale, NJ: Erlbaum.

Fiske, S. T., & Pavelchak. M. A. (1986). Category-based versus piecemeal-based affective responses: Developments in schema-triggered affect. In R. M. Sorrentino & E. T. Higgins (Eds.), *The handbook of motivation and cognition: Foundations of social behavior* (pp. 167–203). New York: Guilford.

Fitts, P. M. (1954). The information capacity of the human motor system in controlling amplitude of movement. *Journal of Experimental Psychology, 47,* 381–391.

Fong, G. T., Krantz, D. H., & Nisbett, R. E. (1986). The effects of statistical training on thinking about everyday problems. *Cognitive Psychology, 18,* 253–292.

Fong, G. T., & Nisbett, R. E. (1991). Immediate and delayed transfer of training effects in statistical reasoning . *Journal of Experimental Psychology: General, 120,* 34–45.

Ford, J. K., Schmitt., N., Schechtman, S. L., Hults, B. M., & Doherty, M. L. (1989). Process tracing methods: Contributions, problems, and neglected research questions. *Organizational Behavior and Human Decision Processes, 43,* 75–117.

Ford, G. T., & Smith R. A. (1987). Inferential beliefs in consumer evaluations: An assessment of alternative processing strategies. *Journal of Consumer Research, 14,* 363–371.

Gabrielli, W. F., & von Winterfeldt, D. (1978). Are importance weights sensitive to the range of alternatives in multiattribute utility measurements? Research Paper 78-6, Social Science Research Institute, University of Southern California.

Gaeth, G. J., & Shanteau, J. (1984). Reducing the influence of irrelevant information on experienced decision makers. *Organizational Behavior and Human Performance, 33,* 263–282.

Gagne, R. M. (1984). Learning outcomes and their effects: Useful categories of human performance. *American Psychologist, 39,* 377–385.

Garner, R. (1987). *Metacognition and reading comprehension.* Norwood, NJ: Ablex.

Gettys, C. F., Pliske, R. M., Manning, C., & Casey, J. T. (1987). An evaluation of human act generation performance. *Organizational Behavior and Human Decision Processes, 39,* 23–51.

Gigerenzer, G., Hell, W., & Blank, H. (1988). Presentation and content: The use of base rates as a continuous variable. *Journal of Experimental Psychology: Human Perception and Performance, 14,* 513–525.

Ginossar, Z., & Trope, Y. (1987). Problem solving in judgment under uncertainty. *Journal of Personality and Social Psychology, 52,* 464–474.

Goldstein, W. M. (1984). *Inconsistent assessments of preferences: Effects of stimulus presentation method on the preference reversal phenomenon.* Unpublished doctoral dissertation, Department of Psychology, University of Michigan.

Goldstein, W. M. (1990). Judgments of relative importance in decision making: Global vs. local interpretations of subjective weight. *Organizational Behavior and Human Decision Processes, 47,* 313–336.

Goldstein, W. M., & Busemeyer, J. R. (1992). The effects of "irrelevant" variables on decision making: Criterion shifts in preferential choice? *Organizational Behavior and Human Decision Processes, 52,* 425–454.

Goldstein, W. M., & Einhorn, H. J. (1987). Expression theory and the preference reversal phenomena. *Psychological Review, 94,* 236–254.

Green, P. E., Helsen, K., & Shandler, B. (1988). Conjoint internal validity under alternative profile presentations. *Journal of Consumer Research, 15,* 392–397.

Green, P. E., & Srinivasan, V. (1978). Conjoint analysis in consumer research: Issues and outlook. *Journal of Consumer Research, 5,* 103–123.

Green, P. E., & Srinivasan, V. (1990). Conjoint analysis in marketing research: New developments and directions. *Journal of Marketing, 54,* 3–19.

Greeno, J. G. (1978). Natures of problem-solving abilities. In W. K. Estes (Ed.), *Handbook of learning and cognitive processes. Vol. 5, Human information processing* (pp. 239–270). Hillsdale, NJ: Erlbaum.

Gregory, R., Kunreuther, H., Easterling, D., & Richards, K. (1991). Incentive policies to site hazardous waste facilities. *Risk Analysis, 11,* 667–675.

Gregory, R., & McDaniels, T. (1987). Valuing environmental losses: What promise does the right measure hold? *Policy Sciences, 20,* 11–26.

Grether, D. M. (1992). Testing Bayes rule and the representativeness heuristic: Some experimental evidence. *Journal of Economic Behavior and Organization, 17,* 31–57.

Grether, D. M., & Plott, C. R. (1979). Economic theory of choice and the preference reversal phenomenon. *American Economic Review, 69,* 623–638.

Grether, D. M., Schwartz, A., & Wilde, L. L. (1986). The irrelevance of information overload: An analysis of search and disclosure. *Southern California Law Review, 59,* 277–303.

Grether, D. M., & Wilde, L. L. (1983). Consumer choice and information: New experimental evidence. *Information Economics and Policy, 1,* 115–144.

Grether, D. M., & Wilde, L. L. (1984). An analysis of conjunctive choice. *Journal of Consumer Research, 10,* 373–385.

Griffin, D., & Tversky, A. (1991). The weighing of evidence and the determinants of confidence. Unpublished manuscript, Stanford University.

Groen, G. J., & Parkman, J. M. (1972). A chronometric analysis of simple addition. *Psychological Review, 79,* 329–343.

Guadagni, P. M., & Little, J. D. C. (1983). A logit model of brand choice based on scanner data. *Marketing Science, 2,* 203–238.

Hammond, K. R. (1986). A theoretically based review of theory and research in judgment and decision making. Report 260, Center for Research on Judgment and Policy, Institute of Cognitive Science, University of Colorado.

Hammond, K. R. (1990). Functionalism and illusionism: Can integration be usefully achieved? In R. M. Hogarth (Ed.), *Insights in decision making: A tribute to Hillel J. Einhorn* (pp. 227–261). Chicago: University of Chicago Press.

Hammond K. R., Hamm, R. M., Grassia, J., & Pearson, T. (1987). Direct comparison of the efficacy of intuitive and analytical cognition in expert judgment. *IEEE Transactions on Systems, Man, and Cybernetics, 17,* 753–770.

Hammond, K. R., Stewart, T. R., Brehmer B., & Steinmann, D. O. (1975). Social judgment theory. In M. F. Kaplan & S. Schwartz (Eds.), *Human judgment and decision processes* (pp. 271–312). New York: Academic Press.

Harrison, G. (1989). Theory and misbehavior of first price auctions. *American Economic Review, 79,* 749–762.

Hauser, J. R. (1986). Agendas and consumer choice. *Journal of Marketing Research, 23,* 199–212.

Hauser, J. R., & Gaskin, S. P. (1984). Application of the "Defender" consumer model. *Marketing Science, 3,* 327–351.

Hauser, J. R., & Wernerfelt, B. (1990). An evaluation cost model of consideration sets. *Journal of Consumer Research, 16,* 393–408.

Hawkins, S. A., & Hastie, R. (1990). Hindsight: Biased judgements of past events after the outcomes are known. *Psychological Bulletin, 107*, 311–327.

Hayes-Roth, B., & Hayes-Roth, F. (1979). A cognitive model of planning. *Cognitive Science, 3*, 275–310.

Hegarty, M., Just, M. A., & Morrison, I. R. (1988). Mental models of mechanical systems: Individual differences in qualitative and quantitative reasoning. *Cognitive Psychology, 20*, 191–236.

Hendrick, C., Mills, J., & Kiesler, C.A. (1968). Decision time as a function of the number and complexity of equally attractive alternatives. *Journal of Personality and Social Psychology, 8*, 313–318.

Henrion, M., Fischer, G. W., & Mullin, T. (in press). Divide and conquer? Effects of decomposition on the accuracy and calibration of subjective probability distributions. *Organizational Behavior and Human Decision Processes*.

Hershey, J. C., & Schoemaker, P. J. H. (1980). Prospect theory's reflection hypothesis: A critical examination. *Organizational Behavior and Human Performance, 25*, 395–418.

Hershey, J. C., & Schoemaker, P. J. H. (1985). Probability versus certainty equivalence methods in utility measurment: Are they equivalent? *Management Science, 31*, 1213–1231.

Hirt, E. R., & Castellan, N. J. (1988). Probability and category redefinition in the fault tree paradigm. *Journal of Experimental Psychology: Human Perception and Performance, 14*, 122–131.

Hjorth-Andersen, C. (1984). The concept of quality and the efficiency of markets for consumer products. *Journal of Consumer Research, 11*, 708–718.

Hjorth-Andersen, C. (1986). More on multidimensional quality: A reply. *Journal of Consumer Research, 13*, 149–154.

Hockey, G., Gaillard, A., & Coles, M. (Eds.) (1986). *Energetics and human information processing*. Dordrecht, the Netherlands: Martinus Nijhoff.

Hogarth, R. M. (1981). Beyond discrete biases: Functional and dysfunctional aspects of judgmental heuristics. *Psychological Bulletin, 90*, 197–217.

Hogarth, R. M. (1987). *Judgment and choice* (2nd ed.). New York: Wiley.

Hogarth, R. M., & Einhorn, H. J. (1992). Order effects in belief updating: The belief-adjustment model. *Cognitive Psychology, 24*, 1–55.

Hogarth, R. M., Gibbs, B. J., McKenzie, C. R. M., & Marquis, M. A. (1991). Learning from feedback: Exactingness and incentives. *Journal of Experimental Psychology: Learning, Memory, and Cognition, 17*, 734–752.

Holland, J. H., Holyoak, K. J., Nisbett, R. E., & Thagard, P. R. (1986). *Induction: Processes of inference, learning, and memory*. Cambridge, MA: MIT Press.

Huber, G. P. (1983). Cognitive style as a basis for MIS and DSS design: Much ado about nothing. *Management Science, 29*, 567–579.

Huber, J. (1983). The effect of set composition on item choice: Separating attraction, edge aversion, and substitution effects. In R. P. Bagozzi & A. M. Tybout (Eds.), *Advances in consumer research* (Vol. 10, pp. 298–304). Ann Arbor: Association for Consumer Research.

Huber, J., & Klein, N. M. (1991). Adapting cutoffs to the choice environment: The effects of attribute correlation and reliability. *Journal of Consumer Research, 18,* 346-357.

Huber, J., Payne, J. W., & Puto, C. P. (1982). Adding asymmetrically dominated alternatives: Violations of regularity and the similarity hypothesis. *Journal of Consumer Research, 9,* 90–98.

Huber, J., & Puto, C. P. (1983). Market boundaries and product choice: Illustrating attraction and substitution effects. *Journal of Consumer Research, 10,* 31–44.

Huber, O. (1980). The influence of some task variables on cognitive operations in an information-processing decision model. *Acta Psychologica, 45,* 187–196.

Huber, O. (1989). Information-processing operators in decision making. In H. Montgomery & O. Svenson (Eds.), *Process and structure in human decision making* (pp. 3–21). Chichester: Wiley.

Huber, V. L., Neale, M. A., & Northcraft, G. B. (1987). Decision bias and personnel selection strategies. *Organizational Behavior and Human Decision Processes, 40,* 136–147.

IMSL (1987). *User's manual, STAT/LIBRARY™: Fortran subroutines for statistical analysis.* Houston, TX: IMSL, Inc.

Irwin, J. R., Slovic, P., Lichtenstein, S., & McClelland, G. H. (1993). Preference reversals and the measurement of environmental values. *Journal of Risk and Uncertainty, 6.*

Jacoby, J., Chestnut, R. W., Weigl, K. C., & Fisher, W. (1976). Pre-purchase information acquisition: Description of a process methodology, research paradigm, and pilot investigation. In B. B. Anderson (Ed.), *Advances in consumer research* (Vol. 3, pp. 306–314). Chicago, IL: Association for Consumer Research.

Jacoby, J., Mazursky, D., Troutman, T., & Kuss, A. (1984). When feedback is ignored: Disutility of outcome feedback. *Journal of Applied Psychology, 69,* 531–545.

Jacoby, J., Speller, D. E., & Kohn, C. A. (1974). Brand choice behavior as a function of information load. *Journal of Marketing Research, 11,* 63–69.

Jagacinski, C. M. (1991). Personnel decision making: The impact of missing information. *Journal of Applied Psychology, 76,* 19–30.

Janis, I. L. (1982). Decision making under stress. In L. Goldberger & S. Breznitz (Eds.), *Handbook of stress: Theoretical and clinical aspects* (pp. 69–87). New York: Free Press.

Janis, I. L. (1989). *Crucial decisions.* New York: Free Press.

Janis, I. L., Defares, P. B., & Grossman, P. (1983). Hypervigilant reactions to threat. In H. Selye (Ed.), *Selye's guide to stress research* (Vol. 3, pp. 1–42). New York: Van Nostrand Reinhold.

Janis, I. L., & Mann, L. (1977). *Decision making.* New York: Free Press.

Jarvenpaa, S. L. (1989). The effect of task demands and graphical format on information processing strategies. *Management Science, 35,* 285–303.

Jarvenpaa, S. L. (1990). Graphic displays in decision making: The visual salience effect. *Journal of Behavioral Decision Making, 3,* 247–262.

John, D. R., & Cole, C. A. (1986). Age differences in information processing: Understanding deficits in young and elderly consumers. *Journal of Consumer Research, 13,* 297–315.

Johnson, E. J. (1979). Deciding how to decide: The effort of making a decision. Unpublished manuscript, University of Chicago.

Johnson, E. J. (1988). Expertise and decision under uncertainty: Process and performance. In M. Chi, R. Glaser, & M. Farr (Eds.), *The nature of expertise* (pp. 209–228). Hillsdale, NJ: Erlbaum.

Johnson, E. J., Camerer, C. F., Sen, S., & Rymon, T. (1991). Behavior and cognition in sequential bargaining. Unpublished working paper, Wharton School, University of Pennsylvania.

Johnson, E. J., & Meyer, R. J. (1984). Compensatory choice models of noncompensatory processes: The effect of varying context. *Journal of Consumer Research, 11,* 528–541.

Johnson, E. J., Meyer, R. J., & Ghose, S. (1989). When choice models fail: Compensatory representations in negatively correlated environments. *Journal of Marketing Research, 26,* 255–270.

Johnson, E. J., & Payne, J. W. (1985). Effort and accuracy in choice. *Management Science, 31,* 394–414.

Johnson, E. J., Payne, J. W., & Bettman, J. R. (1988). Information displays and preference reversals. *Organizational Behavior and Human Decision Process, 42,* 1–21.

Johnson, E. J., Payne, J. W., & Bettman, J. R. (1990). Heuristic processes in judgment. Unpublished working paper, Wharton School, University of Pennsylvania.

Johnson, E. J., Payne, J. W., Schkade, D. A., & Bettman, J. R. (1991). Monitoring information processing and decisions: The Mouselab system. Unpublished manuscript, Center for Decision Studies, Fuqua School of Business, Duke University.

Johnson, E. J., & Russo, J. E. (1981). Product familiarity and learning new information. In K. Monroe (Ed.), *Advances in consumer research* (Vol. 8, pp. 151–155). Ann Arbor, MI: Association for Consumer Research.

Johnson, E. J., & Russo, J. E. (1984). Product familiarity and learning new information. *Journal of Consumer Research, 11,* 542–550.

Johnson, E. J., & Schkade, D. A. (1989). Bias in utility assessments: Further evidence and explanations. *Management Science, 35,* 406–424.

Johnson, M. D. (1984). Consumer choice strategies for comparing non-comparable alternatives. *Journal of Consumer Research, 11,* 741–753.

Johnson, M. D. (1986). Modeling choice strategies for noncomparable alternatives. *Marketing Sciences, 5,* 37–54.

Johnson, M. D. (1988). Comparability and hierarchical processing in multi-alternative choice. *Journal of Consumer Research, 15,* 303–314.

Johnson, R. D., & Levin, I. P. (1985). More than meets the eye: The effect of missing information on purchase evaluations. *Journal of Consumer Research, 12,* 169–177.

Just, M. A., & Carpenter, P. A. (1984). Using eye fixations to study reading comprehension. In D. E. Kieras & M. A. Just (Eds.), *New methods in reading comprehension research* (pp. 151–182). Hillsdale, NJ: Erlbaum.

Kahn, B., Moore, W. L., & Glazer, R. (1987). Experiments in constrained choice. *Journal of Consumer Research, 14,* 96–113.

Kahneman, D. (1973). *Attention and effort.* Englewood Cliffs, NJ: Prentice-Hall.

Kahneman, D., & Knetsch, J. L. (1992). Valuing public goods: The purchase of moral satisfaction. *Journal of Economics and Environmental Management, 22,* 57–70.

Kahneman, D., & Lovallo, D. (1992). Timid choices and bold forecasts: A cognitive perspective on risk taking. *Management Science, 38.*

Kahneman, D., Slovic, P., & Tversky, A. (Eds.) (1982). *Judgment under uncertainty: Heuristics and biases.* Cambridge: Cambridge University Press.

Kahneman, D., & Snell, J. (1990). Predicting utility. In R. M. Hogarth (Ed.), *Insights in decision making: A tribute to Hillel J. Einhorn* (pp. 295–310). Chicago: University of Chicago Press.

Kahneman, D., & Tversky, A. (1972). Subjective probability: A judgment of representativeness. *Cognitive Psychology, 3,* 430–454.

Kahneman, D., & Tversky, A. (1973). On the psychology of prediction. *Psychological Review, 80,* 237–251.

Kahneman, D., & Tversky, A. (1979a). Intuitive prediction: Biases and corrective procedures. In S. Makridakis & S. C. Wheelwright (Eds.), Forecasting. *TIMS Studies in Management Science, 12,* 313–327.

Kahneman, D., & Tversky, A. (1979b). Prospect theory: An analysis of decision making under risk. *Econometrica, 47,* 263–291.

Kahneman, D., & Tversky, A. (1982). Variants of uncertainty. In D. Kahneman, P. Slovic, & A. Tversky (Eds.), *Judgment under uncertainty: Heuristics and biases.* Cambridge: Cambridge University Press.

Kaplan, C. A., & Simon, H. A. (1990). In search of insight. *Cognitive Psychology, 22,* 374–419.

Keen, P. G. W., & Scott-Morton, M. S. (1978). *Decision support systems: An organizational perspective.* Reading, MA: Addison-Wesley.

Keeney, R. L. (1988). Structuring objectives for problems of public interest. *Operations Research, 36,* 396–405.

Keeney, R. L. (1992). *Value-focused thinking: A path to creative decision-making.* Cambridge, MA: Harvard University Press.

Keeney, R. L., & Raiffa, H. (1976). *Decisions with multiple objectives: Preferences and value tradeoffs.* New York: Wiley.

Keeney, R. L., von Winterfeldt, D., & Eppel, T. (1990). Eliciting public values for complex policy decisions. *Management Science, 36,* 1011–1030.

Keinan, G. (1987). Decision making under stress: Scanning of alternatives under controllable and uncontrollable threats. *Journal of Personality and Social Psychology, 52,* 639–644.

Keller, K. L., & Staelin, R. (1987). Effects of quality and quantity of information on decision effectiveness. *Journal of Consumer Research, 14,* 200–213.

Keller, L. R., & Ho, J. L. (1988). Decision problem structuring: Generating options. *IEEE Transactions on Systems, Man, and Cybernetics, 18,* 715–728.

Keren, G. (1991). Additional tests of utility theory under unique and repeated conditions. *Journal of Behavioral Decision Making, 4,* 297–304.

Klayman, J. (1983). Analysis of predecisional information search patterns. In P. C. Humphreys, O. Svenson, & A. Vari (Eds.), *Analyzing and aiding decision processes* (pp. 401–414). Amsterdam: North Holland.

Klayman, J. (1985). Children's decision strategies and their adaptation to task characteristics. *Organizational Behavior and Human Decision Processes, 35,* 179–201.

Klayman, J., & Ha, Y. (1987). Confirmation, disconfirmation, and information in hypothesis testing. *Psychological Review, 94,* 211–228.

Klein, N. M. (1983). Utility and decision strategies: A second look at the rational decision maker. *Organizational Behavior and Human Performance, 31,* 1–25.

Klein, N. M., & Bither, S. (1987). An investigation of utility-directed cutoff selection. *Journal of Consumer Research, 14,* 240–256.

Klein, N. M., & Yadav, M. S. (1989). Context effects on effort and accuracy in choice: An inquiry into adaptive decision making. *Journal of Consumer Research, 15,* 411–421.

Kleinmuntz, B. (1990). Why we still use our heads instead of formulas: Toward an integrative approach. *Psychological Bulletin, 107,* 296–310.

Kleinmuntz, D. N. (1987). Human decision processes: Heuristics and task structure. In P. A. Hancock (Ed.), *Human factors psychology* (pp. 123–157). New York: Elsevier.

Kleinmuntz, D. N. (1990). Decomposition and the control of error in decision-analytic models. In R. M. Hogarth (Ed.), *Insights in decision making: A tribute to Hillel J. Einhorn* (pp. 107–126). Chicago: University of Chicago Press.

Kleinmuntz, D. N., & Schkade, D. A. (1990). Cognitive processes and information displays in computer-supported decision making: Implications for research. Unpublished working paper, Sloan School of Management, MIT.

Knetsch, J. L., & Sinden, J. A. (1984). Willingness to pay and compensation demanded: Experimental evidence of an unexpected disparity in measures of value. *Quarterly Journal of Economics, 99,* 507–521.

Kotovsky, K., Hayes, J. R., & Simon, H. A. (1985). Why are some problems hard? Evidence from Tower of Hanoi. *Cognitive Psychology, 17,* 248–294.

Kottemann, J. E., & Davis, F. D. (1991). Decisional conflict and user acceptance of multicriteria decisionmaking aids. *Decision Sciences, 22,* 918–926.

Kramer, R. M. (1989). Windows of vulnerability or cognitive illusions? Cognitive processes and the nuclear arms race. *Journal of Experimental Social Psychology, 25,* 79–100.

Krieger, A. M., & Green, P. E. (1988). On the generation of Pareto optimal, conjoint profiles from orthogonal main effects plans. Unpublished working paper, Wharton School, University of Pennsylvania.

Kruglanski, A. W. (1989). The psychology of being "right": The problem of accuracy in social perception and cognition. *Psychological Bulletin, 106,* 395–409.

Langley, P., Simon, H. A., Bradshaw, G. L., & Zytkow, J. M. (1987). *Scientific discovery.* Cambridge, MA: MIT Press.

La Rochefoucauld, Duc de. (1678). *Reflections: or sentences and moral maxims.*

Larrick, R. P., Morgan, J. N., & Nisbett, R. E. (1990). Teaching the use of cost–benefit reasoning in everyday life. *Psychological Science, 1,* 362–370.

Latané, B., Williams, K., & Harkins, S. (1979). Many hands make light the work: The causes and consequences of social loafing. *Journal of Personality and Social Psychology, 37,* 822–832.

Levin, I. P., & Gaeth, G. J. (1988). How consumers are affected by the framing of attribute information before and after consuming the product. *Journal of Consumer Research, 15,* 374–378.

Lewicki, P. (1986). Processing information about covariations that cannot be articulated. *Journal of Experimental Psychology: Learning, Memory, and Cognition, 12,* 133–146.

Libby, R., & Libby, P. A. (1989). Expert measurement and mechanical combination in control reliance decisions. *Accounting Review, 64,* 729–747.

Lichtenstein, S., Fischhoff, B., & Phillips, L. D. (1982). Calibration of probabilities: The state of the art to 1980. In D. Kahneman, P. Slovic, & A. Tversky (Eds.), *Judgment under uncertainty: Heuristics and biases* (pp. 306–334). Cambridge: Cambridge University Press.

Lichtenstein, S., Gregory, R., Slovic, P., & Wagenaar, W. A. (1990). When lives are in your hands: Dilemmas of the societal decision maker. In R. M. Hogarth (Ed.), *Insights in decision making: A tribute to Hillel J. Einhorn* (pp. 91–106). Chicago: University of Chicago Press.

Lichtenstein, S., & Slovic, P. (1971). Reversals of preference between bids and choices in gambling decisions. *Journal of Experimental Psychology, 89,* 46–55.

Lichtenstein, S., & Slovic, P. (1973). Response-induced reversals of preference in gambling: An extended replication in Las Vegas. *Journal of Experimental Psychology, 101,* 16–20.

Lindberg, E., Garling, T., & Montgomery, H. (1989). Differential predictability of preferences and choices. *Journal of Behavioral Decision Making, 2,* 205–219.

Lindman, H. R. (1971). Inconsistent preferences among gambles. *Journal of Experimental Psychology, 89,* 390–397.

Lipman, B. L. (1991). How to decide how to decide how to...Modeling limited rationality. *Econometrica, 59,* 1105–1125.

Loomes, G. (1991). Evidence of a new violation of the independence axiom. *Journal of Risk and Uncertainty, 4,* 91–108.

Lopes, L. L. (1982). Toward a procedural theory of judgment. Unpublished manuscript, University of Wisconsin.

Lopes, L. L. (1984). Risk and distributional inequality. *Journal of Experimental Psychology: Human Perception and Performance, 10,* 465–485.

Luce, R. D. (1959). *Individual choice behavior.* New York: Wiley.

Luce, R. D. (1977). The choice axiom after twenty years. *Journal of Mathematical Psychology, 15,* 215–233.

Lynch, J. G., Marmorstein, H., & Weigold, M. F. (1988). Choices from sets including remembered brands: Use of recalled attributes and prior overall evaluations. *Journal of Consumer Research, 15,* 169–184.

Lynch, J. G., & Srull, T. K. (1982). Memory and attentional factors in consumer choice: Concepts and research methods. *Journal of Consumer Research, 9,* 18–37.

McAllister, D., Mitchell, T. R., & Beach, L. R. (1979). The contingency model for selection of decision strategies: An empirical test of the effects of significance, accountability, and reversability. *Organizational Behavior and Human Performance, 24,* 228–244.

McClelland, G. H. (1978). Equal versus differential weighting for multiattribute decisions. Unpublished working paper, University of Colorado.

McConkie, G. W., & Rayner, K. (1976). Asymmetry of the perceptual span in reading. *Bulletin of the Psychonomic Society, 8,* 365–368.

McCord, M. R., & De Neufville, R. (1986). "Lottery equivalents": Reduction of the certainty effect problem in utility assessment. *Management Science, 32,* 56–60.

MacGregor, D. G., & Slovic, P. (1986). Graphical representation of judgmental information. *Human–Computer Interaction, 2,* 179–200.

MacGregor, D. G., & Lichtenstein, S. (1991). Problem structuring aids for quantitative estimation. *Journal of Behavioral Decision Making, 4,* 101–116.

McNeil, B. J., Pauker, S. G., Sox, H. C., & Tversky, A. (1982). On the elicitation of preferences for alternative therapies. *New England Journal of Medicine, 21,* 1259–1262.

Magat, W. A., Payne, J. W., & Brucato, P. F. (1986). How important is information format? An experimental study of home energy audit programs. *Journal of Policy Analysis and Management, 6,* 20–34.

Malhotra, N. K. (1982). Information load and consumer decision making. *Journal of Consumer Research, 8,* 419–430.

March, J. G. (1978). Bounded rationality, ambiguity, and the engineering of choice. *Bell Journal of Economics, 9,* 587–608.

Marschak, J. (1968). Decision making: Economic aspects. In D. L. Stills (Ed.), *International encyclopedia of the social sciences* (Vol. 4, pp. 42–55). New York: Macmillan.

Marx, M. H., & Hillix, W. A. (1963). *Systems and theories in psychology.* New York: McGraw-Hill.

Maule, A. J. (1989). Positive and negative decision frames: A verbal protocol analysis of the Asian disease problem of Tversky and Kahneman. In H. Montgomery & O. Svenson (Eds.), *Process and structure in human decision making* (pp. 163–180). Chichester: Wiley.

Mellers, B. A., Chang, S., Birnbaum, M. H., & Ordóñez, L. D. (1992). Preferences, prices, and ratings in risky decision making. *Journal of Experimental Psychology: Human Perception and Performance, 18,* 347–361.

Mellers, B. A., Ordóñez, L. D., & Birnbaum, M. H. (1992). A change of process theory for contextual effects and preference reversals in risky decision making. *Organizational Behavior and Human Decision Processes, 52,* 331–369.

Meyer, R. J. (1981). A model of multiattribute judgments under attribute uncertainty and information constraint. *Journal of Marketing Research, 18,* 428–441.

Meyer, R. J., & Eagle, T. C. (1982). Context-induced parameter instability in a disagregate-stochastic model of store choice. *Journal of Consumer Research, 19,* 62–71.

Meyer, R. J., & Johnson, E. J. (1989). Information overload and the non-robustness of linear models: A comment on Keller and Staelin. *Journal of Consumer Research, 15,* 498–503.

Milgrom, P., & Roberts, J. (1991). Adaptive and sophisticated learning in normal form games, *Games and Economic Behavior, 3,* 82–100.

Miller, J. G. (1960). Information input overload and psychopathology. *American Journal of Psychiatry, 116,* 695–704.

Mitchell, R. C., & Carson, R. T. (1989). *Using surveys to value public goods: The contingent valuation method.* Washington, DC: Resources for the Future.

Mitchell, T. R., & Beach, L. R. (1990). "... Do I love thee? Let me count...". Toward an understanding of intuitive and automatic decision making. *Organizational Behavior and Human Decision Processes, 47,* 1–20.

Montgomery, H. (1983). Decision rules and the search for a dominance structure: Towards a process model of decision making. In P. C. Humphreys, O. Svenson, & A. Vari (Eds.), *Analyzing and aiding decision processes* (pp. 343–369). North Holland: Amsterdam.

Montgomery, H., & Svenson, O. (1983). A think-aloud study of dominance structuring in decision processes. In R. Tietz (Ed.), *Aspiration levels in bargaining and economic decision making* (pp. 366–383). Berlin: Springer-Verlag.

Mowen, J. C., & Gentry, J. W. (1980). Investigation of the preference-reversal phenomenon in a new product introduction task. *Journal of Applied Psychology, 65,* 715–722.

Mross, E. F., & Hammond, K. R. (1989). Annotated bibliography for cognition and stress. Report No. 295, Center for Research on Judgment and Policy, Institute of Cognitive Science, University of Colorado.

Muller, T. C. (1984). Buyer response to variations in product information load. *Journal of Applied Psychology, 69,* 300–306.

Murphy, A. H., & Winkler, R. L. (1977). Reliability of subjective probability forecasts of precipitation and temperature. *Journal of the Royal Statistical Society,* C (Applied Statistics), *26,* 41–47.

Navon, D., & Gopher, D. (1979). On the economy of the human processing system. *Psychological Review, 86,* 214–255.

Newell, A. (1980). Harpy, production systems, and human cognition. In R. Cole (Ed.), *Perception and production of fluent speech* (pp. 299–380). Hillsdale, NJ: Erlbaum.

Newell, A., & Simon, H. A. (1972). *Human problem solving.* Englewood Cliffs, NJ: Prentice-Hall.

Newman, J. R. (1977). Differential weighting in multiattribute utility measurement: Where it should and where it does make a difference. *Organizational Behavior and Human Performance, 20,* 312–325.

Nisbett, R. E., Krantz, D. H., Jepson, C., & Kunda, Z. (1983). The use of statistical heuristics in everyday inductive reasoning. *Psychological Review, 90,* 339–363.

Nisbett, R. E., & Wilson, T. D. (1977). Telling more than we can know: Verbal reports on mental processes. *Psychology Review, 84,* 231–259.

Nisbett, R. E., Zukier, H., & Lemley, R. E. (1981). The dilution effect: Nondiagnostic information weakens the implications of diagnostic information. *Cognitive Psychology, 13,* 248–277.

Norman, D. A. (1988). *The psychology of everyday things.* New York: Basic Books.

Olshavsky, R. W. (1979). Task complexity and contingent processing in decision making: A replication and extension. *Organizational Behavior and Human Performance, 24,* 300–316.

Onken, J., Hastie, R., & Revelle, W. (1985). Individual differences in the use of simplification strategies in a complex decision-making task. *Journal of Experimental Psychology: Human Perception and Performance, 11,* 14–27.

Paese, P. W., & Sniezek, J. A. (1991). Influences on the appropriateness of confidence in judgment: Practice, effort, information, and decision-making. *Organizational Behavior and Human Decision Processes, 48,* 100–130.

Payne, J. W. (1975). Relation of perceived risk to preferences among gambles. *Journal of Experimental Psychology: Human Perception and Performance, 104,* 86–94.

Payne, J. W. (1976). Task complexity and contingent processing in decision making: An information search and protocol analysis. *Organizational Behavior and Human Performance, 16,* 366–387.

Payne, J. W. (1980). Information processing theory: Some concepts applied to decision research. In T. S. Wallsten (Ed.), *Cognitive processes in choice and decision behavior* (pp. 95–115). Hillsdale, NJ: Erlbaum.

Payne, J. W. (1982). Contingent decision behavior. *Psychological Bulletin, 92,* 382–402.

Payne, J. W., Bettman, J. R., & Johnson, E. J. (1988). Adaptive strategy selection in decision making. *Journal of Experimental Psychology: Learning, Memory, and Cognition, 14,* 534–552.

Payne, J. W., Bettman, J. R., & Simonson, I. (in progress). Attraction effects in risky choice.

Payne, J. W., & Braunstein, M. L. (1971). Preferences among gambles with equal underlying distributions. *Journal of Experimental Psychology, 87,* 13–18.

Payne, J. W., & Braunstein, M. L. (1978). Risky choice: An examination of information acquisition behavior. *Memory & Cognition, 6,* 554–561.

Payne, J. W., Braunstein, M. L., & Carroll, J. S. (1978). Exploring predecisional behavior: An alternative approach to decision research. *Organizational Behavior and Human Performance, 22,* 17–44.

Payne, J. W., Johnson, E. J., Bettman, J. R., & Coupey, E. (1990). Understanding contingent choice: A computer simulation approach. *IEEE Transactions on Systems, Man, and Cybernetics, 20,* 296–309.

Payne, J. W., Laughhunn, D. J., & Crum, R. (1980). Translation of gambles and aspiration level effects in risky choice behavior. *Management Science, 26,* 1039–1060.

Payne, J. W., Laughhunn, D. J., & Crum, R. (1981). Further tests of aspiration level effects in risky choice behavior. *Management Science, 27,* 953–958.

Payne, J. W., Laughhunn, D. J., & Crum, R. (1984). Multiattribute risky choice behavior: The editing of complex prospects. *Management Science, 30,* 1350–1361.

Peters, T. J. (1987). *Thriving on chaos.* New York: Alfred A. Knopf.

Peterson, D. K., & Pitz, G. F. (1986). Explicit cue weighting in a prediction task. *Organizational Behavior and Human Decision Processes, 39,* 84–97.

Petty, R. E., & Cacioppo, J. T. (1986). The elaboration likelihood model of persuasion. In L. Berkowitz (Ed.), *Advances in Experimental Social Psychology* (Vol. 19, pp. 123–205). New York: Academic Press.

Phelps, R. H., & Shanteau, J. (1978). Livestock judges: How much information can an expert use? *Organizational Behavior and Human Performance, 21,* 209–219.

Pitz, G. F., Sachs, N., & Heerboth, J. (1980). Procedures for eliciting choices in the analysis of individual decisions. *Organizational Behavior and Human Performance, 26,* 396–408.

Plott, C. R., & Levine, M. E. (1978). A model of agenda influences on committee decisions. *American Economic Review, 68,* 146–160.

Politser, P. E. (1989). Cognitive guidelines for simplifying medical information: Data framing and perception. *Journal of Behavioral Decision Making, 2,* 149–166.

Polister, P. E. (1991). Do medical decision analyses' largest gains grow from the smallest trees? *Journal of Behavioral Decision Making, 4,* 121–138.

Puto, C. P. (1987). The framing of buying decisions. *Journal of Consumer Research, 14,* 301–315.

Ranyard, R. H. (1976). Elimination by aspects as a decision rule for risky choice. *Acta Psychologica, 40,* 299–310.

Rasmussen, J. (1988). A cognitive engineering approach to the modeling of decision making and its organization in process control, emergency management, CAD/CAM, office systems, and library systems. In W. B. Rouse (Ed.), *Advances in Man–Machine Systems Research, 4,* 165–243.

Ratneshwar, S., Shocker, A. D., & Stewart, D. W. (1987). Toward understanding the attraction effect: The implications of product stimulus meaningfulness and familiarity. *Journal of Consumer Research, 13,* 520–533.

Ravinder, H. V., & Kleinmuntz, D. N. (1991). Random error in additive decompositions of multiattribute utility. *Journal of Behavioral Decision Making, 4,* 83–97.

Rayner, K. (1975). The perceptual span and peripheral cues in reading. *Cognitive Psychology, 7,* 65–81.

Reber, A. S. (1989). Implicit learning and tacit knowledge. *Journal of Experimental Psychology: General, 118,* 219–235.

Reder, L. M. (1987). Strategy selection in question answering. *Cognitive Psychology, 19,* 90–138.

Restle, F. (1961). *Psychology of judgment and choice: A theoretical essay.* New York: Wiley.

Roedder, D. L. (1981). Age differences in children's responses to television advertising: An information-processing approach. *Journal of Consumer Research, 8,* 144–153.

Rothstein, H. G. (1986). The effects of time pressure on judgment in multiple cue probability learning. *Organizational Behavior and Human Decision Processes, 37,* 83–92.

Rumelhart, D. L., & Greeno, J. G. (1971). Similarity between stimuli: An experimental test of the Luce and Restle choice models. *Journal of Mathematical Psychology, 8,* 370–381.

Russo, J. E. (1977). The value of unit price information. *Journal of Marketing Research, 14,* 193–201.

Russo, J. E. (1978). Eye fixations can save the world: Critical evaluation and comparison between eye fixations and other information processing methodologies. In H. K. Hunt (Ed.), *Advances in consumer research* (Vol. 5, pp. 561–570). Ann Arbor, MI: Association for Consumer Research.

Russo, J. E., & Dosher, B. A. (1983). Strategies for multiattribute binary choice. *Journal of Experimental Psychology: Learning, Memory, and Cognition, 9,* 676–696.

Russo, J. E., Johnson, E. J., & Stephens, D. M. (1989). The validity of verbal protocols. *Memory and Cognition, 17,* 759–769.

Russo, J. E., & Leclerc, F. (1991). Characteristics of successful product information programs. *Journal of Social Issues, 47,* 73–92.

Russo, J. E., & Rosen, L. D. (1975). An eye fixation analysis of multialternative choice. *Memory and Cognition, 3,* 267–276.

Russo, J. E., Staelin, R., Nolan, C. A., Russell, G. J., & Metcalf, B. L. (1986). Nutrition information in the supermarket. *Journal of Consumer Research, 13,* 48–70.

Samuelson, W., & Zeckhauser, R. (1988). Status quo bias in decision making. *Journal of Risk and Uncertainty, 1,* 7–59.

Schkade, D. A., & Johnson, E. J. (1989). Cognitive processes in preference reversals. *Organizational Behavior and Human Decision Processes, 44,* 203–231.

Schkade, D. A., & Kleinmuntz, D. N. (in press). Information displays and choice processes: Differential effects of organization, form, and sequence. *Organizational Behavior and Human Decision Processes.*

Schkade, D. A., & Payne, J. W. (1992). Where do the numbers come from? How people respond to contingent valuation questions. Unpublished working paper, University of Texas.

Schneider, D. (1991). Social cognition. *Annual Review of Psychology, 42,* 527–561.

Schneider, S. L., & Lopes, L. L. (1986). Reflection in preferences under risk: Who and when may suggest why. *Journal of Experimental Psychology: Human Perception and Performance, 12,* 535–548.

Schulze, W. D., & McClelland, G. H. (1990, November). The robustness of values from contingent valuation surveys. Paper presented at meetings of the Society for Judgment and Decision Making, New Orleans.

Shanteau, J. (1988). Psychological characteristics and strategies of expert decision makers. *Acta Psychologica, 68,* 203–215.

Shepard, R. N. (1964). On subjectively optimum selection among multi-attribute alternatives. In M. W. Shelley & G. L. Bryan (Eds.), *Human judgments and optimality* (pp. 257–281). New York: Wiley.

Shields, M. D. (1980). Some effects of information load on search patterns used to analyze performance reports. *Accounting, Organizations and Society, 5,* 429–442.

Shields, M. D. (1983). Effects of information supply and demand on judgment accuracy: Evidence from corporate managers. *Accounting Review, 58,* 284–303.

Shugan, S. M. (1980). The cost of thinking. *Journal of Consumer Research, 7,* 99–111.

Shugan, S. M. (1987). Estimating brand positioning maps using supermarket scanning data. *Journal of Marketing Research, 24,* 1–18.

Siegler, R. S. (1983). How knowledge influences learning. *American Scientist, 71,* 631–638.

Siegler, R. S. (1988). Strategy choice procedures and the development of multiplication skill. *Journal of Experimental Psychology: General, 117,* 258–275.

Siegler, R. S., & Crowley, K. (1991). The microgenetic method: A direct means for studying cognitive development. *American Psychologist, 46,* 606–620.

Siegler, R. S., & Jenkins, E. (1989). *How children discover new strategies.* Hillsdale, NJ: Erlbaum.

Silk, A. J., & Urban, G. L. (1978). Pre-test-market evaluation of new packaged goods: A model and measurement methodology. *Journal of Marketing Research, 15,* 171–191.

Simon, H. A. (1955). A behavioral model of rational choice. *Quarterly Journal of Economics, 69,* 99–118.

Simon, H. A. (1956). Rational choice and the structure of the environment. *Psychological Review, 63,* 129–138.

Simon, H. A. (1967). Motivational and emotional controls of cognition. *Psychological Review, 74,* 29–39.

Simon, H. A. (1978). Rationality as process and as product of thought. *American Economic Review, 68,* 1–16.

Simon, H. A. (1981a). *The sciences of the artificial* (2nd ed.). Cambridge, MA: MIT Press.

Simon, H. A. (1981b). Studying human intelligence by creating artificial intelligence. *American Scientist, 69,* 300–309.

Simon, H. A. (1990). Invariants of human behavior. *Annual Review of Psychology, 41,* 1–19.

Simon, H. A., & Hayes, J. R. (1976). The understanding process: Problem isomorphs. *Cognitive Psychology, 8,* 165–190.

Simonson, I. (1989). Choice based on reasons: The case of attraction and compromise effects. *Journal of Consumer Research, 16,* 158–174.

Simonson, I., & Tversky, A. (1992). Choice in context: Tradeoff contrast and extremeness aversion. *Journal of Marketing Research, 29,* 281–295.

Slovic, P. (1967). Influence of response mode upon the relative importance of probabilities and payoffs in risk taking. In *Proceedings of the 75th Annual Convention, American Psychological Association, 2,* 33–34.

Slovic, P. (1972). From Shakespeare to Simon: Speculation – and some evidence – about man's ability to process information. *Oregon Research Institute Bulletin, 12* (3).

Slovic, P., Fischhoff, B., & Lichtenstein, S. (1982). Response mode, framing, theory. *Annual Review of Psychology, 28,* 1–39.

Slovic, P., Fischhoff, B., & Lichtenstein, S. (1981). Informing the public about the risks from ionizing radiation. *Health Physics, 41,* 589–598.

Slovic, P., Fischhoff, B., & Lichtenstein, S. (1982). Response mode, framing, and information processing effects in risk assessment. In R. Hogarth (Ed.), *New directions for methodology of social and behavioral science: The framing of questions and the consistency of response* (pp. 21–36). San Francisco: Jossey-Bass.

Slovic, P., Griffin, D., & Tversky, A. (1990). Compatibility effects in judgment and choice. In R. M. Hogarth (Ed.), *Insights in decision making: A tribute to Hillel J. Einhorn* (pp. 5–27). Chicago: University of Chicago Press.

Slovic, P., & Lichtenstein, S. (1968). The relative importance of probabilities and payoffs in risk taking. *Journal of Experimental Psychology, Monograph supplement, 78,* part 2.

Slovic, P., & Lichtenstein, S. (1971). Comparison of Bayesian and regression approaches to the study of information processing in judgment. *Organizational Behavior and Human Performance, 6,* 649–744.

Slovic, P., & MacPhillamy, D. (1974). Dimensional commensurability and cue utilization in comparative judgment. *Organizational Behavior and Human Performance, 11,* 174–194.

Smith, J. F., & Kida, T. (1991) Heuristics and biases: Expertise and task realism in auditing. *Psychological Bulletin, 109,* 472–489.

Smith, J. F., Mitchell, T. R., & Beach, L. R. (1982). A cost–benefit mechanism for selecting problem solving strategies: Some extensions and empirical tests. *Organizational Behavior and Human Performance, 29,* 370–396.

Smith, V. K., Desvousges, W. H., Fisher, A., & Johnson, F. R. (1988). Learning about radon's risk. *Journal of Risk and Uncertainty, 1,* 233–258.

Sproles, G. B. (1986). The concept of quality and the efficiency of markets: Issues and comments. *Journal of Consumer Research, 13,* 146–148.

Stevenson, M. K., Busemeyer, J. R., & Naylor, J. C. (1990). Judgment and decision-making theory. In M. D. Dunnette & L. M. Hough (Eds.), *Handbook of industrial and organizational psychology* (2nd ed., Vol. 1, pp. 283–374). Palo Alto, CA: Consulting Psychologists Press.

Stewart, T. R., & Ely, D. W. (1984). Range sensitivity: A necessary condition and test for the validity of weights. NCAR 3141-84/14, National Center for Atmospheric Research, Boulder, CO.

Stone, D. N., & Schkade, D. A. (1991a, November). Attribute scaling and explicit incentives in multiattribute choice. Paper presented at the Judgment and Decision Making Society Meeting, San Francisco, CA.

Stone, D. N., & Schkade, D. A. (1991b). Numeric and linguistic information representation in multiattribute choice. *Organizational Behavior and Human Decision Processes, 49,* 42–59.

Sujan, M. (1985). Consumer knowledge: Effects on evaluation strategies mediating consumer judgments. *Journal of Consumer Research, 12,* 16–31.

Sundstrom, G. A. (1987). Information search and decision making: The effects of information displays. *Acta Psychologica, 65,* 165–179.

Svenson, O., & Edland, A. (1987). Changes of preferences under time pressure: Choices and judgments. *Scandinavian Journal of Psychology, 28,* 322–330.

Taylor, S. E., & Brown, J. D. (1988). Illusion and well-being: A social psychological perspective on mental health. *Psychological Bulletin, 103,* 193–210.

Tetlock, P. E. (1985). Accountability: The neglected social context of judgment and choice. *Research in Organizational Behavior, 7,* 297–332.

Tetlock, P. E. (1991). An alternative metaphor in the study of judgment and choice: People as politicians. *Journal of Theory and Psychology, 1,* 451–475.

Tetlock, P. E., & Boettger, R. (1989). Accountability: A social magnifier of the dilution effect. *Journal of Personality and Social Psychology, 57,* 388–398.

Tetlock, P. E., & Kim, J. I. (1987). Accountability and judgment processes in a personality prediction task. *Journal of Personality and Social Psychology, 52,* 700–709.

Thomas, E. A. C. (1983). Notes on effort and achievement-oriented behavior. *Psychological Review, 90,* 1–20.

Thorngate, W. (1980). Efficient decision heuristics. *Behavioral Science, 25,* 219–225.

Thorngate, W., & Maki, J. (1976). Decision heuristics and the choice of political candidates. Unpublished working paper, University of Alberta.

Thuring, M., & Jungermann, H. (1990). The conjunction fallacy: Causality vs. event probability. *Journal of Behavioral Decision Making, 3,* 61–74.

Todd, P., & Benbasat, I. (1991). The influence of decision aids on choice strategies: An experimental analysis of the role of cognitive effort. Unpublished manuscript, Queen's University, Kingston, Ontario, Canada.

Tversky, A. (1969) Intransitivity of preferences. *Psychological Review, 76,* 31–48.

Tversky, A. (1972). Elimination by aspects: A theory of choice. *Psychological Review, 79,* 281–299.

Tversky, A. (1977). Features of similarity. *Psychological Review, 84,* 327–352.

Tversky, A. (1988a, October). Context effects and argument-based choice. Paper presented at the Association for Consumer Research Conference, Maui, Hawaii.

Tversky, A. (1988b). Discussion. In D. E. Bell, H. Raiffa, & A. Tversky (Eds.), *Decision making: Descriptive, normative, and prescriptive interactions* (pp. 599–612). Cambridge: Cambridge University Press.

Tversky, A., & Kahneman, D. (1974). Judgment under uncertainty: Heuristics and biases. *Science, 185,* 1124–1131.

Tversky, A., & Kahneman, D. (1981). The framing of decisions and the psychology of choice. *Science, 211,* 453–458.

Tversky, A., & Kahneman, D. (1983). Extensional vs. intuitive reasoning: The conjunction fallacy in probability judgment. *Psychological Review, 90,* 293–315.

Tversky, A., & Kahneman, D. (1986). Rational choice and the framing of decisions. *Journal of Business, 59,* S251–S278.

Tversky, A., & Kahneman, D. (1988). Rational choice and the framing of decisions. In D. E. Bell, H. Raiffa, & A. Tversky (Eds.), *Decision making: Descriptive, normative, and prescriptive interactions* (pp. 167–192). Cambridge: Cambridge University Press.

Tversky, A., & Kahneman, D. (1990). Cumulative prospect theory: An analysis of decision under uncertainty. Unpublished working paper, Stanford University.

Tversky, A., & Kahneman, D. (1991). Loss aversion in riskless choice: A reference-dependent model. *Quarterly Journal of Economics, 106,* 1039–1062.

Tversky, A., & Sattath, S. (1979). Preference trees. *Psychological Review, 86,* 542–573.

Tversky, A., Sattath, S., & Slovic, P. (1988). Contingent weighting in judgment and choice. *Psychological Review, 95, 371–384.*

Tversky, A., & Shafir, E. (1991). Decisions under conflict: An analysis of choice aversion. Unpublished working paper, Department of Psychology, Stanford University.

Tversky, A., & Simonson, I. (1992) Context-dependent preferences: The relative advantage model. Working paper, Department of Psychology, Stanford University.

Tversky, A., Slovic, P., & Kahneman, D. (1990). The determinants of preference reversal. *American Economic Review, 80,* 204–217.

Viscusi, W. K., Magat , W. A., & Huber, J. (1986). Informational regulation of consumer health risks: An empirical evaluation of hazard warnings. *Rand Journal of Economics, 17,* 351–365.

Von Winterfeldt, D., & Edwards, W. (1986). *Decision analysis and behavioral research.* Cambridge: Cambridge University Press.

Wade, S. E., & Reynolds, R. E. (1988). Developing metacognitive awareness. *Journal of Reading, 33,* 6–15.

Waller, W. S., & Mitchell, T. R. (1984). The effects of context on the selection of decision strategies for the cost variance investigation problem. *Organizational Behavior and Human Performance, 33,* 397–413.

Wallsten, T. S. (1990) The costs and benefits of vague information. In R. M. Hogarth (Ed.), *Insights in decision making: A tribute to Hillel J. Einhorn* (pp. 28–43). Chicago: University of Chicago Press.

Wallsten, T. S., & Barton, C. (1982). Processing probabilistic multidimensional information for decisions. *Journal of Experimental Psychology: Learning, Memory, and Cognition, 8,* 361–384.

Wallsten, T. S., Budescu, D. V., Rapoport, A., Zwick, R., & Forsyth, B.

(1986). Measuring the vague meanings of probability terms. *Journal of Experimental Psychology: General, 115*, 1–18.

Ward, W. C., & Jenkins, H. M. (1965). The display of information and the judgment of contingency. *Canadian Journal of Psychology, 19,* 231–241.

Watson, S. R., & Buede, D. M. (1987). *Decision synthesis: The principles and practice of decision analysis.* Cambridge: Cambridge University Press.

Weber, E. U., Goldstein, W. M., & Busemeyer, J. R. (1991). Beyond strategies: Implications of memory representations and memory processes for models of judgment and decision making. In W. F. Hockley & S. Lewandowsky (Eds.), *Relating theory and data: Essays on human memory in honor of Bennett B. Murdock* (pp. 75–100). Hillsdale, NJ: Erlbaum.

Weber, M., Eisenführ, F., & von Winterfeldt, D. (1988). The effects of splitting attributes on weights in multiattribute utility measurement. *Management Science, 34,* 431–445.

Wedell, D. H. (1991). Distinguishing among models of contextually induced preference reversals. *Journal of Experimental Psychology: Learning. Memory, and Cognition, 17,* 767–778.

Wedell, D. H., & Bockenholt, U. (1990). Moderation of preference reversals in the long run. *Journal of Experimental Psychology: Human Perception and Performance, 16,* 429–438.

Weldon, E., & Gargano, G. M. (1985). Cognitive effort in additive task groups: The effects of shared responsibility on the quality of multiattribute judgments. *Organizational Behavior and Human Decision Processes, 36,* 348–361.

Weldon, E., & Mustari, E. L. (1988). Felt dispensability in groups of coactors: The effects of shared responsibility and explicit anonymity on cognitive effort. *Organizational Behavior and Human Decision Processes, 41,* 330–351.

Wells, G. L. (1985). The conjunction error and the representativeness heuristic. *Social Cognition, 3,* 266–279.

Wickens, C. D. (1986). Gain and energetics in information processing. In G. Hockey, A. Gaillard, & M. Coles (Eds.), *Energetics and human information processing* (pp. 373–389). Dordrecht, the Netherlands: Martinus Nijhoff.

Wilkins, L. T. (1967). *Social deviance.* Englewood Cliffs, NJ: Prentice-Hall.

Williams, C. A. (1966). Attitudes toward speculative risks as an indicator of attitudes toward pure risks. *Journal of Risk and Insurance, 33,* 557–586.

Wood, R. E., & Locke, E. A. (1990). Goal setting and strategy effects on complex tasks. In B. M. Staw & L. L. Cummings (Eds.), *Research in organizational behavior* (Vol. 12, pp. 73–109). Greenwich, CT: JAI Press.

Wright, P. L. (1974). The harassed decision maker: Time pressures, distractions, and the use of evidence. *Journal of Applied Psychology, 59*, 555–561.

Wright, P. L. (1975). Consumer choice strategies: Simplifying vs. optimizing. *Journal of Marketing Research, 11*, 60–67.

Wright, P. L. (1977). Decision times and processes on complex problems. Unpublished manuscript, Stanford University.

Wright, P. L., & Weitz, B. (1977). Time horizon effects on product evaluation strategies. *Journal of Marketing Research, 14*, 429–443.

Wright, W. F., & Aboul-Ezz, M. E. (1988). Effects of extrinsic incentives on the quality of frequency assessments. *Organizational Behavior and Human Decision Processes, 41*, 143–152.

Yates, J. F., & Carlson, B. W. (1986). Conjunction errors: Evidence for multiple judgment procedures, including signed summation? *Organizational Behavior and Human Decision Processes, 37*, 230–253.

Yates, J. F., Jagacinski, C. M., & Faber, M. D. (1978). Evaluation of partially described multiattribute options. *Organizational Behavior and Human Performance, 21*, 240–251.

Zakay, D. (1985). Post-decisional confidence and conflict experienced in a choice process. *Acta Psychologica, 58*, 75–80.

Zakay, D., & Wooler, S. (1984). Time pressure, training and decision effectiveness. *Ergonomics, 27*, 273–284.

Zipf, G. K. (1949). *Human behavior and the principle of least effort.* Cambridge, MA: Addison-Wesley.

Name index

Aboul-Ezz, M. E., 156
Alba, J. W., 3, 28, 236, 253, 260
Albert, D., 28, 56, 60, 96, 102–103, 151, 183
Alloy, L. B., 193
Anderson, J. R., 11, 67, 107, 120, 122, 173, 180, 205, 215
Anderson, N. H., 11, 259, 261
Andriole, S. J., 231
Anzai, Y., 207
Arch, D. C., 265
Arkes, H. R., 8, 111, 213, 236, 238
Aschenbrenner, K. M., 28, 49, 56, 60, 96, 102–103, 151, 183
Ashton, A. H., 238
Ashton, R. H., 111, 156, 238
Atkinson, R. C., 206
Avrunin, G. S., 59, 62, 78, 179

Barnes, V. E., 68, 100, 101
Baron, J., 24, 59, 74, 199, 206
Baron, R. M., 160
Barron, F. H., 230
Barton, C., 39
Batsell, R. R., 55
Bazerman, M. H., 209
Beach, L. R., 68, 73, 75, 100–102, 104, 113, 126, 233, 254
Beattie, J., 24, 59, 74, 199
Bedard, J. C., 34–35, 37, 55–56
Behn, R. D., 231, 236
Bell, D. E., 44, 234
Ben Zur, H., 38–39, 161
Benbasat, I., 88, 234
Berg, J. E., 42, 111
Berman, M. L., 266
Bettman, J. R., 23, 35, 38–39, 43, 45, 49–50, 52, 57–58, 60–61, 77, 81,

83–84, 87–88, 123–124, 131–132, 134, 136–138, 140–142, 154, 159, 163–164, 171–174, 178, 180, 191, 195, 198–199, 208, 210–215, 225–266, 228, 242, 261, 264–265, 268–269, 274, 277
Biehal, G. J., 173
Biggs, S. F., 34–35, 37, 55–56
Billings, R. S., 34, 44, 160
Birnbaum, M. H., 22, 45, 258–259, 261
Bither, S., 103, 126
Blank, H., 66
Blattberg, R. C., 239
Bockenholt, U., 28, 44, 56, 60, 96, 102–103, 151, 183
Boettger, R., 255
Bostic, R., 44
Boyle, K. J., 244
Bradshaw, G. L., 21, 120
Braunstein, M. L., 34–35, 49, 62, 144, 146, 148–150, 152–154, 265–266
Brehmer, B., 104, 209–210
Breznitz, S. J., 38–39, 161
Brookshire, D. S., 243
Brown, J. D., 90
Brucato, P. F., 223
Brucks, M., 147, 265
Budescu, D. V., 52
Buede, D. M., 7, 228
Burke, S. J., 181
Busemeyer, J. R., 22, 24, 122

Cacioppo, J. T., 16
Calvin, W. H., 5
Camerer, C. F., 257
Capon, N., 201
Card, S. K., 79, 266–267
Carlson, B. W., 67

Subject index

ability to execute strategies (*see* inability to execute strategies)
acceleration of processing, 38, 161–162, 164–166 (*see also* time pressure)
accountability (*see* need for justification)
accuracy (*see also* failures in adaptivity; assessing accuracy and effort)
  anticipated vs. experienced, 91–92, 227–228
  assessments of, 92, 178–180, 208–210
  constraints on, 96–97
  and correlation between attributes, 60, 194–195, 198
  criteria for, 88
  and decision strategies, 13, 23, 71, 92–94, 128 143, 161–162, 166–167, 195
  and decision task properties, 13, 71, 97–99, 122, 128–143, 148, 162, 164–165, 167, 194–195, 198, 211–213
  definition of, 88–91
  and dispersion in probabilities, 128–133, 137–143, 162, 164–165, 195, 198, 211–213
  and dominated alternatives present or absent, 128–133, 137–143
  and expected utility or expected value, 89–90
  and feedback on accuracy and effort, 211–213
  and framing effects, 67, 114
  and goals for accuracy vs. effort, 157, 159–160
  and hindsight bias, 209
  and inability to execute strategies, 215, 218

and incentives, 14, 111–112, 156–157, 213, 230, 238, 249–250
and information display effects, 227–228
and intuition vs. analysis, 104–105, 215
and need for justification, 254–255
and number of alternatives, 133–137, 139–142, 148
and number of attributes, 36, 133–137, 139–142
and overconfidence, 92, 209, 237–238
process vs. outcome views, 89
relative accuracy measure, 90–91, 118, 128, 156, 210
sufficiency as criterion for decision quality, 89–90
task vs. context effects, 137
and time pressure, 39, 137–143, 162, 164, 167
and use of heuristics vs. normative strategies, 5, 60, 129, 137, 139, 143, 148, 194, 248
accuracy–effort framework for deciding how to decide (*see also* accuracy; accuracy–effort tradeoffs; assessing accuracy and effort; cost–benefit frameworks for deciding how to decide; effort; perceptual frameworks)
  and accuracy–effort tradeoffs, 13, 94–95, 98–99, 156, 178–180, 210, 214
  assessing accuracy and effort, 207–213
  constraints on accuracy and effort, 96–97, 99
  and constructive processing,